Rethinking health psychology

Health Psychology

Series editors:
Sheila Payne and Sandra Horn

Rethinking health psychology

Michele L. Crossley

Open University Press
Buckingham • Philadelphia

Open University Press
Celtic Court
22 Ballmoor
Buckingham
MK18 1XW

email: enquiries@openup.co.uk
world wide web: www.openup.co.uk

and
325 Chestnut Street
Philadelphia, PA 19106, USA

First Published 2000

ISBN   0 335 20431 7 (hb)   0 335 20430 9 (pb)

A catalogue record of this book is available from the British Library

Library of Congress Cataloging-in-Publication Data
Crossley, Michele L., 1969–
    Rethinking health psychology / Michele L. Crossley.
        p.   cm. – (Health psychology)
    Includes bibliographical references and index.
    ISBN 0-335-20430-9 (pb) – ISBN 0-335-20431-7 (hb)
    1. Medicine and psychology. 2. Clinical health psychology. I. Title.
II. Series.

R726.5.C78   2000
616'.001'9 – dc21

                                                                    00-035682

Copy-edited and typeset by The Running Head Limited,
www.therunninghead.com

Printed and bound in Great Britain by
Marston Book Services Limited, Oxford

Again for Nick

And in loving memory of my Nanna, Irene
Troughton, 31 August 1922–11 February 2000

> The very last time we saw you
> The thing you most wanted to do
> Get the tomatoes potted
> So they'd be ready for us,
> For summer.
> But now,
> We'll have to plant our own.
> And when they blossom
> How can they without you?
> When they blossom
> In summers forever,
> Then,
> We'll watch
> And think of you.

'Thinking of you' by Michele Louise Crossley

Contents

 # Acknowledgements

Thank you to all my friends, colleagues and the series editors, Sheila Payne and Sandra Horn, who have provided valuable comments and criticisms of this book.

I think the main person I have to acknowledge here, though, is Nick, who's had to eat, sleep and breathe health psychology while I've been writing this book! So I'd like to take this opportunity to thank him formally. Thanks Nick.

 # Series editors' foreword

This new series of books in health psychology is designed to support post-graduate and postqualification studies in psychology, nursing, medicine and paramedical science, as well as the establishment of health psychology within the undergraduate psychology curriculum. Health psychology is growing rapidly as a field of study. Concerned as it is with the application of psychological theories and models in the promotion and maintenance of health, and the individual and interpersonal aspects of adaptive behaviour in illness and disability, health psychology has a wide remit and a potentially important role to play in the future.

In this timely book, Michele Crossley examines and challenges the subject matter and methods of contemporary mainstream health psychology. The largely quantitative approach and its concern with concepts such as healthy and unhealthy behaviour, prevention, aetiology and prediction, is set along-side a critical (hermeneutic) paradigm, which uses qualitative methods to explore experiences of and meaning in health and illness, and considers the moral aspects of promoting some behaviours as desirable and seeking to change others. The differences between the two approaches are considered in the context of some of the major topics in the field: health promotion, pain and disease, mental illness, interpersonal relationships in healthcare, and death and dying.

This book is not a comfortable read; it is thought-provoking, challeng-ing and exciting – and a welcome addition to the series.

Sheila Payne and Sandra Horn

Opening thoughts

'Psychology,' wrote Wittgenstein, 'contains experimental methods and conceptual confusions.' It is because researchers have cultivated *empirical* at the expense of *conceptual* sophistication that they do not realise how serious this fault really is.

(Ingleby 1981: 24)

One 'cherished illusion' that must be lost if we are to understand the nature of human action and behaviour in relation to health related phenomena, is the 'myth' which keeps contemporary psychology 'on the move': 'the belief that what we need is simply more "findings" – that round the corner lies some vital new fact which will settle the arguments once and for all'.

(Ingleby 1981: 23)

CHAPTER
1

Approaches to health psychology

All that night long I read and reread the material I'd collected on breast cancer, looking for something that wasn't there . . . I kept searching for information. What I failed to realise at that time was that the physical facts of disease can never fully address its impact, the totality of what it is like to live with cancer. Knowledge alone couldn't control what was happening to me, but I clung to the notion that informing myself could keep me from being pulled under by its strong current.

(Mayer 1994: 21)

Introduction

In very broad terms, contemporary health psychology can be said to consist of two main 'voices': the dominant voice of traditional 'mainstream' health psychology, and the lesser known but gradually emerging voice of 'critical' health psychology. Another way in which these two approaches can be described is as 'scientific' and 'hermeneutic', respectively (Habermas 1971). These various terms will be used interchangeably throughout this book to depict the two distinct approaches to health psychology. The aim of this chapter is to demonstrate in what ways these two approaches differ from each other. It will be suggested that these differences are quite fundamental, impacting on the very definition of *what* exactly the subject matter of health psychology consists of, and *how* such material should be studied. By outlining some of these fundamental differences, we will set the stage for the rest of this book. This involves an attempt to set out in a coherent fashion in what ways a critical health psychological approach would proceed differently in addressing some of the major topics covered in mainstream health psychology textbooks (e.g. health promotion, pain, stress, illness, relationships with health professionals and death and dying). The more general aim of this book is to identify and characterize a different vision of health psychology that can be offered by adopting a critical approach. To begin this task, we need to ask some fundamental questions. What is wrong with mainstream health psychology? What solutions are offered by a critical approach? Do these solutions solve the problems? Through a process of critical appraisal, this book seeks to address these questions.

Before proceeding further, however, our first step is to outline some basic definitions of 'mainstream' and 'critical' health psychology, and then to elucidate the assumptions, theoretical models and dominant methods associated with these approaches. We will begin with mainstream health psychology, and then proceed to critical health psychology.

Defining mainstream health psychology

Mainstream health psychology is that which is most often taught in universities and practised by clinicians, researchers and consultants. Reflecting the conditions of social psychology (see Pancer 1997), mainstream health psychology is a predominantly American enterprise dominated by American general textbooks such as Sheridan and Radmacher (1992), Sarafino (1994) and Taylor (1995). Ogden's (1996) health psychology textbook offers a useful addition to the literature in so far as it is a European-based text but it remains thoroughly wedded to the aforementioned books in terms of style and presentation. This style is one which draws heavily on a 'discourse of scientific progress', presenting investigation into health psychology as a strictly objective enterprise which builds on a 'body of knowledge' that has already been 'discovered' (Bartlett 1998: 23). The basic aims of mainstream health psychology are twofold: (1) to predict health- and illness-related behaviour through the development and testing of theories and (2) to control, manage or change such behaviour through the application of such theories. This is health psychology portrayed as a science, with objective researchers and practitioners who 'uncover the truth' about health- and illness-related behaviour and help individuals adjust to the demands of health and illness in contemporary society.

Mainstream health psychology: background

The emergence of the discipline of health psychology in the 1970s, like the emergence of any approach, can only be understood in relation to what it emerged *as a response to* and *critique of*. This was the 'biomedical' model which dominated the study of disease during the nineteenth and much of the twentieth century. The biomedical model can be characterized as one in which the study of disease is reduced to narrowly defined biological, chemical, cellular or genetic factors which cause physical changes in the body. This narrow definition of disease is further promulgated in methods of treatment which focus solely on changing the physical state of the body such as surgery, radiotherapy, drug and genetic interventions. From this perspective, the human body is a machine and the doctor or surgeon is the mechanic who fixes it when something goes wrong.

In the traditional biomedical model, psychological factors have very little role to play in the disease process. This relates to the conception of mind and body underlying the biomedical model. In this model, mind and body are seen as functioning independently of each other. This is often referred to as the 'mind–body split' (or mind–body dualism) which originated with the philosopher René Descartes (Descartes 1969). From this perspective there exists a basic division between the non-material mind (comprising thoughts, beliefs, feelings, etc.) and the material brain and body (physical matter such as the brain, skin, bones, organs, etc.). Any changes in physical matter were thought to operate independently of the mind and vice versa. This notion that psychological processes were unimportant to the onset and/or progression of disease was, however, to come under attack during the twentieth century from a number of emerging disciplines such as psychosomatic medicine, behavioural health, behavioural medicine and, most recently, health psychology (Ogden 1996: 3).

During the latter part of the twentieth century, as acute contagious diseases gave way to chronic illness and disability, there has been an increasing appreciation of the need to consider social and psychological influences on health and disease. In the 1970s Engel, a psychiatrist, put forward his influential 'biopsychosocial' model as a critique of the traditional biomedical model. The intention of the biopsychosocial model was to provide a framework in which knowledge about the biological, psychological and social aspects of illness could be integrated (Engel 1977). Engel's model was based on 'systems theory', which postulated reciprocal and dynamic interactions between different levels of the human system, from the biochemical to the sociocultural. This model was welcomed by social scientists because it highlighted the importance of psychological and social factors in the study of health and disease. It represented a move away from the simple linear model of disease manifest in the biomedical model and implied a more complex system in which illness was caused by a multitude of interacting biological, psychological and social factors.

The biopsychosocial model obviously had implications for the development of alternative prevention and treatment models. If psychological factors play a potentially mediating role in the onset and progression of illness, then factors such as beliefs, coping strategies and healthy or unhealthy behaviours could be identified and encouraged or discouraged in the pursuit of health. This conception of the relationship between mind and illness represents a departure from the dualism of the traditional biomedical model, indicating an increasing recognition of the interactional processes taking place between mind and body.

Since the publication of Engel's research, the biopsychosocial model has served as a basic framework for academic and clinical research in many areas such as medicine, nursing and, in particular, health psychology, which emerged as a new discipline at about the same time that Engel developed his model. This is clear in many of the main textbooks in health psychology which claim to be framed within an integrated biopsychosocial approach.

Mainstream health psychology: approach and methods

Most of the research done within the remit of the biopsychosocial model in health psychology has been modelled on traditional scientific method and methodologies. It has been assumed that, by means of accurate observation and rational deduction, objective knowledge of the various factors pertaining to the onset, progression and treatment of health and illness can be obtained. A further assumption, congruent with this perspective, is that such knowledge exists independently of the assumptions, goals and beliefs of the researcher, and independently of the specific social and cultural context in which the research is conducted.

Mainstream health psychological approaches rely heavily on pre-defined models of health- and illness-related behaviours. As is clear from any health psychology textbook, a multiplicity of models exists in relation to any aspect of behaviour under discussion. These models tend to consist of an amalgamation of multiple hypothetical constructs related to biological, social and psychological variables. The empirical data fed into these models is frequently derived from quantitative measures of psychological variables such as behaviours, beliefs, attitudes and perceptions, obtained through lab-based experiments, quasi-experimental designs and structured questionnaires. These measuring instruments, or tools, are designed to elicit and limit responses in accordance with the pre-defined theoretical model.

The use of such models and methods is consistent with the attempt to create a 'rational scientific approach to behavioural and psychosocial data' which, as Engel proposed, would mean the availability of psychosocial variables that could be compared to biomedical variables (Engel 1977: 132). The streamlining of psychosocial measures in this way has had the result that statistical analysis can be conducted on comparable psychosocial (e.g. attitudes, beliefs and coping strategies) and biomedical variables (e.g. the presence, severity or progression of disease). As Yardley (1997: 5) notes, one major advantage of this approach is that it has enabled psychological research to win acceptance from medical clinicians and researchers who are familiar with the language and procedures of scientific investigation. Consequently, psychology now forms a small part of the medical school curriculum.

Defining critical health psychology

A *critical* psychology is one which challenges many of the theories and practices that are common in mainstream psychology. There are many different types of critical psychology but they began mainly to gain ascendance in social psychology about fifteen years ago (see Henriques *et al*. 1984; Gergen 1985; Potter and Wetherell 1987). This influence is now beginning to make its way into most other areas of psychology (see Fox and Prilleltensky 1997). These approaches tend to vary widely in their aim and scope but one of the defining characteristics of a critical approach is its attempt to question the *status quo* of psychology and alter it in fundamental ways (Prilleltensky and Fox 1997: 3). They argue that psychology 'too often settles for too little' (p. 3) and in doing so 'restricts the imagination' and 'hinders efforts to create a better society' (p. 14). Committed to making explicit the values lying behind psychological research, critical psychologists argue that mainstream psychology feeds into individualistic ideologies prevalent in contemporary Western societies, actively preventing and exacerbating the failure to achieve social justice, self-determination and participation, caring and compassion, health and human diversity (p. 8). It is these values which guide the pursuit of a critical psychology.

There are increasing signs of an emerging *critical health psychology*. This is not surprising given that, as a relatively new discipline, health psychology has drawn heavily on mainstream social and clinical psychology, both of which have been influenced by critical thinking in recent years. Classic examples include Radley's (1993b, 1994, 1997) 'cultural' approach towards the study of health and illness which attempts to counter the 'individualistic' bent of mainstream psychology. Other recent developments draw on a combination of phenomenological and discursive approaches such as Yardley's (1997) edited collection, Smith's (1996) and Smith *et al*.'s (1997) recent work and most recently, Murray and Chamberlain's (1999) edited collection on qualitative theories and methods in health psychology. Recent developments in narrative psychology (see Crossley 2000a, especially Chapters 6–8; Kleinman 1988; Frank 1995) are also consistent with a critical health psychology agenda. And postmodernist approaches, drawing mainly on sociological work, are also important (Fox 1993). Despite these developments, however, and despite the fact that critical health psychology approaches are becoming increasingly popular in Britain and Europe, as yet no comprehensive textbook exists to counter the dominance of mainstream approaches. One of the central aims of this book is to redress this balance.

Background

One of the central concerns of critical health psychology is the inadequacy of mainstream health psychology's appropriation of the biopsychosocial model. Most of the major health psychology texts (see Sheridan and Radmacher 1992; Sarafino 1994; Taylor 1995; Ogden 1996) pay lip-service to this model. However, as Cooper *et al*. (1996) point out, the biopsychosocial model is often presented as a '*multiple*, rather than *integrated*, explanatory framework' in which 'biological, social and psychological factors co-exist in a seemingly fragmented way' (p. 4). This means that the biopsychosocial model 'merely reflects the simultaneous juxtaposition of a range of explanatory perspectives and *not* the integrated theoretical model that its status implies' (p. 4). These points indicate that, even though mainstream health psychology was originally formulated as a challenge to biomedical mind–body dualism, this dualism is to a large extent retained because mind, body and society are perceived as separate entitites which, although interacting with each other, remain fundamentally separate (Ogden 1996: 5).

A critical approach helps us to understand how we might develop a more integrated approach which shifts to a different level of explanation. This approach seeks to challenge the problem of mind–body dualism and the fragmentary conception of the individual characteristic of mainstream perspectives in health psychology. The importance of developing such a non-fragmentary conception is that it enables us to develop a deeper understanding of both the psychological dimensions of human experiences (e.g. the complex emotional and 'irrational' forces underpinning human action), and also, relatedly, of the socio-cultural dimension of such experiences. Mainstream health psychology's attempt to emulate a natural scientific style of investigation means that it fails to appreciate these crucial elements of human experience. By contrast, one of the major aims of critical health psychology is to develop an *understanding* of such experiences.

What do we mean by this? From a critical psychological perspective, the attempt to study human beings as 'objects', in the traditional scientific manner, remains fundamentally misguided. This is because such an attempt fails to appreciate the unique 'order of meaning' lying at the heart of human existence (Polkinghorne 1988). This 'order of meaning' relates to the fact that, as human beings, we experience our own and other people's behaviour as *meaningful* and, consequently, are continuously engaged in the process of reflecting on, and interpreting the meaning of such behaviour. This reflective capacity characteristic of human consciousness means that the objects of inquiry facing the psychological investigator are of a very different order to those addressed by the natural science investigator. In a profound sense, the 'object' of the psychologist's focus of inquiry is not an 'object' but a 'subject', with subjective thoughts, feelings and interpretations which affect his/her interaction within the world.

But what does this unique 'order of meaning' consist of? Crucial here is an understanding of the role played by language, one of the primary vehicles through which our experiences are rendered meaningful. One of the basic principles of critical psychology is that individuals understand themselves through the medium of language, through talking and writing, and it is through these processes that individuals constantly engage in the process of *constructing* themselves. Learning language enables individuals to communicate, interact and negotiate with each other. Such communicative processes are essential to the creation of a sense of identity. Creating such a sense of self is all about creating a sense of meaning and meaningfulness. This can only be developed in relation to specific social and cultural worlds which involve orientation to a sense of morality and values, sometimes also called an orientation to 'the good' (see Taylor 1989: 91; Crossley 1999b).

It has been argued that one of the definitive characteristics of human beings is that we *care* about whether or not our lives make sense and what our lives are amounting too. As human beings, we are always 'insiders' because we always have a deep, defining set of commitments and identifications to something, even though those commitments will change across different cultures and sub-cultures. This means that we always take some 'stand' on our lives by appropriating certain roles, traits or values (Richardson and Fowers 1997: 282). We always make 'strong evaluations' (Taylor 1989: 3), even if not necessarily consciously, evaluating the quality of our desires, motivations and the worth of the ends we seek in terms of how they fit into our overall sense of a decent or worthwhile life. According to this perspective, such orientations towards meaningfulness form an inescapable part of human agency and social life. Human agency only takes place within a 'space of questions' in which the individual engages with the meanings and moral values inculcated into her by the culture in which she lives. As will become apparent throughout this book, understanding such an 'order of meaning' in relation to human experiences of health and illness, involves a complex appreciation of the interrelationship between identity, values and morality. Our interpretations of health and illness only make sense in relation to particular social and cultural contexts and remain obscure if we attempt to isolate them from or treat them independently of such contexts.

According to a critical health psychology perspective, this is exactly what mainstream health psychology approaches attempt to do. Such approaches do not necessarily deny that meanings, moralities, evaluations and commitments are important in understanding the forces motivating and making sense of people's behaviours. But the attempt to create an 'objective' approach to psychological data congruent with that of biomedical data, means that such considerations have to be factored out and held constant in the attempt to formulate and test pre-existing models of health- and illness-related behaviour. The predominant use of quantitative methods and statistical forms of analysis in mainstream approaches is geared towards a theoretical orientation in which validity (i.e. correspondence with reality) is determined by 'testability' and the ability to precisely record and match 'outcomes' against model-based predictions. Such models tend to consist of variables which can be measured through existing assessment tools. These tend not to incorporate less easily quantifiable material such as values, meaning and subjective moral orientations. This creates a temptation to define reality and validity in terms of what is measurable and to let the rest fall by the wayside. Unfortunately, it is arguably the less easily quantifiable dimensions that are most important in considering people's experiences of health and illness.

One of the central features of critical health psychology relates to the need to explore the qualitative nuances of meaning and value inherent in human experiences of health and illness. The attempt to develop understanding (rather than to predict, manage and control), involves a shift towards qualitative research methods such as semi-structured, in-depth interviews and case-studies. It is argued that such methods enable the researcher to explore the 'meaning-system' of specific individuals (Smith 1995), producing detailed, 'information rich' data which is impossible to separate from context if its full meaning is to be appreciated and understood. Such approaches create a 'detailed and profound insight into a particular, perhaps unique, account or experience rather than a set of broad generalisations about commonalities between different people' (Yardley 1997: 36). Hence, the rationale is to exploit one of the principal merits of qualitative methods – the analysis of meaning in depth and in context (p. 36). This kind of analysis is required if the proposed shift towards a 'different level of explanation' is to be achieved. Indeed, I have written this book in the manner and spirit of qualitative inquiry. This involves in-depth focus on a limited number of studies and investigations. Although this reduces the amount of sources drawn upon, I see this as a cost necessary to the pursuit of a deeper and more critical analysis.

The central points of difference between a mainstream and critical health psychological approach are set out below:

Mainstream ('scientific') health psychology
- biopsychosocial model
- quantitative methods
- unhealthy and healthy behaviour
- beliefs
- aetiology
- prediction
- targeting
- prevention

Critical ('hermeneutic') health psychology
- phenomenological-discursive model
- qualitative methods
- meaning
- morality
- experiences of health and illness

◆ contextual
◆ relational
◆ understanding

A preliminary framework for this book: rethinking 'technical' questions as moral issues

The work of critical theorist Jurgen Habermas (1973, 1991) is centrally concerned with a critique of 'instrumental reason', a form of knowledge unique
to, yet within, dominant modern technological society. Habermas argues
that modern society is based on a damaging confusion of *praxis* and *techne* –
these are Greek words meaning 'culture' and 'technology' respectively. Contemporary Western societies tend to be dominated by a collapsing of the cultural and moral dimensions of life into merely technical and instrumental
considerations. The implication of this is that advances in technology tend to
'produce technical recommendations, but they furnish no answer to practical (or moral) questions' (Habermas 1973: 254). Accordingly, too many
spheres of life become dominated by a practical and instrumental viewpoint
which construes problems in terms of means–ends, cost–benefit analyses,
and seeks to maximize our control and mastery over events. Although this
increases our *instrumental* prowess, it undermines our ability to evaluate the
moral worth of ends and goals (Richardson and Fowers 1997: 272).
    Another critical theorist, Horkheimer (1974), similarly argued that the
modern glorification of instrumental reason actually turns into its opposite,
an 'eclipse of reason'. When a stance of scientific neutrality regards all values
as 'merely subjective' it undermines our ability to reason together about the
'inherent quality of our way of life and about what ends we might best seek.
As the means of control and influence grow, life gets more organised and
complicated but we lose the ability to set priorities and impose needed
limits' (Richardson and Fowers 1997: 272).
    From a critical psychology standpoint, it can be argued that mainstream
health psychology is an example *par excellence* of such dominant 'instrumental reason'. As will be shown throughout this book, mainstream health
psychology treats issues of health and illness, risk and safety, pain, stress,
survival, relationships and death as largely 'technical' problems that can be
'managed' by various forms of intervention and control. It has already been
suggested that one of the main aims of mainstream health psychology is to
promote healthy behaviours in order to maintain health and, in the case of
already existing disease, to promote healthy behaviours and ways of thinking in order to prolong life. One of the ways in which it does this is by
targeting beliefs that predict 'unhealthy' behaviours – or beliefs that are
allegedly related to 'disease-free' survival – and attempting to change them
accordingly. The very statement of such aims, however, makes clear that
they are based on the assumption that concepts of health and unhealth,

disease and non-disease, are clear cut and can be professionally and objectively defined. Perhaps even more problematically, it is simplistically assumed that the technical goals of health psychology (promoting health and survival, ridding the population of disease, pain, and ultimately death?) are desirable. Such a focus, as Habermas predicted, although increasing *instrumental* and technical prowess, fails to engage with the moral questions associated with the worth of such goals.

Engagement with such issues constitutes a central task of critical health psychology. A critical health psychologist must be able to open herself to questions such as: Why should we try and change 'risky' behaviours? How important is safety? How important is health? How important is survival? What are we losing in the pursuit of a 'risk-free', healthy, disease-free population? Perhaps people want pain? Perhaps people need disease? How important is life? Perhaps people need (and want) death? If we could eliminate pain, disease, death, suffering – would we, should we? Over and against the right to healthcare, we must ask whether people have a more fundamental right to what Kugelman (2000a) calls the 'liberty to contend with the pains and pleasures that define life as human'.

It is all too easy to invoke common sense and undermine critical questions by making rhetorical reference to what 'every sensible right-minded' person would want given the opportunity. The fact is, however, if we actually turn to examine the voices and narratives of people who are engaging in 'risky' health-related behaviours, living with disease, or facing the possibility of their imminent death, the 'rational' and common-sense status of such values quite often breaks down, as people live their lives in accordance with different moral values and objectives. A detailed exploration of such 'alternative rationalities and moralities', as outlined in this book, should make us increasingly reticent about the value neutrality of a health psychology geared towards the management and control of health and illness. It may also make us profoundly uncomfortable with the idea that the 'professional' way of seeing things is necessarily the 'right' way and instil scepticism with regard to the endorsement and imputation of such values onto the community at large.

This is particularly the case if such values are perceived in a critical light. For instance, some critical psychologists argue that the underlying values and institutions of modern societies 'reinforce misguided efforts to obtain fulfilment while maintaining inequality and oppression' (Prilleltensky and Fox 1997: 4). Because 'psychology's values, assumptions and norms have supported society's dominant institutions since its birth as a field of study, the field's mainstream contributes to social injustice and thwarts the promotion of human welfare' (p. 4). In accordance with this perspective, it could be argued that mainstream health psychology 'strengthens values and institutions that prevent many people from living meaningful lives' (p. 5). Restricting its input to immediately practical interventions, such as various 'coping' and 'management' strategies, it 'endorses individualism and de-emphasises values related to mutuality, connectedness and a psychological sense of community' (p. 9).

For example, consider the multitude of 'addictive' health problems faced by many of us in contemporary society: eating or not eating, smoking, using drugs, having unsafe sex . . . These are all reduced to 'individual' problems of 'coping style' or 'personality type'. Such individualistic reductionism fails to appreciate the way in which such 'addictive' problems relate to the social, economic and cultural context of contemporary life (see Chapter 3). This is reinforced and perpetuated by locating solutions to such problems in the hands of professionals such as psychologists, counsellors and doctors. In this way, we become more and more reliant on professionals as our lifeworlds are 'colonized' and all of our problems come to be defined in terms of professional agendas.

Critical psychological perspectives argue that, by reinforcing the core values of individualism in this way, professions such as health psychology implicitly serve to reinforce capitalist power. Stealthily and silently, we are working to create a world in which the existential, moral and ethical issues related to life and health, can be reduced to anaesthetized individualistic problems solved by administrative and technical solutions. Through this process, we fail to pursue more fundamental questions regarding issues of health, life and death, thereby hindering more significant, longer-term benefits for both individuals and society as a whole.

It should be noted here that such negative perspectives on the power-infused nature of professions such as mainstream health psychology, have themselves been subject to criticism from other perspectives (see Chapter 2). Researchers such as Giddens (1992) and Beck (1992), for instance, have argued against the predominantly negative view of individualistically focused strategies of management and control. Rather than resulting in a society replete with narrow-minded people divorced from wider concerns, such authors argue that individualistically based interventions (such as therapy and counselling) often encourage people to experience enhanced feelings of control and confidence, thus increasing their ability to engage with social, moral and ethical issues (Crossley 1999b, 2000b).

From this perspective, the rise of professions such as mainstream health psychology should not necessarily be viewed as a negative phenomenon in terms of the capacity for psychological and social development. This is especially the case when we consider that the very nature of a discipline that claims to be a science involves a commitment to the ideal of a self-critical, ever-changing nature of its subject matter. In this sense, the project of a critical health psychology is, in theory at least, entirely compatible with the goals and ambitions of the discipline of health psychology more generally (Rappaport and Stewart 1997: 304). This means that, taken as a whole, mainstream and critical health psychology enable both the means to intervene

technically in the pursuit and promotion of health and health-related behaviours, and the interpretive and discursive skills to debate and consider
the moral and ethical dimensions of such actions. Researchers adopting
such a perspective are likely to be less critical of health psychology *per se*
and more likely to adopt a 'revisionist' position in which a critical, questioning perspective is not *necessarily* perceived as at odds with the aims of
a more mainstream approach. From this perspective it may be possible
to work alongside mainstream approaches, adding a crucial cultural and
evaluative dimension to the study of health behaviour, in order that it can
be more deeply understood and subject to more successful interventions.
Some, however, would argue that such developments in critical health
psychology simply involve a more sophisticated attempt to increase existing 'technologies of power and surveillance' within health psychology, thus
constituting a 'qualitative change in the microphysics of power' (Poster,
cited in Osborne 1995).

A critical agenda – asking questions, not necessarily promoting solutions

All of these issues lead us to further questions regarding the role of psychology generally and, more specifically, the role of health psychology in
contemporary society. Is it the role of the health psychologist to operate
in the manner of a government lackey, administering technical solutions
to society's problems? Or is there, as most critical health psychologists
would argue, the need for a more academic and considered approach?
From this standpoint, a critical approach provides a means of stepping
back from the professional 'modernizing' tendency to rush in and do the
job. It introduces a much needed sense of caution, a heavy dose of modesty
and a proper academic scepticism with regard to the limitations of our
knowledge.

Hence, from a critical health psychology perspective, a central aim is the
development of understanding, not necessarily the attempt to predict,
manage and control (although understanding could also be used in pursuit
of these objectives).

In keeping with other critical psychological perspectives, a critical health
psychology should not seek to settle matters relating to assumptions, social
values, and moralities, but should 'question the ways in which they are being
settled' (Rappaport and Stewart 1997: 305). Highlighting the value of questioning, a critical approach 'seeks to name the questions rather than to
provide the answers', encouraging health psychologists to 'ask questions
about the meaning and functions of our own work' (p. 303). This book is
based on the premise that such an attempt to develop a deeper, more academic study of health psychology is much needed in a discipline dominated
by the modernizing administrative mentality.

Chapter summary

By the end of this chapter you should understand the following issues and concepts:

◆ The two main approaches to health psychology: 'mainstream' (scientific) approaches and 'critical' (hermeneutic) approaches.
◆ The importance of critical health psychology's focus on reflexivity, meaning, language, and connections between health, identity and morality.
◆ The tendency of mainstream health psychology to reduce questions of health and illness to instrumental, technical problems of management and control – and the problems with this.
◆ Mainstream health psychology's tendency to perpetuate and feed into the problems of contemporary society.
◆ The possibility of integration and rapprochement between mainstream and critical health psychology approaches.

Discussion points

◆ Mainstream health psychology perpetuates the problems of contemporary society by reinforcing individualism and alienation. Discuss.
◆ Are mainstream and critical health psychology approaches mutually exclusive? To what extent can they be used in tandem? Outline some of the main advantages and disadvantages of attempting to achieve such rapprochement.

Key reading

Crossley, M. (2000a) *Self, Trauma and the Construction of Meaning*, Chapter 1. Buckingham: Open University Press.
Ogden, J. (1996) *Health Psychology*, Chapter 1, pp. 1–9. Buckingham: Open University Press.
Prilleltensky, I. and Fox, D. (1997) Introducing critical psychology: values, assumptions and the status quo, Chapter 1, pp. 3–21, in D. Fox and I. Prilleltensky (eds) *Critical Psychology: An Introduction*. London: Sage.
Radley, A. (1994) *Making Sense of Illness: The Social Psychology of Health and Disease*, Chapter 1. London: Sage.

Yardley, L. (1997) (ed.) *Material Discourses of Health and Illness*, Chapters 1 and 2. London: Routledge.

Further reading

Any other introductory chapter in a 'mainstream health' psychology text, e.g. Sarafino (1994) or Sheridan and Radmacher (1992).

Health and illness in contemporary society

Introduction

In the last chapter we looked at some of the major differences associated with the two main theoretical approaches in contemporary health psychology. It is important to emphasize, however, that the academic study of health psychology does not exist in a vacuum. Rather, the developments, changes and critiques taking place within the discipline are related to debates in other academic disciplines (such as sociology), changes in various professions (such as nursing, health promotion and medicine) and wider economic, social and cultural changes. In Britain, for example, the restructuring of the National Health Service (NHS) has been particularly pertinent to these developments. The aim of this chapter is to present an overview of these forces with a view to locating contemporary approaches to health psychology within their relevant context.

In addition, it is also important to highlight the fact that, from a critical perspective, the social, economic and historical context of healthcare is intrinsic to people's experiences of health and illness. Understanding this context is not just peripheral to what is perceived as the 'real' substantive matter of health psychology from within a mainstream approach. This notion perpetuates the scientific rhetoric that the findings of health psychology remain largely independent of context, value-free, and can be imported from one culture to another without problems. Hence, the social and cultural changes discussed in this chapter are not just interesting background material. Rather, they present a crucial framework through which health and ilnesss are experienced and constituted in contemporary Britain. The way in which these cultural changes are manifested in various dimensions of health and illness will be charted over the course of this book.

Background

Developments in both the practical context of healthcare provision (such as health reforms in the NHS) and the academic study of health psychology, reflect broader intertwined transformations in culture and the economy. These transformations are sometimes referred to as the shift from 'modernism' to 'late' or 'post' modernism, or alternatively, the shift from 'Fordism' to 'post-Fordism' (Nettleton 1996: 214).

The term 'modernism' is often used to describe the modern age which, from a Marxist perspective, is the historical period following the Middle Ages. Some other social theorists use the term modernity in opposition to 'traditional' or less developed societies (Best and Kellner 1991: 2). Modernity refers to a variety of economic, political, social and cultural transformations. It can be characterized by the changes in society which came about through the process of industrialization and advancing capitalism, sometimes referred to as 'modernization' – a term denoting processes of individualization, secularization (the decline in religion), commodification (the dominance of market value), urbanization, bureaucratization and rationalization (the celebration of 'reason' as the source of progress in knowledge and society). All of these processes have together constituted the modern world.

Postmodernity, as its name suggests, describes the period following modernity (sometimes also referred to as the period of 'high modernity'). We are allegedly living in the postmodern era now. The beginning of the postmodern era can be located historically towards the end of the 1970s and is characterized by the increasing proliferation of hi-tech developments such as computers, the internet, virtual reality and hyperspace, all of which create the capacity for new forms of communication and knowledge, and consequent changes in social and economic formations.

The related notion of a shift from a 'Fordist' to a 'post-Fordist' culture refers to the way in which economic production is organized and the social, political and cultural consequences of this (Nettleton 1996: 216). For instance, a Fordist regime of production is one which, like Henry Ford's original black car, engages in mass production of a standardized product which is matched by equal levels of mass consumption. The production process is 'large-scale, inflexible and capital intensive . . . characterized by rigid hierarchical and bureaucratic management structures' (p. 216). By contrast, post-Fordism is characterized by production techniques which are designed to respond to consumer demand and increasingly fragmented market tastes.

The focus on consumerism is very important because it highlights the fact that the production of goods and services no longer focuses on catering for *needs*, but instead emphasizes *preference* and *consumer satisfaction* (Bury 1998: 4). In the light of such diversified consumption, it is perhaps not surprising that the social and cultural context of postmodernity produces changes in psychological experience, creating a new sense of space and time, and new modes of experience and culture (Giddens 1991).

These transformations in economic, cultural, social and psychological life are important to our analysis of health, illness and medicine in contemporary British society. In terms of the provision of health services, for instance, since the 1970s this has shifted from mass universal needs being met by monolithic, paternalistic, professionally led bureaucracies, to a situation of welfare pluralism, quasi-markets and consumer sovereignty (Nettleton 1996). In addition, the role of health, illness and medicine has taken on increasing salience over the last few decades in a manner which has contributed to the refashioning of contemporary culture, self and society (Bury 1998: 5). One of the main aims of this chapter is to highlight the ways in which three processes central to the transformations of modern society, and pointing towards the development of postmodernity, are reflected in changes in the delivery, planning, researching and experiences of health and illness. These three processes, which will each be addressed in turn, consist of 'objectification', 'rationalization' and 'subjectification' (p. 2).

Objectification and the biomedical model

One of the central processes associated with modernism is that of 'objectification'. This refers to a process in which 'forms of knowledge originally embedded within everyday life become progressively separated and subjected to specialist development' (Featherstone 1992: 162). In terms of medicine and health-related professions, processes of objectification are apparent in so far as the development of expertise in various professions tends to sequestrate (take away) medicine and health from everyday life and practices, transferring it into an 'object' of medical (or related health professional) discourse.

The dominant biomedical model underlying medical training and practice has often been used to highlight the nature and implications of such 'objectifying' processes. As we saw in Chapter 1, the biomedical model can be characterized as one in which the study of disease is reduced to narrowly defined biological, chemical, cellular or genetic factors which cause physical changes in the body. This view of medicine can be seen as 'the culmination of a long-term socio-historical process characterized by – and given impetus by – tensions existing at the levels of both practical application and philosophical abstraction' (Cooper et al. 1996: 5).

During the sixteenth century, for instance, medical knowledge was founded on a classical education which incorporated both classical texts on anatomy and physiology and a knowledge and understanding of philosophy. This reflected the importance of philosophical theories for the development and understanding of medical practice. In the contemporary medical curriculum, however, these philosophical aspects have largely lost their significance. 'Over the years there has been a trend towards skill and away from wisdom, towards training and away from education' (Charlton 1993: 476). Charlton argued that the scientific focus underpinning contemporary medical education has led to a situation in which doctors have a single mode of thought characterized as the 'medical morality' (Cooper *et al.* 1996: 6). Although such medical morality is undoubtedly valuable, at the same time, it limits the doctor in his/her ability to practise humanely. As Kleinman, himself a medical doctor, has argued, the ability to practise humanely (through listening to people's experiences of illness) constitutes 'a core task of doctoring' which has been 'atrophied in biomedical training' (Kleinman 1988: xiii). An unintended outcome of this transformation of the medical care system is that it drives the practitioner's attention away from the experience of illness. Frank (1991), an academic who has himself had cancer, develops Kleinman's argument by illustrating that the dominant biomedical model operates not just to divert the physician's attention away from the experience of illness and suffering, but also the patient's (see Chapter 5).

The hegemony (dominance) of biomedical knowledge was firmly established with the ascendancy of scientific techniques and methods in medicine during the mid- to late eighteenth century. It gained increasing influence with the advent of laboratory science and 'germ theory' towards the end of the nineteenth century, both of which were instrumental in achieving control over contagious diseases (Cooper *et al.* 1996: 6). The development of 'cell theories' provided a context in which disease could be understood, leading King (1982: 297) to argue that progresses in bacteriology probably did more to underscore the importance of science in medicine than any other advance. Hence began a process of formalization of the biomedical model as medical schools increasingly incorporated this new scientific representation of disease into their teaching. This formalization reached its peak in the mid-twentieth century. From then on, perceived from the standpoint of the biomedical model:

> healthy people become manifestations of healthy cellular activity; ill people become manifestations of dysfunctional cellular (i.e. bacteriological) activity. The patient becomes a 'problem' to be solved, and the solution to that problem lies in adopting a scientific, mechanistic approach that precludes any consideration of social, psychological or behavioural influences.
>
> (Cooper *et al.* 1996: 7)

Thus the formalization of the biomedical model served to objectify disease in a manner which reduced it to the physical structures of pathological anatomy, disregarding the experiential features of 'illness' located in the patient's individual biography. As Spiro (1986: 5), himself a doctor, has argued, laboratory medicine turns the physician into a scientist studying the cell and its subcellular, DNA structure and processes, rather than looking and listening to the patient.

But how has medicine gained such power to define and construct the nature of disease in this way? Some Marxist perspectives associate the rise of the medical (and other professions) with the emergence of capitalism (Johnson 1977; Navarro 1978). From this perspective, the key to professional autonomy and power is the ability, as a monopoly producer, to define and satisfy the needs of the consumer in a manner that appears altruistic. This ability increases the greater the distance is between provider and consumer in terms of resources and knowledge. As patients have no organized and universal knowledge base (enshrined in examination and registration requirements), they are unable to counter the power of doctors (or other professions). Hence, 'the uncertainty of lay knowledge compared to the coherence of medical expertise compounds the inequalities of power between them' (Hardey 1998: 70).

Professions are, of course, dependent on the state for their social position. Unlike other occupations, however, professions 'are deliberately granted autonomy, including the exclusive right to determine who can legitimately do its work and how the work should be done' (Freidson 1970: 56). This autonomy is established as a result of competition with other occupations. In practice, the state leaves 'technical' or clinical matters to the jurisdiction of the profession (Hardey 1998: 69). For example, in Britain, the General Medical Council (GMC) performs this role, providing medicine with considerable scope to organize and set its own work and standards. Once a profession is established, it continues to patrol the boundaries of its work and develop strategies to retain or further exert professional dominance (Hardey 1998: 69). For instance, medicine, like any other producer, has been able to foster its monopoly by controlling the supply of new doctors into the profession, which in turn helps to legitimate relatively high status and salaries. Similarly, Lawrence (1995) has argued that medicine is a 'bounded profession' in so far as, historically, the medical profession has marginalized practitioners who have not conformed with the dominant biomedical view of disease and illness. Hence, 'marginal medicine' became precisely that, 'marginal to the dominant theories and approaches of an increasingly assertive and "bounded" group of highly organised experts' (Bury 1998: 7). (However, this is changing – see Chapter 7 on alternative medicine.) Moreover, in Britain, the National Health Service has played a significant role in consolidating the public dominance of medicine by placing the profession at the centre of public policy so that authority has both been sustained and circumscribed (Hardey 1998: 69).

The dominance of professions, particularly the medical profession, is also expressed and reinforced through what are sometimes called the 'micro-level' of medical encounters (Hardey 1998: 83). This includes everyday medical practices and interactions such as the consultant's 'ward round' in hospital. As Hardey (1998) argues, this has long been an expression of power over medical students, nurses and patients. An Audit Commission report published in 1993, for instance, found that patients often felt insecure in asking questions and that they often did not get sufficiently good quality information from medical encounters (Hardey 1998: 84).

None of this is to argue that individual doctors are to be held responsible for the objectification associated with the hegemony of biomedical culture. As Martin (1993: 13) argues, medical culture has a powerful system of socialization that exacts conformity as the price of participation. It is also a cultural system whose ideas and practices pervade popular culture and in which we all participate to some extent. In addition, it is also important to note that the application of science to medicine was originally intended as a progressive move, as part of a political reform movement which attacked the authority of élite physicians and the aristocracy in general. As such, at the time of its inception, medical thought was allied with 'progressive bourgeois approaches to new technologies' (Bury 1998: 6). For instance, despite contemporary critiques of hospitals as 'depersonalizing' and 'objectifying institutions', the development of hospitals originally formed an important part of the attempt to democratize medicine, 'a new kind of medical space . . . attuned to the revolutionary dream of "medicine in liberty"' (Osborne 1995: 38). Nevertheless, reflecting one of the central processes of modernism, medical professionalization led to a process of objectification in which the individual patient or lay person was rendered largely 'invisible and obliged to be passive in the face of expert advice' (Bury 1998: 8). Central to these developments, was a sense of 'separation', 'differentiation' and loss of meaning (p. 8). As with all dominant approaches, however, this conception of disease and medical practice harboured within it the seeds of its own challenge.

Deconstructing the biomedical model

During the 1970s academic discourse, particularly social constructionist theories emerging in sociology (see Berger and Luckman 1967), argued that what we take to be 'fact', 'knowledge' and 'reality', are a result of interactions between people and their interpretations of these interactions. Through language and social practice 'the world is ordered into objects that are apprehended as reality, and then internalised again as objective truth' (Radley 1994: 33). Our common sense and scientific knowledge about health, illness and disease come about through social constructions mediated through social relations, comprising examples of what Berger and Luckman (1967) described as 'objectifications of the social world'. As Lupton makes clear, this does not mean that disease and illness do not exist, but that these states and experiences are known and interpreted via social activity and should therefore be examined using social and cultural analysis

(Lupton 1994: 11). This is especially required given the powerful role played by medical knowledge (backed up by powerful medical practices and institutional structures) in contemporary understandings of health and disease. The power of medicine to define reality of disease has led us to experience 'this knowledge not as constructed, but as objective, as if it came from elsewhere than the social world' (Radley 1994: 33). This is what Berger and Luckman refer to as the experience of *reification*.

These kinds of approaches began to challenge the biomedical model's assumption of its own objectivity and the very possibility of 'objective knowledge', thus calling into question the fundamental assumptions on which the biomedical model was based and moving the debate towards an exploration of the value-laden nature of the biomedical model. Much of this work had a distinctly 'anti-medical' flavour. For instance, Zola (1977) argued critically against three fundamental values which underlay 'medical science': 'activism', 'instrumentalism' and 'worldliness'. 'Activism' is a value which reflects medicine's powerful need to *act on* the body and the environment rather than to *adjust* to bodily and environmental changes. Closely related to this, 'instrumentalism' refers to the notion that the practitioner must be seen to be doing something, anything, if his/her credibility is to be maintained. Hence it is preferable to write a prescription for medication rather than send the patient out of the surgery with nothing to show for his/her visit. As Spiro (1986: 4) argues, one reason for the overuse of technology in medicine comes from the emphasis during training that 'an answer can be found for everything if the physician will only look far and deep enough, and with enough instruments'. Finally, 'worldliness' refers to the fact that medicine exhibits a preference for secular, as opposed to religious/spiritual explanations and responses to illness.

This 'anti-medical' position finds expression in some contemporary research influenced by the work of French historian and philosopher Michel Foucault (although Foucault himself did not necessarily intend his work to be critical of medicine). Here, one finds a critique of the 'objectifying gaze' of medicine which brings patients under the control of the powerful expert and monopoly of the medical profession. Only the doctor can know the truth about illness through the language of disease. Accordingly, the patient becomes passive, a 'docile body' in Foucault's terms, caught in the web of medical knowledge and power (Bury 1998: 7). Strong anti-medical themes are also evident in postmodern approaches to health such as Fox's (1993) who, with strong echoes of Zola, defines medicine as a characteristically 'modernist' enterprise in which there is an 'unacknowledged will to mastery' (p. 122). Feminist critics such as Oakley (1984) and Martin (1993) have similarly emphasized the way in which contemporary medicine increasingly monopolizes womens' bodies, especially in relation to reproductive health, 'sequestrating' childbirth from the everyday world of women and lay practices, resulting in a 'destructive travesty of parenthood' (Martin 1993).

It is important to note that not all perspectives influenced by social constructionist arguments necessarily endorse such 'anti-medical' critiques. For instance, some critical approaches to health psychology (which are influenced by social constructionism, as we saw in the last chapter) are more critical of biomedical approaches than others. The most important implication of such approaches is that they have 'provided a way of freeing ourselves from the everyday assumptions (reifications) of medicine' (Radley 1994: 33). This allows a shift from the position of biomedicine as *the* way of understanding health and illness, towards the existence of multiple models.

Another important point to note is the fact that challenges to the monopolizing power of medicine and the biomedical model have not been confined to academic debates, but have also gained ground in other professions such as nursing (Cooper *et al.* 1996), health psychology (as we have already discussed in Chapter 1), 'alternative' forms of medical treatment (see Chapter 7) and 'alternative' modes of care such as palliative care (see Chapter 8). The conceptions of disease and illness promoted within these various perspectives have not just been the result of altruistic practitioners campaigning for the 'good' of the patient. Just as the medical profession managed to gain monopoly power over the definition and treatment of disease through the development of resources and knowledge institutionalized and circumscribed through professional organizations and structures (e.g. entrance exams, registration requirements), so too has nursing attempted to professionalize over the course of this century (Cooper *et al.* 1996).

Similarly, the fact that psychology as a discipline has tried so desperately to define itself as a 'natural science', and the related fact that it is so wedded to scientific method and quantitative forms of investigation and analysis, can be understood in the context of psychology's attempt to professionalize this century. In a society that places such high value on the methodology of science, the practice of anything recognized as belonging to that category reflects positively on the prestige and social status of the practitioner. Hence, developing their investigative practices in this way has been a means whereby psychologists have sought to establish and improve their own status as professionals and as scientists (Danziger 1990: 119).

Likewise, the development of specialist areas of medicine such as palliative care constitutes an attempt to increase professional autonomy and power by defining the palliative care profession as a monopoly producer in terms of the definition and satisfaction of the needs of the terminally ill 'consumer'. In this way the professions carve out and ensure a stake in the future market economy of healthcare.

Rationalization and health reforms in the National Health Service

This notion of a 'market economy of healthcare' points towards a shift from modernism to post-modernism in so far as it hints at the breakdown of a health service led by monolithic, paternalistic, professionally led bureaucracies (characteristic of modernism's objectifying processes), towards a situation of welfare pluralism, quasi-markets and consumer sovereignty (characteristic of 'postmodernity'). This leads us to a consideration of the second process central to the transformation of modern society – *rationalization* – which involves 'the gradual adoption of a calculating attitude towards more and more aspects of life' (Lyon 1994: 24). Rationalization has been defined as a process by which significant changes are made in established arrangements in resource allocation and organizational structure, and the criteria and objectives of service provision (Flynn 1992: 4). Rationalization is also related to increasing bureaucratization which marks a shift from modernity to postmodernity.

The process of rationalization is manifest in the so-called 'restructuring' of the National Health Service (NHS) in Britain which began in the late 1980s. This refers to a series of changes in the culture and organization of the NHS which has incorporated new corporate planning procedures, the enforcement of cash limits, performance indicators, compulsory tendering for contracts, efficiency savings, the hiving-off of statutory services, greater use of marketing and consumer-relations techniques, a challenge to professional dominance and the formation of an enterprise culture (Nettleton 1996: 215). At the centre of these developments has been the incorporation of 'market principles' and a climate of market competition partly created by the NHS and Community Care Act (1989). The intention and implementation of this Act were to reduce distinctions between NHS, voluntary and private sector provision of healthcare. As a result 'purchasers' of healthcare now contract for services, encouraging all sectors to compete on equal terms for funding. Hence, successful bidders are likely to be those offering the most cost-effective care of the highest standard (Butler 1992; Clark 1993).

The introduction of market principles into the NHS is sometimes referred to as the creation of an internal or managed market because it involved a separating out of the roles of purchasers and providers of healthcare. This purchaser–provider split was achieved by setting up NHS Trusts to take responsibility for the management of hospital and community services (the providers). By contrast, health authorities were accorded the responsibility of purchasing services for the people living in their areas (hence, the purchasers). Primary care also experienced radical changes in so far as some general practitioners became independent fundholders, which basically meant that, like the health authorities, GPs became purchasers of services on behalf of the clients attached to their practice. These purchasers can buy services from NHS providers, the voluntary or private sector. In this competitive climate it is not surprising that service providers are today being forced to become much clearer about what exactly they are offering and to engage in assessments of the quality and auditing of their services.

This climate of market competition has been related to increasing patient consumerism. For instance, the 1990 contract for general practitioners (DOH 1989b), the White Paper *Working for Patients* (DOH 1989a) and *The Patient's Charter* (DOH 1991) all espouse the principles of consumerism, indicating that patients are customers with implicit purchasing power (Hardey 1998: 84). As Nettleton (1996) argues, the NHS Management Executive have incorporated these principles of post-Fordist consumerism into their marketing strategies with the slogan 'Everything we do is driven by you'. And under the internal market, purchasers of healthcare (health authorities and GP fundholders) have been given the responsibility for meeting the needs of the population they serve in ways that are open to public scrutiny for the first time in the history of the service (Doyal 1998: 12).

Part of the purchasing process requires purchasers to carry out needs assessments in order to determine the needs of the community they serve. As this process involves consultation with various community groups, it is another way in which individuals and groups are given the opportunity 'to have their voices heard by those who can take action on their behalf' (p. 13). Providers of services (NHS Trusts, voluntary and private sector agencies) are thus being forced to rationalize their activities in a manner which facilitates the development of services in ways that are more sensitive and appropriate to the needs of users (Doyal 1998: 12). Following on from earlier developments, the annual planning document for the NHS as a whole, *Priorities and Planning Guidance for 1996–1997*, clearly emphasizes the importance of 'lay voices', recommending that health authorities should 'give greater voice and influence to users of NHS services locally and the development of NHS policy both nationally and locally' (NHS Executive 1995). In a similar vein, the Labour government is in the process of broadening the composition of health authority and Trust boards in favour of greater local community representation and to transforming Community Health Councils into 'Local Health Advocates'. The membership of the latter is intended to reflect the interests of the community, to provide a means whereby health authority plans can be scrutinized and to ensure that patients' views are heard (Milewa *et al.* 1998: 509).

Accordingly, it could be argued that the 'restructuring process' has increased the importance of the 'lay voice' and opened up possibilities for developing services more sensitive to the varied needs of NHS users (Doyal 1998: 12). In this way, traditional patterns of power and control have been partially disrupted and new mechanisms set up to express the views of the wider community (p. 4).

In particular, at the level of policy, these changes represent a challenge by the state to overt medical domination (Hardey 1998: 84). Patients are being redefined as experienced subjects who can contribute knowledge and take an active part in decisions (p. 84). In a classic post-Fordist move, health service provision is no longer being determined by *need* (as defined by a monopoly medical profession) but is instead focusing on *preference* and *consumer satisfaction* (Bury 1998: 4). Medical dominance is also being challenged with the rise of 'evidence-based medicine' which, as part of the move towards greater effectiveness and efficiency, involves rapid growth in the monitoring and evaluation of clinical practice. As Doyal (1998) argues, such developments have particular significance for groups such as women because historically 'some of the most serious examples of ineffective treatment have been inflicted on female patients' (p. 12). For instance, as a direct result of the monitoring and evaluation of clinical practice, many fewer women have radical mastectomies. Likewise, the value of continuing to perform large numbers of hysterectomies has been widely questioned (Coulter *et al.* 1988). And many aspects of the new obstetrics have also been criticized both for their ineffectiveness and potential damage to mothers and babies (Doyal 1998: 12).

The move towards greater medical accountability and the reduction of medicine's monopoly power may, at first glance, appear as a positive and democratizing shift. However, it is important to come back to the point that the process of rationalization goes hand-in-hand with increasing bureaucratization. This means that the reduction in medical power is not necessarily transferred to lay people (although they may play a greater role in defining need due to the process of needs assessments) but to other professional groups such as health service management.

The restructuring of the NHS has represented a radical shift in forms of management. From the 1960s to 1983, management of the health service operated in accordance with a 'diplomacy model' (Harrison *et al.* 1990). In this model the Health Service Manager's role was not to lead or change the direction of the Health Service, but to smooth out conflicts and enable professionals to get on with the job of caring for patients (Nettleton 1996: 218). One of the key characteristics of this model was that doctors had more influence than managers in so far as they had clinical freedom to make decisions about individual patients. Hence, through the aggregation of their decisions, they determined the shape of the service (p. 218). The 1980s, however, witnessed the displacement of the diplomacy style of management with the emergence of a 'new managerialism'. Emulating private-sector style management, this has been characterized as 'more interventionist, dynamic and innovative' (p. 218). This style of management was endorsed by the Griffiths report (DHSS 1983), the outcome of a review of management in the NHS conducted by a team of business leaders. Griffiths, managing director of Sainsbury's supermarkets, led the team which concluded that 'private sector' styles of management were needed in the NHS. In particular, there was a need for 'continuous evaluation of performance against defined objectives, outputs and standards' (Nettleton 1996: 218).

This new style of management has meant that the structures of control in the NHS have shifted from a form of medical autonomy towards more management control. This has enabled the government to tackle directly the dilemma of how to impose its political priorities on an organization in which professional judgement has historically determined the local delivery of services (Cousins, cited in Nettleton 1996: 219). The ethos and practice of the new managerialism has therefore facilitated the implementation of central government objectives (p. 221). Of course, this attempt to shift the boundaries of control from medicine to management has not been achieved without resistance from doctors. However, the rise of the 'audit' society, by which is meant an infiltration of all kinds of monitoring activities in the form of measures of activities and outputs, may be gradual, increasing incrementally over time and therefore not necessarily resisted when introduced. Nevertheless, such auditing procedures 'represent a radical departure from previous arrangements concerning professional autonomy, because they entail managerial encroachment on the determination of work content, productivity, resource use and quality standards' (Flynn 1992: 183). These disruptions to traditional patterns of medical power and domination are sometimes referred to as a process of 'proletarianization' in which doctors are increasingly losing control over the context and content of medical work due to the bureaucratization and corporatization of healthcare (Hardey 1998: 84). In the United States, similar processes are characterized as 'deprofessionalization' (Haug 1988).[1]

Audit is frequently justified on the grounds that it 'empowers popular control' (i.e. users of health services) in so far as those who use public resources (such as doctors) are placed under scrutiny. But it is important to clarify the dominant theoretical models on which such evaluating processes are based before such populist messages are endorsed. As Nettleton points out, many of the central concerns of the new managerialism – audit, accountability, organizational rationality and efficiency – have been given concrete expression and academic legitimacy with the rise of an emergent occupational group, health economists (Nettleton 1996: 221).

The goal of health economists is to introduce 'economic rationality' into the NHS. To this end a whole series of economic style cost–benefit measures have been introduced such as Quality Assurance (QA), Performance Indicators (PIs), Diagnostic Related Groups (DRGs) and Quality Adjusted Life Years (QALYs). All of these measures are based on and developed in relation to the theoretical 'rational model' of the individual presupposed by health economy research. Such models, culled from economic theory, are also frequently appropriated by mainstream health psychology as a way of predicting people's behaviour.[2] This model of the individual presupposes that s/he will make the most efficient use of available resources to maximize the attainment of given ends. Critical approaches generally regard such models as a naïve and simplistic way of explaining and understanding human action. Perhaps more important to point out at this stage, however, is the implicit assumption within such models that successful clinical 'outcomes' can be defined largely in terms of economic rationality. Such assumptions carry within them the potential of squandering non-quantifiable action which, in terms of medical practice, may be that which is most humane. These are some of the problems encountered as clinical freedom is progressively circumscribed by bureaucratic assessment.

Whereas objectifying processes and the rise of professional expertise (medical dominance) separated key areas of experience from everyday life, 'the rationalizing process re-enters the everyday world and infuses it with a new and powerful dynamic' (Bury 1998: 9). This is because expert knowledge is 'fed back in order to rationalise, colonise and homogenise everyday life' (Featherstone 1992: 162). In terms of contemporary medicine, this means, as Armstrong argues, that medicine has moved out from its 'citadel' in the hospital and clinic (in which it objectified the patient's body and experience of illness) to survey normal populations (Armstrong 1994). Such movement 'signifies a broadening of medicine's remit beyond its original "objectifying" tendency to a new "postmodern" set of processes' (Bury 1998: 12). The development of professions such as health economics and mainstream health psychology have been part of this postmodern process in which medicine has extended its gaze to include not just the patterning of disease (i.e. pathological bodies) but also the investigation of the healthy population for early signs of abnormality. As Bury argues, scientific methods and powerful statistical techniques therefore go beyond the examination of medical cases to the study of an endless array of 'normal' processes (p. 10). This is manifest in the proliferation of concepts such as 'well being', 'quality of life' and 'life satisfaction' which, since the 1960s, have entered the social and medical lexicon in the attempt to measure virtually all aspects of experience.

The important point to note here is that not only do such processes result in an extension of the surveillance potential of medical science but, perhaps more importantly, everyday life itself undergoes a powerful transformation through such rationalizing processes (p. 11). In the face of monopolistic medical provision, the individual is reduced to a passive or docile patient who is accorded minimal voice in his/her illness and treatment. However, as we have seen in the case of health reforms in Britain, as rationalizing and measuring processes proliferate (in the form of the 'new managerialism' and the rise of professions such as health psychology and health economy), there is a shift towards seeing the patient as an active consumer. This has the implication that 'health rather than illness becomes the watchword . . . as more and more areas of life become subject to rational calculation and choice' (p. 11). Through this process, lay people come to absorb expert knowedge and attempt to organize their lives in a manner whereby they actively choose healthy lifestyles in order to minimize health risks. As will become apparent in Chapter 3, the focus on lifestyle and health-related behaviours such as smoking, alcohol consumption, drug use, food, diet, exercise and sex, constitutes one example of the way in which everyday life has become subject to the expertise of professions allied to medicine such as health psychology.

Subjectification

This leads us on to a consideration of the third process integral to the transformation of contemporary society, that of 'subjectification'. The extension of the medical gaze into everyday life tends to complicate the object, the focus of medical and health-related investigations. That is to say, the more the lay person is enjoined to be active in calculating and acting on health-related risks, 'the more a complicated form of subjectivity comes to the fore' (Bury 1998: 12). Whereas modernist medicine could rely on professional expertise and the docile body, the proliferation of health-related information and practices tends to create individuals who are less willing to believe in the authoritative voice of science and are more actively resistant to professionally defined knowledge and interventions. Such transformations are particularly important for understanding the rise of critical approaches to health psychology. If mainstream health psychology can be characterized as part and parcel of the 'rationalizing' processes of modernism, then critical approaches can similarly be seen as bound up with the 'subjectifying' processes of postmodernism, the proliferation of voices and widespread scepticism regarding the dominance and authority of scientific and professional ways of defining reality.

Numerous researchers have argued that 'postmodernity' has created a characteristic sense of personal identity and selfhood (see Taylor 1989; Giddens 1991; Smith 1994; Crossley 2000a). These arguments have an important bearing on our experiences of health and illness in contemporary Western society in comparison with earlier periods such as the 1950s–1970s. Taylor, for instance, argues that in modernist times, people lived within 'unchallengeable frameworks' of meaning in which courses of action were decided in accordance with what can be characterized as a 'substantive' definition of rationality and morality. Basically, this meant that people's sense of the 'good' was perceived in terms of its alliance with a pre-existent order created by God or, in more recent times, in accordance with scientific truth and reality. Accordingly, during earlier periods of the twentieth century, the medical profession, based firmly within a biomedical scientific agenda, exercised monopoly control over the definition and meaning of 'disease', creating seemingly 'unchallengable frameworks' of meaning (see Cooper et al. 1996; Hardey 1998). From this biomedical perspective, any 'meanings' accorded to illness by the patient were deemed largely irrelevant and the patient was encouraged to be a passive and docile object for medical examination and treatment (Kleinman 1988).

In postmodern societies, by contrast, our 'frameworks of meaning' have themselves become problematic. Most of us live with a sense that *the* framework of meaning no longer exists. This is partly related to the decline in religion and traditional institutions and partly to the rise of the modern capitalist economy (see also Lasch 1980, 1984; Holifield 1983; Bellah *et al.* 1985; Cushman 1990; Giddens 1991; McLeod 1997: 1–27). The implication is that, in contrast to the 'substantive' order of rationality and morality characteristic of earlier times, today we live with a more procedural and reflexive model in which our action is judged in terms of the standards by which we and the community to which we belong, construct, rather than discover, order (Taylor 1989: 156). Our lives take on the 'object of a quest' (see McIntyre 1981) in so far as we continuously try to negotiate and *make* its meaning while traversing our various roads.

As we have already seen in this chapter, over the past twenty years or so, rapid changes in economy, society and culture, manifest in the health arena through massive health reforms, have served to challenge biomedical dominance and led to the redefinition of patients as experienced subjects who can contribute knowledge and take an active part in decisions (Hardey 1998: 84). Here we witness a classic move from a substantive order of rationality and morality, where supreme faith was placed in medicine and science, to a breakdown in such faith and the related move towards a procedural model in which subjectivity and reflexivity come to play a far greater role.

There are basically two opposing strands of thought regarding the increasing subjectification and reflexivity accompanying experiences of health and illness. These have already been touched upon very briefly in Chapter 1. On the one hand, some researchers welcome this postmodern move, optimistically celebrating difference and possibility, and highlighting the importance of individual agency. On the other hand, other researchers are more sceptical, viewing increasing subjectification as a sign of deepening organization and surveillance in contemporary experiences of health and illness, through which the possibility of agency and freedom is minimized (Bury 1998: 16). The following outline aims to depict the main contours of these two strands of thought in more detail.

Representing the more pessimistic point of view with regard to these changes, it has been argued that the focus on subjectivity and reflexivity constitutes an important indicator of the way in which the operation of power has shifted in contemporary society. In order to appreciate these arguments, it is necessary to elaborate on what these researchers, inspired by the work of Foucault, actually mean by 'power'. For Foucault, modern power is non-authoritarian, non-conspiratorial and non-orchestrated. Yet it produces and normalizes bodies to serve prevailing relations of domination and subordination (Bordo 1993: 26). In order to understand this new conception of power it is necessary to understand an important conceptual change. We must stop thinking of power as the possession of individual groups – as something people have. Instead, it must be seen as a dynamic or network of non-centralized forces. Hence, power is sustained not from above, but through multiple processes of different origin and scattered location which serve to regulate the most intimate and minute elements of the construction of space, time, desire and embodiment. When power works from below in this way, dominant forms of morality and selfhood are maintained through individual self-surveillance and self-correction to norms. As Foucault argues: 'There is no need for arms, physical violence, medical constraints. Just a gaze. An inspecting gaze, a gaze which each individual under its weight, will end by interiorising to the point that he is his own overseer, each individual thus exercising this surveillance over, and against himself' (Foucault, cited in Bordo 1993: 303).

Hence, some researchers argue that the current focus on health and health promotion (see Chapter 3), encouraging us to find out information and act on knowledge concerning healthy diets, environmental stressors, and various forms of biological, mental and ecological preservation, constitutes a new form of power over individuals which, rather than undermining medical dominance, actually serves to reinforce it (Armstrong 1987). This can be seen in the way in which professions such as health psychology develop in alliance with medicine, aiming to facilitate the pursuit of bio-medically defined agendas by adding a psychological dimension to the study of disease. Likewise, the current critique of such approaches, represented by various forms of critical health psychology, which aim to enhance the understanding of lay experiences of health and illness, can be seen as an increasingly elaborated professional discourse which stands 'in no absolute or necessary opposition to medical enlightenment itself' (Osborne 1995: 42). The appeals to subjectivity in these approaches can be viewed as ushering in a new form of power and domination, in Bury's terms (1998: 13) a 'pastoral power'. In this context, it is possible to see how 'medicine has become a privileged site . . . for the pursuit of enlightened subjectivity in general' (Osborne 1995: 43). Hence, it is argued, what is at stake here 'is . . . not the antinomy of the medical model so much as a deepening of the probity of clinical rationality' (p. 42). According to such arguments, critical approaches, in their attempt to increase understanding of the individual and his/her relationship to society in relation to health issues, involve a qualitative advance in the 'technologies of surveillance' and thus 'a qualitative change in the microphysics of power' (Poster, cited in Osborne 1995: 43).

Central to this process, as we have already seen in Chapter 1, is the way in which the skills and lives of lay people are undermined and encroached upon by various professions through a process of 'colonising the life-world' (Habermas 1987). Such professional infiltration is related to the conditions of late-modernity in which, according to theorists such as Lasch (1984), people are forced to make sense of themselves and their lives in contexts where they experience loss of a sense of history, continuity and feelings of belonging due to the decline in traditional institutions. This sense of loss leads to a sense of insecurity and is related to the rise of a 'cult of expertise' in which people become dependent on various professions and forms of therapy to survive the vicissitudes of the lonely, modern world. Such reliance creates what Lasch calls a 'culture of narcissism' or, in his more recent work, a 'culture of survivalism' in which people come to appropriate the 'rationality' underpinning various professional agendas (e.g. medicine, health promotion, counselling, social work) into their lives. It is useful at this point to recall the three key fundamental values characterizing 'modernist' professions such as medicine outlined earlier in this chapter – 'activism', 'instrumentalism' and 'worldliness'. Not surprisingly, given that medicine (and other professions) emerged in the context of capitalism, such rationality reflects the core values of capitalism and is imbued with notions of self-discipline, self-denial, self-control and willpower (Crawford 1984). The basic point of Lasch's argument is that the adoption of such professionally defined 'survivalist' strategies create 'minimalist' selves who, because of their lack of a sense of belongingness and community, have to reduce problems of life and health, often reflecting deeper existential, moral and ethical issues, to matters of administrative management.

Researchers such as Cushman (1990) and Crawford (1994) have highlighted the negative contours of such processes in relation to experiences of self and health, arguing that the increased concern with health and lifestyle (as promoted by professions such as health psychology and health promotion) results in 'privatized' consumerist individuals who are only interested in 'managing' their own health and well-being. This creates an environment in which issues of health and illness are perceived as largely divorced from wider social, moral and ethical considerations (see also Førde 1998). From this perspective, individuals are encouraged to see 'the project' of health in terms of self-determination alone, thus accentuating the potential for 'victim-blaming' and the perception of illness as largely the fault of the individual, something which could have been avoided if only health had been correctly maintained.

While acknowledging such possibilities, however, other researchers have put forward a less pessimistic view with regard to the contemporary structure of professions and power and their impact on individual experiences of self and health (see Giddens 1991; Beck 1992; Melucci 1996a, 1996b). Giddens, for instance, throws some doubt on Lasch's idea of the 'minimal self', arguing that this depiction of the negative features of contemporary selfhood is based on an inadequately passive conception of the human agent. This conception fails to take account of the fact that all human agents stand in a position of *appropriation* in relation to the social world, which is to say that they respond *reflexively* and *creatively* to the changes going on around them. Hence, although it is true that contemporary life may impoverish individual action (through lack of a sense of community and belongingness), it is also true that it creates greater opportunities and new possibilities for individuals that were not even conceivable in previous eras. Giddens extends this critique to what he sees as Lasch's overly negative interpretation of the rise of professional culture. The idea that the appropriation of professional forms of rationality simply creates 'management' type selves, lacking in depth, fails to appreciate the potentially empowering nature of individual involvement with professional interventions (such as therapy) which, ideally, enable individuals to respond creatively and reflexively to ongoing changes in their environments.

From this perspective, the rapid expansion of information and information exchange characteristic of late-modernity potentially facilitates a process of lay 're-skilling', rather than the more passive picture suggested by professional 'colonization'. This is especially the case in relation to health and illness because of the increasing expansion of health-related material aimed at 'consumers' by those in the mass media and health promotion. Added to this, the rise of the internet and the 'network society' (Castells 1996) potentiates immediate access to international health resources and to knowledge previously inaccessible to the lay public. Through e-mail and internet sites, lay people can get in touch with self-help and pressure groups and access information about alternative modes of treatment and therapies (see Chapters Six and Seven). In this way, the dependence of lay people on professions such as medicine and psychology can be reduced as they become increasingly knowledgeable and thus empowered to take control over their own health and illness.

Hence, far from the 'narcissistic' and moral closure predicted by theorists such as Lasch, Giddens argues that increased access to knowledge and information has led to a widespread resurgence of interest in moral, political and ethical affairs. This includes issues such as abortion, euthanasia, death, survival, trauma, terminal illness, disability, quality of life, animal rights, environmental activism, etc. – all of which engage with reflexive concerns related to life, self and the body. With specific regard to health and illness, they involve the kind of questions we shall repeatedly encounter throughout this book: how can or should a person live with terminal illness? Do I have the right to risk my life and health by engaging in risky behaviours? Do I have the right to risk the lives of others? Do I have the right to decide when I should die if I am afflicted by a terminal illness? These are all questions that Giddens characterizes as issues of 'life politics'. They are the kind of questions that only develop when a certain level of knowledge and certainty has been reached.

For instance, the question of whether or not I have the right to risk my own life by smoking comes about only when we have access to knowledge scientifically proving the relationship between smoking and increased mortality. Likewise, the kinds of questions asked by critical approaches to health psychology, critical as they are of mainstream health psychology, can only be asked because the latter, along with medical research, has provided a crucial basis for the technical and administrative management of disease. Nevertheless, from such a basis, more reflexive concerns regarding theory, philosophy, morality and ethics, as manifest in critical approaches, can and need to spring forth. It is only because psychology is fast becoming an increasingly administrative science, responding to the (health) management problems of contemporary society, that we need to stand back and ask whether this is appropriate. Is this all we demand of a psychological science? Or should we be expecting something more? The increasing concern with 'life political' issues characteristic of postmodern societies calls for a remoralizing of psychological and social issues related to health, and demands a renewed sensitivity to questions that have been undermined by the rationalizing processes of modernism.

Chapter summary

By the end of this chapter you should understand the following issues and concepts:

- The way in which contemporary approaches to health psychology are located in the wider social and economic context, e.g. the shift from modernism to postmodernism and the implications this has for experiences of health and illness.
- The three major processes central to the transformation of modern society, i.e.
  1 objectification
  2 rationalization
  3 subjectification
- The way in which these three processes are reflected in changes in the planning, delivery and researching of health and illness, e.g.
- Processes of objectification and the biomedical model.
- Rationalization and health reforms in the NHS. Challenges to medical control ('deprofessionalization') and the implications this has for the 'democratizing' of healthcare provision. NB: mainstream health psychology is connected to the 'rationalizing' process of 'modernism'.
- Subjectification – a more complicated subjectivity comes to the fore. Professional and scientific authority is no longer passively accepted by the public. NB: critical health psychology is connected to the subjectifying process of postmodernism.

Discussion points

◆ In what ways do the rationalizing changes introduced in the NHS challenge traditional structures of power and control in healthcare provision? Discuss the positive and negative implications of such changes.
◆ The postmodern shift towards increased subjectification and reflexivity creates the potential for a more 'democratic' form of healthcare and service delivery. Critically discuss.
◆ Outline the ways in which mainstream and critical health psychology connect with changes occurring in contemporary Western societies.
◆ Critical health psychology simply deepens the surveillance potential of health professionals and the State over lay people. Discuss.

Key reading

Bury, M. (1998) Postmodernity and health, pp. 1–29 in G. Scrambler and P. Higgs (eds) *Modernity, Medicine and Health*. London: Routledge.
Hardey, M. (1998) *The Social Context of Health*, Chapter 3, pp. 47–66. Buckingham: Open University Press.
Nettleton, S. (1996) *The Sociology of Health and Illness*, Chapter 8, pp. 194–227. Cambridge: Polity Press.

Further reading

NHS Executive (1995) *Priorities and Planning Guidelines, 1996–1997*. Leeds: NHS Executive.

Notes

1 It should be noted here that Freidson (1994) has argued against the proletarianization thesis in relation to the medical profession, on the grounds that it is not non-professional managers and bureaucrats involved in management, but actually members of the medical profession who are increasingly taking up managerial and administrative posts. In this way medical dominance is maintained. As Weiss and Fitzpatrick (1998: 317) point out, however, the accuracy of this prediction depends entirely on whether this new élite view their role as managers representing organizational and 'audit' objectives, or as professionals defending traditional professional values such as clinical autonomy.

2 Indeed, it is interesting to note that the September 1998 issue of *The Psychologist* contained three articles inciting psychologists and psychology graduates to become more involved in the process of NHS clinical audit (Baker and Firth-Cozens 1998; Cape and Hewer 1998; Hearnshaw and Robertson 1998). Here, we see psychology truly as an 'administrative science', conducting research solely in accordance with managerially defined objectives and in terms of its utility in specific administrative contexts (Danziger 1990: 105).

Rethinking psychological approaches to health promotion

In a state of shock we went up to the foetal medicine department where a doctor talked to us about a foetal blood test with a 1 in 100 chance of inducing miscarriage balanced against the 1 in 250 chance that the cysts indicated something nasty. As odds went they were reasonable ones and had I been standing in the bookie's thinking about putting money on a healthy baby there would have been no problem. But under the circumstances the odds were meaningless. In these situations all odds are the same odds, or rather, evens. Either the worst will happen or it won't: the baby will die or it won't. The odds always feel like 50:50.

And as it was then so it was for me now. Either they'd cure me [from cancer] or they wouldn't. Everything was 50:50. When the official odds were 92% they were really 50:50.

(Diamond 1998: 139)

Psychology and health promotion

Health promotion is based on the premise that the behaviours we engage in, and the circumstances in which we live, impact on our health. Over the last century, 'health behaviours' have played an increasingly important role in health and illness. About 50 per cent of premature deaths in Western countries can be attributed to lifestyle (Hamburg *et al.* 1982). In particular, four behaviours, the so-called 'holy four' (McQueen 1987), are identified as being associated with disease: smoking, alcohol 'misuse', poor nutrition and low levels of exercise. More recently, high-risk sexual activity has been added to the 'risk factor' list (Bennett and Murphy 1997: 8). These behaviours are related in a complex fashion to wider social and structural variables such as gender, socio-economic status and ethnicity (pp. 12–16).

The practical and theoretical literature on health promotion has challenged the biomedical model, recognizing that the causes of disease are commonly attributable to a complex mixture of biological, psychological and social causes. Accordingly, much health promotion is premised on a biopsy-chosocial model (Downie *et al.* 1990; Bunton and Macdonald 1992; Cooper *et al.* 1996: 89) and health promotion interventions tend to be wide-ranging, including 'individual behaviour change, community support for health, the creation of healthy environments and changes in national and global economic and fiscal policies' (Cooper *et al.* 1996: 89). Indeed, recent years tend to have witnessed the formalization of a multidisciplinary approach in the development of a range of models of health promotion (p. 13).

Having said that, however, this chapter will focus on psychology's contribution towards health promotion. It will be argued that the theories and models relied on by mainstream health psychologists have focused very narrowly on cognitive processes and individual behaviour change. However, the rise of more critical approaches has led to the challenge of these theories and models, resulting in the development of alternative conceptions of health-related behaviour and a subsequent questioning of the role played by psychology in health promotion.

Mainstream health psychology and health promotion

'Risk' and 'risk behaviour' have become keywords in psychological investigations of many different types of health-related behaviours such as eating, drinking, smoking, drug use and having sex. National health strategies established in the UK in the 1990s have sought to improve the health of the population by reducing the prevalence of such health-damaging behaviours.

Mainstream psychological approaches have traditionally been concerned with delineating the predictive factors contributing towards engagement in certain health-related behaviours. On the basis of specific models of health-related behaviour, they have designed health education and promotion interventions which aim to change people's behaviour in order to produce a 'healthier' population. Some of the best known theoretical models used within mainstream health psychology are the 'Health Belief Model' (HBM), 'Protection Motivation Theory' (PMT), the 'Theory of Reasoned Action' (TRA) and the 'Health Action Process Approach' (HAPA) (see Sheridan and Radmacher 1992; Sarafino 1994; Ogden 1996).

These models are all based on the assumption that an individual's perceptions, beliefs and knowledge contribute, in varying degrees, to the performance (or non-performance) of health-related behaviours. The HBM, for instance, theorizes that health-related behaviours are the product of numerous 'perceptual' variables such as 'perceived susceptibility', 'perceived severity', 'perceived costs' and 'perceived barriers'. Taking cigarette smoking as an example, the HBM would predict that whether or not a person engages in such behaviour depends on a number of variables such as how susceptible she perceives herself to be with regard to cancer or coronary heart disease (CHD); how serious she perceives cancer/CHD to be and the balance between her perception of the costs and benefits of smoking.

One of the major problems with models such as the HBM, recognized during the very early stages of its development, was a failure to appreciate the way in which individual perceptions and ways of thinking are related to social and cultural context. To overcome this limitation, later approaches such as the TRA and HAPA attempted to place more emphasis on the relationship between individuals and the social world by incorporating additional 'socially' related variables into theoretical models of health behaviours. For instance, continuing the smoking example, this would include additional considerations such as 'subjective norms' which would include factors such as parental smoking and peer-group pressure and the effect they have on individual perception (Ogden 1996: 91). It is in relation to this addition of social context that later models such as the TRA and HAPA have been characterized as '*social* cognition' models, in contrast to earlier models such as the HBM and PMT which were simply called 'cognition' models. This distinction serves to illustrate the varying extent to which the models place individual beliefs and perceptions within a social context (p. 20).

A consistent feature of all of these models is their assumption that a person's engagement with health-related behaviours depends on a rational process of weighing up the potential costs and benefits of such behaviour. This is not surprising given that these approaches draw heavily on theories drawn from economics. In accordance with such assumptions, the vast majority of health promotion and educational interventions designed within mainstream health psychology tend to espouse information and education as the foundation of behaviour change. The provision of information and practical skills, sometimes disseminated through selected peer or community leaders to act as motivators for the implementation of healthy behaviours, remains the central *modus operandi* of health promotion work drawing on mainstream psychological approaches.

Critical approaches to health-related behaviours and health promotion: health, identity and culture

One of the central critiques of a critical health psychological approach is that mainstream health psychology's theoretical models produce an image of the individual that is overly rational and thus inadequately psychological and social. That is to say, insufficient attention is paid to the fact that human beings are often motivated by 'irrational', unconscious forces and emotions. In addition, health-related behaviours such as eating, smoking, drug-use and exercise, embody latent social, cultural and value-laden meanings that individuals incorporate into their ways of thinking, but are not necessarily consciously aware of. If we look carefully at how people conduct and talk about their health-related activities, it becomes apparent that their 'decisions' to act in certain ways do not conform to rational, logical, value-free ways of thinking, but have their own alternative logic and validity that is related in a complex fashion to the cultural and moral environment in which they live (Calnan 1987: 8; Nettleton 1996: 41; Crossley and Crossley 1998).

This emphasis on the unconscious and habitual 'meanings' of health-related behaviours from a critical psychological approach is crucial, and points to the shift in focus from theoretically pre-defined models of 'health' and 'risk' behaviours, towards how people themselves subjectively conceptualize 'healthy' or 'risky' behaviours (Yardley 1997). This is important not only in terms of developing a more detailed understanding of the meaning of such behaviours. It also impacts directly on psychology's contribution towards health promotion practices. The 'need to promote a willing partnership between users and professionals in the promotion of health is enshrined in the NHS and Community Care Act' (Jacobson *et al.* 1991: 15). If health promotion strategies are to be effective, 'the cooperation of those receiving such strategies is essential and, in turn, if those receivers are to cooperate, then health promotion "knowledge" must be made accessible and meaningful' (Cooper *et al.* 1996: 13). In order to achieve this, it is necessary to take account of the complex psychological and psychosocial dynamics of such behaviours and thus to formulate strategies in a language that is meaningful to individuals (Watney 1990). This cannot be achieved if our theoretical models render us incapable of adequately understanding and explaining the full complexity of health-related behaviours.

Mainstream health psychology's failure to address the meaning of health-related behaviour is manifest in its fragmentary approach. Research from this perspective tends to be broken down into *specific* and allegedly *discrete* forms of behaviour which constitute separate areas of speciality and sub-speciality. For example, it is customary in mainstream health psychology textbooks to find various health-related or 'risky' behaviours (such as smoking, drinking, eating, exercising and having sex) each addressed in a separate chapter (see Sheridan and Radmacher 1992; Sarafino 1994; Ogden 1996). These various behaviours are addressed in a manner which apes the objective or factual nature of medical anatomy and physiology textbooks. For example, in Ogden's (1996) textbook, each of the main health-related behaviours is broken down and presented in a logically precise and definitive fashion: '*What is* (smoking, drinking, exercising, etc.)? *Who* does/doesn't do it? *Why* do/don't they do it? *What factors predict* whether they do/don't do it? And finally, *what factors predict relapse* from a particular behaviour?

As we saw in Chapter 1, this is health psychology portrayed as an objective science, presenting neat, tidy and allegedly value-free psychological knowledge. The same fragmentation is apparent in the study of addictive behaviours in which various addictions such as cigarette smoking, drug use and alcohol use are studied largely in isolation from each other.

To a limited extent this fragmentary approach may be beneficial in so far as it enables technical progress in relation to particular specialisms. On the other hand, however, such a narrow and instrumental focus has considerable drawbacks because it results in a loss of attention to the potentially unifying nature of such behaviours. For instance, consider the fact that addictive behaviours tend to be functionally interchangeable or 'cross-addictive' (i.e. there are consistent interrelationships between behaviours such as overeating, drinking, smoking, etc.) (Ogden 1996: 109). So far, mainstream psychological approaches have had very little to say about what such 'cross-addictions' tell us about the wider nature and meaning of addictions. This is because of mainstream health psychology's 'respectful attitude towards diagnostic tags' (Balint 1957: 39) which tends to result in a superficial rendition of symptoms that is of limited use in helping us get to grips with the real, underlying problems signified by such symptoms. As Balint advised, there is a need to aim at a 'more comprehensive, deeper diagnosis [one] which is not content with comprehending all the physical [or behavioural] signs and symptoms but tries to evaluate the pertinence of [those] symptoms' (p. 55). This argument receives added weight when we consider the proliferation of behaviours that have been bidding for addictive status in recent years: sex, food, shopping, love, relationships, computer games, the internet . . . We are reaching a point where 'almost any pattern or habit can become an addiction' (Giddens 1992: 75).

Critical health psychology has initiated this move towards the elucidation of a deeper understanding of healthy and unhealthy behaviours in contemporary society. As we suggested in Chapter 1, such understanding requires a more sophisticated appreciation of the way in which people's behaviour is intrinsically connected to the cultural and social world through symbols which are packed full of value-laden meanings and an orientation to 'the good'. And as we discussed in Chapter 2, in contemporary society (often referred to as 'post' or late modernity), visions of 'the good' no longer seem very concrete or readily available. This has created a characteristic sense of personal identity and selfhood in contemporary life where we seem to be on a continuous search or 'quest' for 'the good' (see Taylor 1989; Giddens 1991; Crossley 2000a); Cushman (1990) characterizes this kind of self (that most of us live with today) as a self which feels empty, experiencing a sense of absence that we cannot quite put our finger on. This feeling of emptiness tends to be experienced interiorly, as if it represented a lack of personal conviction and worth. Hence, we experience a repetitive need and desire to be filled up, to get rid of our vague feelings of emptiness and loss.

Such theories are important for understanding the connection between identity and health-related behaviours because one of the central ways in which we tend to cope with our feelings of emptiness in contemporary society is by consuming and producing in various ways in the attempt to comfort ourselves and make us feel fuller or more fulfilled. Feelings like 'I need a fix' or 'I need a drink' are often manifest signs of deeper, latent feelings such as loneliness, depression or anxiety. Because the resulting behaviour – drugs, alcohol – fails to clarify the nature of these feelings, the behaviour must be repeated, often compulsively (Odets 1995: 141). Hence, we tend to over-indulge in the consumption of products such as food, cigarettes, drink, watching TV and shopping, or to over-produce by becoming 'addicted' to activities such as work and exercise. In the absence of the deeper range of involvements available in pre-modern settings, such practices represent individual forms of comfort and indulgence. In Lasch's (1984) terms, they comprise the survival strategies through which we adapt to contemporary social life.

Such survival strategies cannot be reduced to the individual because they are related in a complex fashion to the economic structure of a society based on advanced consumer capitalism (Crawford cited in Bordo 1993: 333). On the one hand, as producers of goods and services, we must sublimate, delay and repress our desire for immediate gratification – cultivating the work ethic. On the other hand, as consumers, we must display a boundless capacity to capitulate to desire and indulge in impulse. This means that the regulation of desires becomes an ongoing problem as we find ourselves continuously besieged by temptation while being socially condemned for overindulgence. Food, diet, artificial substances, exercise and sex are central arenas in which this struggle for control is played out. Our lives vacillate between a daytime rigidly ruled by the 'performance principle' and nights and weekends in which we capitulate to unconscious 'letting go' (food, sex, shopping, drink, TV and other addictive 'drugs'). In this way 'the central contradiction of the system inscribes itself on our bodies' (Bordo 1993: 201), highlighting the 'difficulty of finding homeostasis between the producer and consumer sides of the self'.

These insights feed into more recent theories in which it has been suggested that 'health' has become a key concept, a 'dominant cultural motif', in the construction of identity in contemporary postmodern societies (Bordo 1993; Crawford 1994; Radley 1994; Leichter 1997; Woodward 1997; Williams 1998). Crawford, for instance, argued that 'health has become the key organising symbol for the good, moral, responsible self'. Radley has likewise argued that health, as an aim, is inseparable from what people perceive the 'good life' to be. It has an essentially moral and ideological character to it, because it is tied up with what people believe is good, or correct or responsible (Radley 1994: 190). Similarly, Woodward claimed that 'health and the body imagined through it . . . are not only biological and practical . . . but packed with connotations about what it means to be good, respectable and responsible' (Woodward 1997: 127).

These theories all suggest that health has become associated with moral virtue to such an extent that 'the pursuit of health is actually the pursuit of moral personhood' (Crawford 1994). Leichter (1997: 359) similarly proposes that good health now represents more than merely a state of physical and mental well-being. For many, especially the more affluent, it 'symbolizes a secular state of grace'. Hence, the contemporary obsession with lifestyles and health-related behaviours is not just about external bodily configuration, but represents a contemporary 'good' which has psychological and moral depth. Increasingly, the size and shape of the body has come to operate as a marker of personal, internal (dis)order (Bordo 1993: 193) and as a 'cultural metaphor' for self-determination, will and moral fortitude (p. 68).

The corollary of this attempt to create a sense of personal and social order by engaging in healthy lifestyles lies in the values and meanings that come to be attached to opposing unhealthy and risky behaviours. These become practices which symbolize, conversely, lack of control, badness, immorality and irresponsibility. In the last chapter we looked at the way in which postmodernism creates a different kind of self and identity, potentially a more reflexive and interpretive individual who is less likely to accept unquestioningly 'substantive' definitions of reality set down by established forms of authority. This chapter aims to explore how health promotion strategies designed on the basis of mainstream health psychology's theories, fail to appreciate these complex relationships between health-related behaviours and moral identities. Moreover, it is argued that this failure may actually be instrumental in perpetuating and exacerbating the very behaviours it is trying to reduce, manage and control.

Survival strategies: health and risk

Health as a survival strategy

An appreciation of the moral and identity laden nature of concepts of health and risk can be found in studies on the increasing emphasis on lifestyle or self-improvement amongst certain sectors of society in Britain and the US. In the aftermath of the political turmoil of the 1960s, Lasch (1984) comments on how Americans retreated to purely personal preoccupations. Having lost hope in improving their lives by engagement in political affairs, people convinced themselves that what mattered was 'improvement' through lifestyle changes. In contemporary life, this focus on self-improvement is frequently manifest in a concern with health, incorporating diet, fitness and a whole range of holistic mind–body practices.

Theorists argue that through such practices, the body (in fitness and health maintenance regimes) and mind (in fitness and various forms of therapy) become 'sites of control' which provide at least a minimal sense of control and security in an increasingly insecure world (see Bordo 1993; Shilling 1993). People no longer feel they can control events outside themselves – how well they do in their jobs or in their personal relationships, for example – but they can control the food they eat and how far they can run (Bordo 1993: 153). Accordingly, self-improvement through various ways of promoting health, constitutes a major coping mechanism of our times (Leichter 1997: 366).

Control is a central underlying theme associated with a whole range of contemporary bodily practices such as dieting and fitness regimes. In Bordo's (1993) study of contemporary eating practices, typical quotes from women include comments such as 'dieting is the one sector of my life over which I and I alone wield control' (Liu, cited in Bordo 1993: p. 149), and an anorexic patient's comment that 'You make your own body your very own kingdom where you are the tyrant, the absolute dictator' (p. 150). Bordo argues that a similar emphasis on control is apparent in fitness regimes in which people engage in jogging and marathon running, despite painful injuries such as shin splints, knee and calf injuries. Another example is evident in a recent issue of a magazine (sponsored by Adidas) issued to female members of the health club I go to, in which a woman writes:

> I love the elation and the exertion of the workout itself, the pleasure of pushing my body to its limits, achieving my goals and getting stronger, fitter, healthier. And then leaving the gym, freshly showered, flushed, revitalised, my muscles taut and all-systems in top gear. I'm ready to face the world – and beat it.

'Surely', Bordo argues, we must recognize in such statements, a 'central *modus operandi* for the control of contemporary bourgeois anxiety' (p. 150).

The article just mentioned is entitled 'Why I love working out' and is illustrative of the role that fitness regimes are coming to play in people's lives. Based around a 'love' metaphor, with subheadings such as 'initial attraction', 'head over heels' and 'together forever', it opens with the question 'Never really got on with exercise? Maybe you should assess your *relationship*. With the right approach you'll find it becomes a *true passion*' (emphasis added). Continuing the love metaphor:

> Falling in love is really a wonderful thing isn't it? One day you're walking along quite happily on your own, then, suddenly, out of the blue, you meet someone new. You flirt, you date, you get to know him – and then, as if by magic, you wake up one morning and realize you simply can't imagine life without him any more. A few years ago, it happened to me. But it er, wasn't a person I woke up to that day and realised I couldn't live without. It was *exercise* I fell in love with.

This woman continues (emphasis added):

> When I started working out, how I looked was the be-all and end-all. But, like any casual fling, that was shallow and short-lived. My attachment runs far deeper than that now. Exercise is *my sanity and my sanctuary*. It can be an *escape* from my day or a celebration of vitality. It gives me time to think and time not to think.

Here, the emphasis on escape, sanctuary and sanity, and the idea of exercise as a relationship, serves as an explicit reminder of the way in which contemporary bodily practices constitute Laschian type survival strategies, forms of comfort and security which are substitutes for traditional forms of meaning and community.

Risk as a survival strategy

The above brief overview has shown how the focus on lifestyle and health represents a way of making meaning and identity, of providing a sense of control and security, a survival strategy. But what about those who do not pursue health in this way? What about those who engage in more risky behaviours such as smoking, eating junk foods, excess drinking, drug use, unsafe sex? Are these just irrational individual choices? Or are they socially organized behaviours, expressing their own logic, validity, morality and value orientation? In the following overview we will look at numerous empirical qualitative studies which provide detailed insight into the 'alternative lay rationalities' associated with so-called 'risk' behaviours. From this analysis, it will become clear that the risky behaviours targeted by mainstream health psychology, constitute only one part of the 'landscapes of meaning' framing people's everyday lives (see also Graham 1998). When set within the broader landscape of the complex range of emotions, meanings and uncertainties infiltrating people's lives, it will become increasingly apparent that mainstream health psychology's commonly accepted definition of risky behaviours (such as smoking, diet and unsafe sex) becomes relativized and appears somewhat limited and naïve.

Smoking: a self-help strategy

One important illustration of such 'alternative rationalities' can be found in Graham's (1998) study of smoking amongst young single mothers living in households dependent on welfare benefits. Graham argues that smoking, however paradoxically, can be seen as a way of protecting children from the adverse consequences of poverty. When talking about the way they handle the stress and exhaustion of caring for young children, women in low-income households suggest that 'cigarettes provide an important self-help child protection strategy' (Graham 1993: 58). For example, the following are typical comments made by women whom Graham interviewed:

> [I am very likely to smoke] when the baby is screaming and won't shut up.

> [I am very likely to smoke] when I'm making the tea. The two older ones come home from school, the baby's hungry and all four of them are hungry. They are all fighting and screaming and the dinner's cooking in the kitchen. I'm ready to blow up so I light a cigarette. It calms me down when I'm under so much stress . . .

Similarly, for women in violent relationships, smoking operates as a 'risk avoidance strategy'. As one woman commented:

> I don't think I could be as brave if I don't smoke. I'm pretty brave when I have a cigarette in my mouth. I light up a cigarette and get all the courage in the world.
>
> (Greaves 1996: 49)

Graham argues that women are emphasizing that cigarette smoking is a situated routine, 'fashioned in and against the material and relational pressures of everyday life'. For such women 'life is a continuing struggle' and 'cigarettes emerge as one of the few constants, one of the few resources that they can control and rely on' (Graham 1993: 33). Hence:

> I just gotta have cigarettes by my side 'cos they're the only stable thing in my life. Just not having them is the hardest thing. I won't smoke them, but I've gotta have them 'cos they're my best friend.
>
> (Lawson 1993: 12)

> As far as I can see, you can't count on a guy because they are not always there, kids aren't always there . . . I'd say it's [smoking] my security. Because they [cigarettes] are always there.
>
> (Greaves 1996: 65)

Relativity of risk

Another important concept in qualitative studies on lay rationalities related to risky health-related behaviours is that of relativity of risk. A good illustration is Rhodes's (1998) study of safer sexual practices amongst heroin users. Rhodes argues that heroin users' perceptions of HIV risk are part of a 'hierarchy of risk priorities' associated with injecting drug use. On a day-to-day basis, many heroin injectors perceived the risk of overdose to be of far greater concerns than HIV. The following quote from a heroin user is typical:

> Death is like a normal thing, like an everyday thing. If you take heroin you can be dead at any moment and it's not very frightening – you live with that. So it doesn't frighten you much like it would a normal person . . . It was normal that even best friends, they died. I mean, it was very sad, but it was normal, nothing special . . . and I think that's why drug users are not so afraid to get AIDS.
>
> (cited in Rhodes 1998)

Hence, 'perceptions of risk susceptibility and acceptability can be seen as a function of the perceived *immediacy* of risk' (Rhodes 1998).

In a study of HIV-negative gay men, Odets (1995), a therapist who works with gay men, recounts a therapeutic episode which similarly highlights the importance of understanding the 'relativity of risk' concept if we are to make sense of lay rationalities with regard to health-related behaviour. One of his clients was talking about his visit to his physician. At one point his physician said to him:

> 'We should really talk about your cholesterol levels'. I said, 'What about them?' and she said, 'Well, these are among the highest levels I've seen in my entire medical practice', and she was asking about my diet, and so on, and I finally said, 'You know, I don't care what my cholesterol is, and if I think about having a heart attack in 10 or 20 years, it just doesn't mean anything in the context of HIV . . . the whole thing made me incredibly angry . . . here we are in the middle of a plague and practically everyone I know is dying of AIDS . . . and my problem is cheese . . .'
>
> (Odets 1995: 116)

Gay men and unprotected sex

The importance of understanding 'alternative rationalities' and 'relativity of risk' is beginning to be widely discussed in relation to gay men's sexual practices (Boulton et al. 1995; Flowers et al. 1997; Smith et al. 1997). Within the HIV/AIDS field there is a general sense of confusion as to why, despite nearly fifteen years of health education and health promotion directed specifically at gay men, there is still a high incidence of unsafe sex (mainly unprotected anal intercourse (UAI)) amongst this population (see Gold 1995; Odets 1995; Rofes 1998). Smith et al. (1997) argue that the failure of many health interventions is partly attributable to the fact that they have failed to explore 'lay rationalities' – i.e. the meaning and significance that certain sexual practices have for gay men themselves. Odets (1995) puts the matter rather more succinctly: 'What is so important about having a penis in your rectum – or putting yours in someone else's – that millions of gay men continue to do it even at the risk of death?' (p. 189).

UAI among men, Odets continues, 'has real significance aside from its anatomical convenience' because it incorporates strong 'interpersonal and psychological *meaning* for many gay men' (p. 189). These symbolic meanings must be understood if health psychology is to have any impact on such behaviours. Such meanings include, for instance, unprotected sex as a symbol of trust, intimacy and love (de Wit et al. 1994; Lowy and Ross 1994; Smith et al. 1997; Rhodes 1998), unprotected receptive anal intercourse as symbolic submission and unprotected sex as a symbolic assertion of risk and life (Odets 1995: 189). The latter is of particular relevance to this chapter. For instance, Odets cites an incident reported to him by one of his psychotherapy patients, Will, a gay HIV-negative man. Will told the story of meeting a man, Kevin, while on a week's vacation. They spent a lot of time together during the week and had hours of discussion about their lives, families, work, etc. During the course of these conversations Kevin revealed to Will that he was HIV-positive and talked about how lonely he was living in a gay community that largely shunned people with HIV. A few days later, Kevin invited Will to his home for dinner. After dinner, the two men began to make love on the floor. Will described this encounter in the following way:

> After we'd been on the floor for a couple of hours, I rolled Kevin over onto his side – I mean we didn't have any condoms – and I went into him. He was obviously very pleased, but he was startled too, and he said, 'Why are you doing this?' And I said to him, 'Because it's important.'
>
> 'And why, reflecting now, do you think you did this despite your appreciation of the risks?' I asked.
>
> 'Because it was important.' Will sat quietly for a moment. 'It was really a remarkable time. Though I haven't seen him for a year now, I think about him and his life a lot. He is an amazing person, and it was very important.'
>
> (cited in Odets 1995: 199)

Odets uses this example to illustrate that for many gay men, the act of UAI serves as a kind of psychological affirmation of one's life. For many people, he argues, 'absolute safety at the cost of human intimacy may be too high a price' to pay (Odets 1995: 132). This argument is further clarified by reference to a gay man, Woody Castrodale's, description of an HIV-negative support group he facilitated. One man in the group was admitting that he often felt like having unsafe sex. In response to this, another man blurted out 'I can't believe you're talking like this. I don't know about you but I intend to stay alive and you're going to commit suicide.' 'As I was sitting listening to this', writes Woody Castrodale,

> my mind went into a sort of free fall. The more I've been facilitating this group, the more I realise that *I don't want to live without risk – this would not be living.* And sometimes the group makes me think that we're hiding behind these prohibitions about talking about one thing or another as a way to hide out against life. I realised, with regard to this issue of sex, how *complicated* it is. What it comes right down to is life, and death, and sex, and these things mixed up together make quite a brew.
>
> (cited in Odets 1995: 180)

'*I don't want to live without risk – this would not be living.*' This statement demonstrates how UAI has become loaded with a paradoxical symbolic significance; precisely because of its association with risk and death, it comes to symbolize a willingness to live life 'to the full' – at the highest level of risk possible. Similarly, Rhodes's study of unprotected sex amongst injecting drug users showed how such sex took on the meaning of 'real' sex because of its risky associations. As one man commented: 'Sometimes we decided to spoil ourselves and have real sex . . . We both decided to throw caution to the wind and have real sex for once, and we enjoyed it all the more although we knew we were putting me at risk' (cited in Rhodes 1998: 215).

Risky behaviours as symbolic rebellion/transgression

The association of risk with living alluded to above alerts us to the fact that, as certain behaviours become the receptacles for all that is valued and moral – exercise, safe sex, eating healthily, drinking moderately, abstaining from use of artificial stimulants such as cigarettes and other narcotics – a curious process takes place. Not only do their 'opposing' behaviours – non-exercise, unsafe sex, eating junk food, drinking heavily, smoking, using drugs – become associated with a sense of irresponsibility and immorality, but they take on a certain cachet and value of their own precisely because of this association. A deeper psychological understanding of risky behaviours reveals that, although knowledge of their potential lethality or harmfulness may serve as a deterrent, sometimes, by contrast, it may actually provide the primary motivation (often unconscious) to engage in such behaviours. Hence, some people engage in risky health behaviours precisely *because* of their association with risk. By engaging in particular 'unhealthy' practices, the body comes to be used as a vehicle through which the individual can 'embody resistance to cultural norms' (Bordo 1993: 203). It is in this way that risky health-related behaviours constitute a symbolic transgression and rebellion against dominant social and cultural values.

An appreciation of this rebellious dimension of health behaviours remains totally undeveloped within health psychology at present. This is not surprising given that it involves an understanding of the links between issues of health, morality, values, identity, emotions, economy and culture, all of which, as we have seen in this chapter, have remained largely untouched in mainstream health psychology. The section that follows therefore draws largely on research in relation to unsafe sexual practices amongst gay men, but it is hypothesized that the central argument, unhealthy practices as symbolic of rebellion and transgression, is equally applicable to many other such behaviours.

In a similar vein to theorists who have argued that the pursuit of health is the pursuit of 'moral personhood' (Crawford 1994), Odets argues that safer sex has become a 'moral posture' in the gay communities. This has made 'the topic of unprotected sex, or one's feelings about it, a taboo' (Odets 1995: 178). As with all taboos, this means that unprotected sex comes to have a certain aura of risk, rebellion and excitement surrounding it. The notion that such aspects of rebellion are central, perhaps *constitutive*, of risky health behaviours, became increasingly apparent in my study of the emotional and psychological needs of long-term HIV 'survivors' (see Davies 1997; Crossley 1997a; 1997b; 1998a; 1998b; 1998c; 1999b).

A particularly lucid example was evident in an interview with one man when I asked him 'in which areas of his life' he thought being HIV-positive had affected him most predominantly. He replied defensively that 'you've got to be aiming at sex here, haven't you?' When I responded that no, that wasn't necessarily the case, he said 'Well a lot of people do. They want to see if, whether you are doing safe sex and all that, all that sort of business.' At a later point in the interview when we did actually get on to a discussion of sex, he was adamant that being HIV-positive had made him *more* interested in sex than he ever was before. He began by describing how he used to go to Hampstead Heath for sexual 'escapades' and then corrected himself mid-sentence. 'No', he told me, 'listen, I *still* go to the Heath . . . *You* tell Joe Bloggins', he continued, 'that at the age of thirty he can have no more sex, he can have no more company, he can have nothing. See if he can deal with it . . . I have had to deal with it by taking power back for me.' These comments shed further light on his behaviour when, one night, after months of emotional fear and trauma, he told his friend 'I must take back my sexuality'. Hence:

> I borrowed someone's leather jacket and I went up the Heath and I stood by a tree and I would not leave that tree until I had got fucked rotten, to put it bluntly. I had to take it back, take the power back for me, not let the doctors or anybody else [tell me what to do] . . .'
> (cited in Crossley and Crossley 1998)

The comments of this man make it clear that his behaviours constitute a rebellious response to his own internalized perception of what others consider safe and respectable behaviour to be. On numerous occasions, he reveals his assumptions that I (representing the 'general public' and/or health professionals) am judging him – 'you've got to be aiming at sex here', 'well, lots of people do', 'you tell Joe Bloggins', 'not letting the doctors or anybody else' tell him what to do. Hence, his conscious decision to go and 'get fucked rotten' is taken in order to thwart and rebel against acceptable social conventions. His acts constitute attempts to assert himself over and above restricting social conventions. In his own words, 'This is me, who I am, at this point, with my sexuality, with my emotions or whatever it may be.'

Appreciating this rebellious dimension of sexual practices associated with homosexuality, such as anal intercourse, is important because it demonstrates how such acts stand in defiance of more general societal prohibitions against homosexuality (Odets 1995: 195). The same is true of sexual activities associated with 'cruising' behaviour which involve multiple sexual contacts, often with anonymous and objectified bodies in public spaces such as toilets and parks. The important point to note here is that such sexual activities constitute an affront to the conventions of 'normal, responsible, respectable' society. By explicitly engaging in such 'irresponsible' practices, culminating in unprotected anonymous sex, gay men engage in acts which rebelliously deny the values of mainstream culture, thus asserting their own psychological independence and autonomy.

It is likely that similar psychosocial mechanisms constitute a large part of the current vogue for 'bare back' riding (UAI) amongst the gay dance/party subculture (see Rofes 1998). In a recent focus group I held with gay men as part of an evaluation of a community health promotion programme (Crossley and Chapman 1999), the group talked about the way in which people engaged in 'risk' behaviour precisely because of its risk associations. For instance, one man commented as follows:

> There is some evidence of this if you look on the Web for example, this is more in the States than here but in America there is a whole dance/party subculture which at the moment has this whole question about 'bare back riding' as they call it, in other words sex without condoms, and there are whole web sites dedicated to that topic and lots of personals between people who actually want to have unprotected sex, so you could argue I suppose that that is an example of where people are actually going out of their way to seek risky behaviour. I don't think it is quite such an organized thing here though . . .

Picking up on this last comment, another member of the group commented that, from his experience as an Outreach worker, 'The working girls (in Liverpool) have commented they are being offered additional money *not* to use condoms and some have been beaten up when they've refused to do that'. And as another man said, 'If you say this is highly risky people will say "it must be good, I will have a go"' (see Crossley 2000c).

Although the above has focused mainly on risky sexual practices, I have already suggested that similar elements of psychological rebellion and transgression are probably important in understanding the nature of other unhealthy or risky health-related behaviours. Another example of this can be found amongst studies of dieting behaviour. Some studies, for instance, have suggested that relapse from restricted food intake does not just occur as a result of the individual passively giving in to an overwhelming desire to eat. Rather, what happens is that the individual makes an active decision to overeat 'as a form of rebellion against self-imposed food restrictions' (Ogden 1997: 205). This rebellious state of mind has also been described in obese binge eaters who report bingeing as a 'way to unleash resentment' (Loro and Orleans 1981). In order to understand the meaning of such transgressive behaviour more clearly, it is necessary to understand some of the discourses surrounding food in our culture. Bordo lucidly demonstrates that 'unrestrained appetite' and 'gluttony' are constructed as inappropriate for women in our culture. This is one of the reasons why women experience food (especially rich, fattening food like chocolate and ice cream) as exciting, 'dangerous and frightening' (Bordo 1993: 108). Advertisements for such foods depict them as the object of obsession and innermost cravings, and the women who eat them doing so with furtiveness and secrecy. As Bordo argues, 'the depiction of female eating as a private, transgressive act, makes restriction and denial of hunger central features of the construction of femininity and set up the compensatory binge as a virtual inevitability' (p. 130). When the dieter feels low, tired, stressed or needy, she turns to food as a form of emotional self-comfort, rebelling against all the strictures imposed on her from a vague and generalized hostile outside world.

Health and risk as socially structured survival strategies

The above overview of some of the studies investigating why people engage in healthy and risky behaviours, highlight that people's ideas about health, illness and disease have their own rationality – a rationality which arises out of the circumstances in which they live their lives and out of interactions with others which create a sense of morality, values, or an orientation to 'the good' (see Crossley 2000a). Moreover, this orientation to 'the good' implicitly involves individuals in the quest to be filled up, to feel a sense of belonging and meaning in the wake of vague feelings of emptiness and loss that most of us suffer within contemporary Western society (Cushman 1990). Accordingly, such health-related behaviours serve as crucial survival strategies, ways of making sense and meaning, in today's world.

We only need to pay attention to the metaphors used when people are describing why they engage in particular 'healthy' or 'risky' practices to see this. For instance, the woman cited from my exercise magazine earlier in this chapter builds her story of why she exercises on the basis of a love metaphor. She tells us that she has 'fallen head over heels in love' with exercise. It is her 'escape', her 'sanity' and her 'sanctuary'. It gives her strength 'to face the world – *and beat it*'. Note the powerful analogies between young single mothers' accounts of why they smoke. Cigarettes, they tell us, are 'my best friend'. They are a source of 'stability and security', making me feel 'brave' and giving me 'courage in the world'. In her analysis of the cultural construction of food in contemporary society, Bordo (1993) similarly shows how women, in particular, learn to associate food with love and emotional comfort. Bordo discusses how one woman described her hunger as a 'black hole that I had to fill up' (p. 105) and another described food as 'the only thing that will take care of me' (p. 126). Similarly, among some people, engaging in unsafe sex has come to operate as a symbolic gesture of love and commitment, and becoming infected with one's HIV-positive partner's virus 'the ultimate expression of love' as the relationship becomes 'more important than life itself' (see Joffe 1997). And amongst others, unsafe sex has come to symbolize the capacity to exercise free will, to demonstrate to oneself that 'risk is more important than life itself' for to 'live without risk is not to live at all'.

The projective psychological dynamics operating in all these instances are equivalent. Some object, in the form of an inanimate object (cigarettes, food), act, person or relationship (exercise, sexual partner, own free will), is being invested with all the 'good' qualities – control, security, safety, love, friendship, self-assertion – that the individual experiences an (often implicit) need for. These objects are like the infant's first 'transitional object' – the comfort blanket, Teddy, 'Dodo', etc. (Winnicott 1974). They serve as powerful mediators between self and world, ways of providing a sense of order and meaning, thus enabling us to accommodate ourselves to the stresses and demands of life. Viewed from this psychological perspective, healthy and risky lifestyle options constitute two sides of the same coin. Both represent attempted resolutions of the contradictions of a culture which inculcates a chronic sense of emptiness and meaninglessness, producing a subsequent need or desire to get rid of that feeling.

It is however important, when highlighting the psychological equivalence of such survival strategies, to maintain a grasp of the fact that they are socially and culturally structured. That is to say, such psychological survival strategies tend to take on varying forms within different social groupings. For instance, the adoption of healthy survival strategies such as exercising and working out tends to cluster within the middle classes. Studies of middle-class consumption patterns have found that higher-income groups are the largest consumers of health- and body-care products (Savage et al. 1992). And in both Britain and the US, the current fitness craze, sometimes dubbed 'Deprivation Chic', is understood largely as a phenomenon of young, upwardly mobile professionals (Bordo 1993: 153). Accordingly, Leichter (1997: 373), citing a study which showed that 9 per cent of all exercise machines were purchased by the lowest income groups, in comparison with 45 per cent by the highest income households, argues that the search for fitness remains largely the province of a particular class.

By contrast, it should not have escaped your notice that an important feature of studies of various risky behaviours is their tendency to focus on people who occupy materially and/or socially disadvantaged positions (such as single mothers on welfare benefits, gay men, drug users). This is not incidental. Numerous studies have shown that individuals in deprived social groups tend to engage in more health-damaging behaviours such as smoking, drinking excessively, eating fat-rich diets and engaging less in fitness and exercise programmes (Bennett and Murphy 1997: 14; Doyal 1998: 22).[1] Exactly why this is so is a matter of some debate. Some argue that it is due to economic and financial deprivation which limit people's ability to engage in healthier lifestyles. Others, however, argue that such explanations are too simplistic and that a more complex understanding of the way in which material and social deprivation impinges on the individual's lifestyle is required.

For instance, consider the single mother on welfare benefits who chooses a risky behavioural strategy, smoking, rather than going to the gym four or five times a week to work out and pursue a healthy lifestyle. This choice cannot simply be attributed to lack of financial resources. If she can afford to smoke twenty cigarettes a day, she can afford to join the local gym. At the local gym near where I live it costs £318 per year for a 'Gold card' giving you access to all swimming, aerobic and step classes, jacuzzi, sauna, steam facilities, at any time of the day from 6.00 am until 10.00 pm, seven days a week. If you are unemployed or on welfare benefit it costs 50p per hour for crèche facilities. Smoking twenty cigarettes a day costs about £21 per week, approximately £1000 per year. Our single mother would have a lot of change left over if she stopped smoking and substituted it for the health club. Her lack of engagement with 'healthy' behaviours cannot be reduced to matters of economy or finance.

To understand her behaviour it is useful to draw on Crawford's (1994) argument which, as we discussed earlier in this chapter, emphasizes that health-related behaviour is inextricably connected to the social and economic structure of society in so far as the contradictions between production and consumption are inscribed on our bodies. Bearing in mind the material–social distinction between those engaging in 'healthy' and 'risky' behaviours, however, it is important to add another dimension to Crawford's argument. The contradiction between production and consumption is not just inscribed on the bodies of individuals, but also on the social body more generally. Accordingly, whereas 'healthy' middle-class responses such as the health/fitness craze represent an 'extreme development of the capacity for self-denial and repression of desire' (the work ethic in absolute control), more risky solutions represent 'an extreme capacity to capitulate to desire (consumerism in control)' (Bordo 1993: 201).

One central feature of those dedicated to the productive dimension, is their practical and ideological commitment to the 'performance principle' which involves maintaining a sense of control, direction, self-mastery and an ability to 'colonize the future' (Giddens 1992). Within contemporary society, however, with the rise of a welfare dependency culture, many materially/socially disadvantaged groups of people have become largely alienated from this performance principle. Having lost or never experienced the sense of shared meaning and identity deriving from membership within a productive community, many such individuals are faced with a life which lacks direction and meaning.[2] In such populations, an oppositional 'unconscious letting go' principle dominates. As the ability to sublimate, delay and repress immediate needs by projecting into the future is severely compromised, this is manifest in unhealthy behaviours such as smoking, drug use, over-eating and engaging in unsafe sex. In accordance with this argument, our smoking single mother will not go to the gym because she does not see the value and purpose of engaging in such activities which, as we have already suggested, are all about building up an identity based on performance, direction, control and self-mastery – cultivating the work ethic. If such principles are alien to her life, then she is unlikely to perform such activities. In fact, given our earlier argument regarding the transgressive nature of risky health practices, she is likely to inhale more deeply on her cigarette as a way of (consciously or unconsciously) rebelling against the values that her life is alienated from.

It is in relation to this morally value-laden nature of health-related activities that health can be defined:

> . . . not simply something that one *has* or *is*. Rather, it comprises . . . a reiterative set of practices and ritualised performances by which one, literally and metaphorically, materially and culturally, socially and morally, becomes 'viable' at all . . . 'Viable' in the sense that the performative aspects of health demonstrate the social and cultural legitimacy of the body, both to self and others.
>
> (Williams 1998: 444)

This notion of 'viability' draws on the sociologist Pierre Bourdieu's (1992) work on the 'habitus', a concept which refers to 'embodied dispositions which shape how people, or more generally, generations and cultures, perceive and understand the world around them' (Hardey 1998: 122). Such habitus is 'precognitive', which means that it is not consciously thought about, and certain behaviours are just enacted in the form of repetitive habits. According to Bourdieu, habitus is manifest in people's attachment to certain types of food, exercise, work, sport, art, etc., including the various kinds of health-related behaviours that we have been discussing in this chapter. Such bodily activities in the form of habitus comprise 'the most indisputable materialisation of class taste'. Accordingly, we can see how, through the concept of health or risk as habitus, it is possible to see how health comes to operate as a 'positional good' (Leiss 1983). Positional goods help to establish and maintain an individual's position in the social hierarchy and can therefore be seen as part of the habitus of particular social groups (Elias 1978; Bourdieu 1984).

Numerous researchers have argued that it is by 'labouring on the body' in particular ways that dominant relations of power are institutionalized in contemporary consumer culture. Here, the body has increasingly come to serve as a symbol of pleasure, happiness and success (Nettleton 1996: 50). As we have already seen, our beliefs about health and illness are influenced by prevailing social and medical ideologies which 'reflect the values of capitalism and individualism' in so far as 'they are imbued with notions of self-discipline, self-denial, self-control and willpower' (Crawford 1984). It has been argued that, through their conformity to the productive dimension of consumer capitalism, the middle classes produce and disseminate cultural imagery and information which aims to expand and legitimate its own lifestyles (Featherstone 1991). One of the main ways in which this is achieved is by championing healthy lifestyles through various forms of health education and health promotion.

Where does this leave critical health psychology? Should there be health interventions to try and change people's behaviour?

So far in this chapter we have tried to develop an appreciation of 'lay rationalities' regarding health-related behaviours. We have seen that people's ways of thinking and orienting to these behaviours are rather different to the 'rational decision-maker' who objectively weighs up the costs and benefits of various actions, presupposed within mainstream health psychology's theoretical models. As Radley argues, 'people conduct their lives – including those things thought to be "healthy" and "unhealthy" – according to beliefs that involve a range of other concerns apart from health alone' (Radley 1994: 194). We have seen in this chapter that such concerns include rather more 'irrational', less predictable desires such as the pursuit of moral virtue, the immediate need for satisfaction, and the need to feel a sense of belonging, love, excitement and autonomy. An exploration of the psychosocial dynamics involved in the pursuit of healthy and risky behaviours has facilitated an understanding of the way in which the meaning of such behaviours develops in the context of dominant cultural mores.

This process of deconstructing the meaning of various health-related or risky behaviours from the lay point of view, has encouraged us to see beyond the idea that there is one single, authoritative, value-free, objective truth or reality associated with risk and health. So where does this leave critical health psychology in relation to questions regarding the value of various kinds of health-related behaviours and whether we should intervene in order to try and change them? In what ways, if any, can healthy behaviours and lifestyles be seen as 'better' than risky behaviours? Even if we were able to facilitate individuals and communities to shift their behaviours from risk to health, as defined by scientific studies, would that be desirable? Or do the alternative considerations and values discussed throughout this chapter – the need for immediate gratification, love, free will, excitement, etc. – have their own validity which competes with such definitions?

Some theorists, especially those associated with postmodern approaches to health studies (e.g. Fox 1993), have argued that an understanding of 'lay rationalities' serves to challenge 'the process of objectification that is the foundation for . . . expert knowledge' (Cooper *et al.* 1996: 96). Accordingly, from a postmodern perspective, there would, instead, be a 'radical suspicion' of scientific definitions of health which would also mean that there are 'no unquestionable imperatives for activity' (Fox 1993: 137). Fox continues:

[the idea of] a unitary notion of health or illness dissolves in the postmodern mood to be replaced by something which is very fragmentary and indeterminate . . . In place of health or its absence, one is left only with *difference*. I have called this indeterminacy *arche-health*.

(p. 137)

This deconstructed notion of health would lead to health promotion programmes which, rather than consisting of 'indiscriminate and totalizing interventions' are instead:

programmes which enable people to make active decisions about the lives they lead; a celebration of diversity in the target population, rather than a perspective which sees individuals as deviates from some norm of behaviour . . . and programmes which do not detract from the finitude of those who are clients, for example, by an overblown emphasis on 'being healthy' as opposed to 'becoming this or that'.

(p. 137)

Fox's notion of 'becoming this or that' refers to his attempt to validate people's own perceptions of risks and values instead of trying to impose a pre-defined concept of 'health' upon them. So, for instance, taking our earlier example of people having unsafe sex because of the value they place on their relationship over and above their own survival, such behaviour would be valued and appreciated in its own right. Health promoters should have no right or moral sanction to try and change such behaviour.

The critical health psychologist has some sympathy with this argument. This is especially the case with regard to the necessity of taking into account the validity of people's own definitions of health and risk and developing a sceptical attitude towards health promotion interventions which impose simplistic, scientifically defined norms on the population as a whole. On the other hand, there are also major problems with such postmodern perspectives. One of the main problems is that such arguments ignore what we have repeatedly seen throughout this chapter – ways of perceiving health and risk are structured through a person's negotiations with others and, more generally, through their material and social position. If we simply validate the individual's 'alternative rationality', as the postmodern approach encourages us to do, we fail to appreciate the social structuration of such perceptions. In doing so, we potentiate the perpetuation of health inequalities by failing to address the differences in health behaviours manifest across social groupings.

Another related problem here relates to the willingness to feed into the contemporary myth of individual protest and rebellion. As we have already seen in relation to risky behaviours such as smoking and unsafe sex, individuals may feel emotionally and psychologically attached to these behaviours because they are associated with a sense of rebellion against dominant social values. Simply reiterating this sense of rebellion and autonomy, however, obscures the tension that exists between the psychological meaning of a behaviour, which 'may enact fantasies of rebellion and embody a language of protest', and the 'practical life of the disordered body' which, by contrast 'may utterly defeat rebellion and subvert protest' (Bordo 1993: 181). It is notable that people turn to behaviours such as unsafe sex, comfort eating, smoking, drug use, rarely in a state of pleasure and independence, but when they feel desperate, empty, lonely, depressed, stressed, low in self-esteem and worthless. Hence, although such behaviours may heal and soothe the 'empty self' in the immediacy of the present, from a more long-term point of view, all they do is passively placate the individual and ensure the perpetuation of conditions which led to such feelings of inadequacy in the first place.

From a critical psychological perspective, the naïve acceptance and legitimation of lay accounts of reality often serves merely to perpetuate and institutionalize ways of life based on passivity, defeatism and apathy. This denies individuals and communities the possibility of making innovative changes in their lives, reinforcing the myth of individual protest and rebellion, while encouraging individuals to go on smoking, eating, injecting, fucking or loving themselves into oblivion.

Challenging simplistic interventions

A critical health psychology, then, despite appreciating the validity of 'lay rationalities', still attempts to maintain a *critical* eye on those ways of thinking, and is not opposed, in principle, to interventions which attempt to change self-destructive or harmful behaviours. Having said that, however, critical health psychology does seek to challenge mainstream health psychology for the health promotion interventions it has typically produced. This is largely because they are based, as we have argued earlier in this chapter, on simplistic models which fail to take account of the full complexity and meaning of health-related behaviours.

Health promoters, keen to present unequivocal and straightforward messages based on predictability, controllability and regularity, fail to address the anomalies and sophistication of lay thinking (Nettleton 1996: 45). This is one of the main reasons why the efficacy of such health promotion programmes in terms of changing behaviour is so poor (Radley 1994: 193). A typical example is safer sex health promotion campaigns directed towards gay men. Odets (1995: 185) argues that, according to self-report figures, the percentages of gay men practising anal intercourse today, are 'astonishingly close' to those before the epidemic. This 'leaves the possibility that our education may be of little or no value at all in motivating change in the behaviour that all gay men, and their grandmothers, know to be the most dangerous for transmitting HIV' (Odets 1995: 185).

Despite overwhelming evidence that gay men are knowledgeable about HIV/AIDS, promotion and prevention efforts continue to be based on public health and social marketing models which espouse information and education as the foundation of behaviour change. Accordingly, they tend to rely on informing and educating people on instrumental sexual techniques, such as how to use a condom and exhorting people to 'use a condom every time'. Relying on 'ridiculously simple solutions' (p. 132), such approaches not only ignore, but deny, the complex psychological, interpersonal and psychosocial issues that have arisen as a result of the AIDS epidemic and are manifested in various forms of sexual behaviour (p. 186). Such efforts at health promotion support the vision that gay sex is without 'human meaning'. As Odets argues, 'If we were to believe much of our AIDS education, the gay man who simply "plays it safe" can carry on with a "normal" life without a care in the world' (p. 186).

Odets's critique of health education and promotion campaigns directed towards safer sex can also be generalized to other health-related behaviours discussed in this chapter, such as smoking, drinking, eating and drug use. These behaviours are infused with emotional and moral meaning related, in a complex fashion, to the individual's biographical and social background. The vast majority of health promotion campaigns can be characterized as 'scheme' based, in so far as they encourage the development of simple behaviours and ways of thinking (use a condom every time, avoid all sugary foods, substitute a glass of whisky with orange juice, think positively). These simple techniques are useful, at least in the short term, because they enable us to substitute harmful, destructive behaviours, with an (allegedly) less harmful alternative. The problem is, however, that such 'schemes' and techniques are not really very helpful in the long term because they tend to ignore and deny the more complex, less easily controlled emotions and feelings surrounding such behaviours. Focusing on simple, behavioural management techniques facilitates a denial of what our engagement in 'addictive' health-related behaviours actually represents – attempts (often unconscious) to maintain some sense of meaning, direction and control in a world too often experienced as meaningless and empty as we have seen in this chapter. Although 'scheme' based interventions may provide a temporary respite from such feelings, they do so in a manner which has immense costs in terms of preventing us from appraising and addressing the nature of such underlying problems.

Opening out to discussion

Too often, attempts to promote health and to educate the public about health-related issues are rooted in traditional psychological models which encourage us to see 'health' and 'risk' as black and white, objective, value-free choices and issues. This frequently results in a conception of the public as a largely passive mass waiting to receive directive, categorical advice, which will enable them to conduct their lives safely in accordance with scientifically discovered truths. Unfortunately (for health promoters), knowledge about health-related issues is very rarely as clear cut as this ideal would have it, muddied as it invariably is by uncertainties and ambiguities. Even if such knowledge were clear cut and unambiguous, its audience, as we have seen in this chapter, is certainly not.

Despite this, a great deal of health promotion continues to cling to the ideal of objective, value-free knowledge which is translated into action through directive education. 'Directive education is necessary', argued one health promoter, because people 'need to be told *what to do*' (cited in Odets 1995: 195). But, as we have seen in this chapter, it is possible that such authoritative approaches, rooted as they are in a denial of alternative ways of seeing things, actually create a precedent for the very behaviours they are trying to prevent. This is because directive instructions disempower people, leading them to behave secretly, unthinkingly, and often self-destructively (p. 195), or even, as we have already argued, in conscious defiance of prohibitions they feel have been imposed on them. One man in my focus group was very clear on this point when he said that 'I will happily tuck into a T-bone steak *almost on principle* because I feel I can make my own mind up. I suppose, I guess other people feel the same way about sex.' (NB: this remark was made in 1997 during the ban of beef on the bone in Britain and relates to fears of bovine spongiform encephalopathy (BSE).)

A good example can again be taken from the safer sex literature in which there is an 'absolute prohibition against saying that it is *sometimes* acceptable to have anal sex without a condom' (Odets 1995: 194). The 'nearly universal response' to such an admission is that it will 'encourage men to do dangerous things' (p. 194). But, as Odets argues, part of the answer to this objection is obvious – some men *are* doing such dangerous things anyway. Indeed:

> one of the reasons for the dangerous behaviours is our prohibition against discussing obvious possibilities. Our prohibition does not allow men to have the information or develop the judgement to discern when a particular behaviour is likely to transmit HIV and when it is not. Our practice of simply instructing men in behaviours – 'a condom every time' – actively obstructs the development of a capacity for informed judgement and perpetuates society's desire to simply dictate behaviours to gay men.
>
> (p. 195)

In order to provide the opportunity for people to make informed, clear and conscious decisions about their behaviour, such issues must remain open to discussion rather than being prematurely prohibited. Unless this is achieved, 'unprotected sex will remain impulsive and covert among gay men . . . but no less destructive for its public invisibility' (p. 181).

Among the possible topics of discussion would be the kinds of issues we have discussed in this chapter; the desire to be intimate and to love another human being; the need to express one's own autonomy; the need to feel free . . . These issues, and the nature of the choices being made, must be made more conscious and explicit. Is it true, people must be encouraged to ask themselves, that the expression of intimacy, love, connection, autonomy, etc. (through various 'risky' behaviours) is as important, or more important to them, than life itself? If so, what does this tell us about the kinds of lives we are living? Are we desperate? Does our life mean so little to us that we prefer to engage in practices that will probably end it more quickly? Do we really want to survive?

The answers to these questions may not necessarily be what the health promoter wants to hear. But as we advance into a new century, and as risky and addictive behaviours advance with us, it is my contention that we are crying out for a reduction in directive scheme-based interventions, and more in the way of opportunities to discuss the kinds of lives we are leading. It is only in this way that we will develop a sense of sustaining meaning, and lives that are possible of expressing such meaning. Critical health psychology can aid this process, rather than perpetuating, as mainstream approaches have done, the denial and closure that lead to self-destructive and damaging behaviours.

Some would argue that such critical alternatives, opening to discussion, encouraging people to understand why they are behaving in the way they are doing, getting them to address potential feelings of self-destruction, encouraging a sense of responsibility in relation to one's own life and health, are simply a more sophisticated technique of surveillance by which people in socially/materially deprived positions are encouraged to 'interiorize' the connection between health and morality and thus reproduce existing relations of power. This may be so, but resolving this issue depends on whether such internalized power is viewed as positive or negative. As we saw in the last chapter, Giddens sees positive potential in such internalizing processes (Giddens 1991). It may be, for instance, that the strong productive dimension associated with the pursuit of health (colonizing the future, having a sense of control, direction, self-mastery and self-integrity) means that the body is being made to speak, not just for the self, but also for others to whom one is responsible. In this way it is possible to see how an enhanced concern with the individual body and self, can work hand-in-hand with a more communitarian and ethical concern for the larger social body. These are all issues that have remained unaddressed within contemporary health psychology. Adopting a critical approach not only opens up such questions, it also helps us see their absolute relevance to a health psychology geared up for the problems of the contemporary era.

Chapter summary

By the end of this chapter you should understand the following concepts and issues:

- The dominant models of health-related behaviour change in mainstream health psychology, e.g. HBM, PMT, TRA, HAPA. You should understand their limitations, especially related to their assumptions of a rational, logical individual.
- Critical health psychology's assertion that health behaviours encompass an 'alternative rationality' to that assumed in mainstream health psychology's models. This rationality is associated with the 'subjective meaning' of health behaviours and is connected in a complex way to the social, economic and moral environment.
- Healthy and risky behaviours function as 'symbolic goods' and survival strategies (i.e. ways of making meaning, identity, creating a sense of order and connection).
- The intextricable connection between 'health' and identity – health connected to contemporary notions of moral goodness, responsibility, individual control.
- The symbolic connection between risky behaviours and rebellion, transgression against dominant moral values.
- Different health-related behaviours and their connection with economic and social groupings.
- Mainstream health psychology's failure to take such symbolic, value-laden meanings into account may actually exacerbate the behaviours it is attempting to manage and control.
- Critical health psychology's questioning of the value of intervening in health-related matters. Does such psychological intervention make matters worse? Is it encouraging the pursuit of risky health behaviours? Are different kinds of intervention required?

Discussion points

- People engage in risky health practices because they value things other than the abstract concept of health presupposed in dominant health education models and interventions. People should be left to pursue their life and health as they see fit. Discuss.
- Being a bit of a 'fitness freak', as I walked out of the gym one day after having finished a vigorous one-hour circuit training session followed by a half-hour session on the Stairmaster, I stopped to chat

with a friend of mine, a 54-year-old marathon runner currently in training for a triathlon event. I admitted that I was 'absolutely shattered and didn't have an ounce of energy left'. In all seriousness, he turned to me and said 'No, that's not right, Michele, your energy sources are not finite. It's all in here' (tapping his forefinger on his temple). In what way can this behaviour be understood as an 'expression of contemporary bourgeois anxieties' (Bordo 1993)?

♦ By failing to appreciate the morally laden nature of risky health behaviours, mainstream health psychology runs the risk of exacerbating the very behaviours it attempts to reduce, manage and control. Discuss.

♦ Critically discuss the idea that critical health psychology has a moral duty to challenge the 'alternative rationalities' associated with risky health behaviours as a means of improving individual health and reducing social inequalities in health.

Key reading

Crawford, R. (1994) The boundaries of the self and the unhealthy other: reflections on health, culture and AIDS. *Social Science and Medicine*, 38(10): 1347–65.
Cushman, P. (1990) Why the self is empty: toward a historically situated psychology. *American Psychologist*, 45: 599–611.
Ogden, J. (1996) *Health Psychology*, Chapters 2, 3, 5, 6, 7, 8. Buckingham: Open University Press.

Further reading

Bordo, S. (1993) *Unbearable Weight: Feminism, Western Culture and the Body*. Berkeley: University of California Press.
Odets, W. (1995) *In the Shadow of the Epidemic: Being HIV Negative in the Age of AIDS*. Durham, NC: Duke University Press.

Notes

1 Also consistent with these findings are Donovan's (1986), which suggest that groups in society with the least power are more likely to hold fatalistic views on illness causation.

2 NB: This lack of a sense of a productive community is applicable to many gay men and constitutes a central feature of the work of contemporary gay theorists such as Rofes (1998) who argues for the need to 'revive the tribe' and create a new sense of positive identity, a revived sense of the future (post-AIDS), amongst gay cultures.

Mainstream health psychology's study of pain and disease

CHAPTER 4

Introduction

In mainstream health psychology textbooks it is routine to find separate chapters on pain, stress and various diseases such as HIV infection, cancer and coronary heart disease (see Sheridan and Radmacher 1992; Sarafino 1994; Ogden 1996). By contrast, this book takes the unusual step of studying pain, stress and disease together. One of the main reasons for doing this is to highlight the way in which research in these areas has followed similar paths and thus encountered analogous problems in the formulation and reformulation of theoretical and methodological problems. This will be achieved by providing a brief overview of how mainstream health psychology has progressively moved from simplistic mechanical models of pain, stress and disease processes, towards more sophisticated biopsychosocial models. Somewhat problematically, however, it will then be argued that such models, due to a combination of theoretical and methdological limitations, fail to provide an adequate characterization of the way in which pain, stress and disease are actually experienced and reflexively oriented to by individuals. This critique sets the scene for the next two chapters, in which a critical health psychological approach towards experiences of pain, stress and disease, is outlined.

Early mechanical models of pain, stress and disease

Early models of pain, stress and disease are all analogous to the extent that they reduce their object of investigation to biological and physiological changes taking place in the body. This is apparent in the following brief rendition of each of these areas of research.

As Horn and Munafò argue (1997: 1), for the past three hundred years, researchers have emphasized the mechanistic nature of pain. One of the earliest writers on pain, the philosopher Descartes (1664), provided the behaviouristic basis which has had a pervasive influence on all subsequent scientific and philosophical investigation into the phenomena of pain (Horn and Munafò: 1997: 2). Basically, Descartes regarded pain as an automatic response to a painful stimulus, a simple, behaviouristic stimulus–response (s–r) theory. Pain is manifest in the withdrawal of a body part (e.g. a finger) from a noxious stimulus (such as fire). The underlying mechanism of such experience is purely physiological in so far as bodily withdrawal occurs as a result of a direct pathway of messages transmitted between sensory nerves and the brain. This linear model is best expressed in Descartes' assertion that injury causes pain in the same way as a bell-ringing mechanism works, so that 'by pulling at one end of a rope one makes to strike at the same instant a bell which hangs at the other end' (cited in Horn and Munafò 1997: 4). Two of the most influential theories of pain that have developed over the last century or so, Von Frey's (1895) *specificity theory* and Goldshneider's (1920) *pattern theory*, have perpetuated Descartes' mechanistic behaviouristic legacy by similarly attributing pain experience to a simple stimulus–response model (Horn and Munafò 1997: 5).

Some of the earliest studies of stress within psychology were based on an analogous model, conceptualizing stress as deriving from some aspect of the environment (e.g. being stuck in a traffic queue), which caused strain in the individual and resulted in various biochemical and physiological changes (Bartlett 1998: 5). For example, Canon's 'fight or flight' model suggested that external threats in the environment increased activity rate and physiological arousal, thus enabling the individual to escape or fight the source of stress (Ogden 1996: 201). Hans Selye's General Adaptation Syndrome (GAS), developed in 1956, similarly defined stress as a 'non-specific response of the body to any demand made upon it' (Bartlett 1998: 6). In both of these models, stress was defined largely in terms of an automatic 'physiological response pattern which leads to a disruption of normal homeostatic regulatory physiological functioning' (e.g. sympathetic arousal increases the release of stress hormones and increases heart rate, blood pressure and muscle potential) (p. 6).

In an attempt to depart from Canon's and Selye's physiologically based models of stress, Holmes and Rahe (1967) developed 'Life Events' theory which attempted to examine stress as a response to more personal life changes. These authors argued that various life changes constitute stressors by taxing our adaptational resources, causing both physiological and psychological strain (Bartlett 1998: 29). They developed the well-known Social Readjustment Rating Scale (SRRS) to measure the relative stressfulness of various life events. These consist of 43 life event items ranging from those considered to be the most stressful, such as death of spouse and divorce, to more moderate events such as minor violations of the law, Christmas and change in eating habits. Despite the move away from conceptualizing stress as a response to a physiological stressor, however, it is now clear that Holmes and Rahe's model continues to attribute the experience of stress to a simple stimulus–response model.

As we have already seen in Chapter 1, early biomedical models similarly characterized disease as a mechanical response of the body to biological, chemical, cellular or genetic stimuli which cause physical changes in the body. In accordance with this model, for instance, HIV disease would be conceptualized as the body's 'response' to cellular changes induced by the HIV retrovirus stimuli which attack T-helper cells (specifically CD4 positive T-cells), resulting in immunological deficiency, the proliferation of opportunistic infections and gradual progression from HIV infection to AIDS. Similarly, cancer could be conceptualized as the body's response to cellular stimuli such as the uncontrolled growth of abnormal cells which produce tumours.

A role for psychology?

Analogous to studies of disease within the biomedical model, the history of pain research is one in which psychological or subjective factors have been largely ignored. Up until the 1960s, pain research operated on the assumption that 'real' pain consisted of that for which an organic basis could be identified. By contrast, when an organic basis could not be found, pain was categorized as 'psychogenic', 'all in the mind' and 'not real'. Indeed, Horn and Munafò argue that even in contemporary philosophical and scientific pain research, there is a strong aversion to the notion that the experience of pain can be characterized as a private or subjective phenomenon and 'any discussion of internal mental objects . . . is [seen as] meaningless and irrelevant' (Horn and Munafò 1997: 2).

Nevertheless, by the mid-1960s, it was increasingly recognized that earlier models of pain, stress and disease had failed to incorporate a more active role for psychological processes. In terms of pain research, this recognition came from the need to make sense of various anomalies which suggested a more complex relationship between physiological and psychological mechanisms than had previously been imagined. Amongst these were findings that similar tissue damage suffered by different individuals does not necessarily result in the same pain experience. Beecher's (1959) study of American service personnel who were severely wounded in action constitutes a classic example. These men reported very little pain, in some cases none at all, even though comparable injury on a civilian ward would have required extensive pain medication.

Other examples include cases such as 'phantom limb' in which pain and sensation in a limb continues to be 'felt' by the patient, despite the fact that the limb has been amputated (5–10 per cent of amputees report this). And what about patients suffering from chronic pain in which no organic pathology can be found? (Loeser (1980) reported that 70 per cent of patients with chronic low back pain have no discernible physical pathology.) In addition, recent research has developed techniques whereby pain tolerance levels can be increased. For instance, athletes have been trained to tolerate higher levels of pain, and cognitive interventions have been developed which allow acute and chronic patients to endure and modify their pain (Horn and Munafò 1997: 7–9). Investigations into the placebo effect, in which inert substances (e.g. a sugar pill as opposed to a drug containing pharmacological ingredients) have been shown to effect pain relief, also throw up questions regarding the role of psychological processes in the experience of pain (see Ogden 1996, Chapter 12). Cultural differences in pain tolerance and pain threshold have also been found. For instance, people's perceptions of pain vary in different families, social and cultural groupings, and institutional settings such as hospitals or clinics (see Zborowski 1952). As Horn and Munafò (1997: 9) argue, if pain transmission systems were simple and mechanistic, as earlier models suggested, then phenomena like these simply would not occur.

The same has been argued in terms of the study of stress. Bartlett (1998: 7), for instance, has argued that defining stress 'merely in terms of a physiological (or other) response has proved inadequate in accounting for the complexities of the stress process'. Canon, Selye and Holmes and Rahe all developed models which suggested a 'consistent response towards stressors', characterizing individuals as responding passively and automatically to changes in the external world (Ogden 1996: 202).

Such models minimized the role of psychology and failed to take account of individual differences in the stress process. For example, individuals vary considerably in their response to life events . A life event such as illness may, for one person, be regarded as extremely upsetting, whereas for another, it may be a relief from an unpleasant situation. The early models relating to the stress process are unable to account for such differences in perception.

In response to the shortcomings of these earlier models, Lazarus (1966) developed his 'transactional' model of stress in which the individual no longer passively responds to stressors but actively interacts with them. Central to this model is the concept of 'appraisal'. Lazarus argued that stress involved the transaction between an individual and his/her environment and a stress response is elicited only if an individual appraises a potentially stressful event as actually being stressful (Ogden 1996: 205). Lazarus defined two forms of appraisal – *primary* and *secondary*. The former refers to whether or not the event itself is perceived as benign or harmful. The latter refers to the indivdual's assessment of whether s/he feels adequately prepared to cope with the stressor. The result of this process of primary and secondary appraisal determines whether or not a stress response is manifested.

Biomedical models of disease processes have been criticized in the same way as early models of pain and stress. For instance, cancer cells are present in most people but not everyone gets cancer. Also, although research suggests a link between smoking and lung cancer, not all smokers develop lung cancer (Ogden 1996: 266). And how can we account for the fact that those who do have cancer progress at different rates to more advanced stages of the disease and ultimately to death? Or for the fact that some people do not progress at all, surviving the disease and becoming cancer-free? The same questions have been asked of HIV infection. Not everyone exposed to the HIV virus becomes HIV-positive, suggesting that stimuli other than basic biological factors may influence susceptibility to viral infection. In addition, once a person is HIV-infected, the length of time it takes to progress from HIV to AIDS to death remains variable. Research on long-term HIV survivors has also questioned the assumption that everyone who is HIV-positive will necessarily go on to develop AIDS (see Davies 1997). To reiterate our earlier theme, if pain, stress or disease transmission systems were simple and mechanistic, phenomena like these simply would not occur. Perhaps then, psychological and social factors play some role in determining the individual's predisposition, longevity and survival of disease?

The development of psychology and biopsychosocial models of pain, stress and disease

In the light of such questions and reservations regarding the mechanistic nature of pain experience, in their classic 1965 paper entitled 'Pain mechanisms: a new theory' (and then in subsequent work (1982)), Melzack and Wall attempted to introduce a more active psychological dimension to the understanding of pain (see Sarafino 1994; Taylor 1995; Ogden 1996: 223). Their model, known as the 'Gate control theory' (GCT) suggested that although pain could still be understood in terms of a simple stimulus–response pathway, this pathway is complex and mediated by a network of interacting processes. The central feature of the GCT is that the transmission of pain information is modulated at the base of the spinal column by a 'gate'. 'The extent to which this gate is open or closed determines the degree to which nerve fibre transmissions pass to the brain stem and cerebral cortex, and consequently, the degree to which pain is felt' (Horn and Munafò 1997: 3). The more the gate is opened, the greater the perception of pain. By contrast, closing the gate greatly reduces pain perception.

The GCT represented an important advance on simple previous stimulus–response theories of pain. It introduced a role for psychology and characterized pain as a multidimensional process in which many factors are involved in pain perception, not just a single physical cause (Ogden 1996: 225). Most importantly, it led to the creation of a *three process model of pain* in which individual differences in the perception of pain were seen as the product of three interacting dimensions: (1) physiological; (2) 'subjective-affective-cognitive'; and (3) behavioural. This model under-pins many contemporary developments in the study of pain perception which have examined the relationship between the individual's perception of pain and variables such as learned behaviour, attention, coping style, self-efficacy, locus of control, memory, fear/anxiety, depression and personal-ity (see Horn and Munafò 1997: chapter 5 for a concise outline of these studies).

More recent 'interactional' models of stress related to Lazarus's work have similarly characterized stress as a more complex biopsychosocial process which takes greater account of active, psychological functioning. These approaches define stress as the whole process of encountering stress-ful stimuli in the environment and responding to that stress, a process which incorporates a whole range of physiological, behavioural and psychological factors (Ogden 1996: 201). Such models hypothesize that individual dif-ferences in the stress process are best accounted for by a theory of 'person–environment fit' (P–E fit) in which stress occurs as the result of 'a lack of fit between P and E, while successful coping can be viewed as a change in either P or E such that the degree of fit is improved' (Bartlett 1998: 64).

In recent years such stress theories have identified important person and environment-related variables which allegedly act as mediating factors affecting appraisal processes and determining stress responses. Of particu-lar relevance to this book are those factors which determine stress responses and are thought to be related to the initiation and progression of illness. These include P factors such as the 'Type A behaviour pattern' (believed to predispose the individual to coronary heart disease, see Rosenman et al. 1975), the 'Type C' personality (believed to predispose the individual to cancer, see Kissen 1966; Shaffer et al. 1987; Eysenck 1990) 'self-efficacy' (see Bandura et al. 1982, 1988), 'dispositional optimism' (Scheier and Carver 1987), 'negative affectivity' (Watson and Clark 1984), 'hardiness' (Maddi and Kobasa 1984), 'mastery' (Karesek and Theorell 1990), 'locus of control' (Rotter 1966), 'sense of coherence' (Antonovsky 1979). On the E side, vari-ables such as work environment (Warr 1987), social support, age, sex, employment status, social class and urbanization (Jenkins 1991) have been studied as important factors influencing the stress process. All of these various P and E variables are hypothesized as playing some role in mediat-ing stress-induced immunosuppression and physiological changes by affect-ing the stress appraisal process. They do this either by predisposing the individual to the experience of stress, or, by contrast, by buffering against such experiences.

The relatively recent development of approaches such as psychoneu-roimmunology (PNI) in the study of disease processes is similarly pre-dicated on a biopsychosocial model in so far as it suggests complex interrelationships between biological (neurological, immunological) and psychological functioning. Initiation, progression and potential survival from various diseases such as cancer and HIV/AIDS, are modelled as the result of complex interactions between psychosocial processes and activities of the nervous, endocrine and immune systems (Ader and Cohen 1985; Antoni *et al.* 1990; Goodkin *et al.* 1992). The complex array of psychosocial factors thought relevant to disease systems include: behavioural or lifestyle factors (such as cigarette smoking, diet, sexual behaviour, alcohol and drug use – engagement in which can allegedly be predicted by health beliefs (see Chapter 3)); subjective factors related to the stress process such as control, coping styles, personality and hardiness; and social factors such as life events and social support.

From a mainstream health psychology perspective, the aim of research is to identify and manipulate perceptual, behavioural and cognitive dimensions of pain, stress and disease, in order that they can be managed through reduction or alleviation. The various methods of intervention include a range of behavioural and cognitive methods such as biofeedback, relaxation, cognitive therapy, Simonton techniques (which include relaxation, mental imaging and exercise programmes), hypnosis and improving social support.

Theoretical limitations of biopsychosocial models of pain, stress and disease

Horn and Munafò (1997: 12) argue that the great strength of the GCT lies in its ability to integrate psychological, behavioural and physiological elements and present them as different levels of explanation in a single holistic system. But in what sense is pain, studied from this perspective, or relatedly, stress, from an interactional or transactional perspective, or disease, from a PNI perspective, understandable as a holistic system? By contrast, other researchers such as Ogden (1996: 225) have argued that the main weakness of the GCT lies in its perpetuation of Cartesian dualisms between body and mind. This is despite the fact that the GCT (and transactional/interactional stress models, and PNI models of the disease process), attempted to depart from such dualism by providing a more sophisticated understanding of the interaction and integration between psychological and physical processes. At bottom, however, such processes are still seen as fundamentally separate in these models, all of which retain conceptions of the body as a physiological system to which various factors are attached by means of cause and effect relationships (Radley 1997: 52).

Such criticisms reiterate our earlier argument first encountered in Chapter 1. There, we argued that there is a tendency in mainstream health psychology to dress up biopsychosocial or 'three process models' related to various phenomena (in this case pain, stress and disease) as if they constituted holistic and integrated frameworks. In reality, however, such approaches represent no more than multiple explanatory frameworks in which various physical, emotional and behavioural factors are thrown together in a seemingly fragmented way with little theoretical understanding of how they actually connect together.

Bartlett (1998: 74) reiterates this critique in relation to investigations of stress when he argues that the list of variables studied in relation to the stress process, especially those related to the P component of the biopsychosocial model, 'appears almost endless'. As Coyne and Lazarus (1980: 146) have critically argued:

> We have distinct bodies of literature focusing on antecedent environmental conditions of stress, on intervening states and traits and responses to stress. With apologies and compromises, these conflicting definitions side-slip across each other with little coherence and minimal integrative effort. Fractions of variance are accounted for by arbitrary partitioning and sampling of person and environment variables are interpreted as if they represented proportions of causal responsibility. Linear causal relationships, dictated by the constraints of experimental design, are taken as adequate representations of what *occur naturalistically as mutually causative, reciprocal relationships*.
>
> (p. 146, emphasis added)

Accordingly, it is gradually becoming apparent that one of the primary problems in relation to such studies of pain, stress and disease, relates to the failure to engage in integrated theorizing. This failure is a direct result of the over-reliance on hypothetico-deductive theory testing (Bartlett 1998: 145).

Methodological problems with biopsychosocial models of pain, stress and disease

Closely related to such theoretical inadequacies are methodological issues related to the validity of the dominant methods used to measure pain, stress and disease within contemporary mainstream health psychology. Concerns regarding such methodologies were first raised by Wall (1977) over twenty years ago. Criticizing the implicit assumption of pain as a simple sensory experience akin to that of pressure, heat or light, Wall argued that 'If I sense pain it comes in a packet with such changes as fear, loathing, anxiety, dislike, urgency, etc.' (p. 363). Underpinning this simple statement is an appreciation that in order to understand human experiences of pain, it is necessary to appreciate the way in which pain becomes a function of the whole individual, including his present thoughts and fears as well as hopes for the future. In other words, it is necessary to examine the ways in which pain has *meaning* for the individual.

Wall's comments were made in relation to his development of the GCT which, as we have already seen, sought to challenge the notion that pain constituted a simple mechanical response to a stimulus. These comments were particularly pertinent to the psychophysical methods used in pain research at the time. These consisted mainly of four different methods of inducing pain in laboratory settings – thermal, electrical, chemical and mechanical – all of which implicitly assumed that pain was a sensory experience like pressure or heat (Horn and Munafò 1997: 93). Increasing recognition that the experience of pain involved a more complex relation between physiology and psychology, however, led to the development of more sophisticated pain assessment tools such as the Pain Discomfort Scale (Jensen et al. 1991), the Pain Disability Index (Tait et al. 1990) and the 'Pain Anxiety Symptoms Scale' (McCracken et al. 1992).

In an analogous fashion, recognition that the experience of stress involved complex interactive dynamics between physiology and psychosocial processes, is what originally led Holmes and Rahe to their formulation of the Social Readjustment Rating Scale. The same thinking lies behind the development of many other life events scales such as the Life Experiences Survey (LES), the PERI Life Events Scale, the Unpleasant Events Schedule (UES) and the Daily Hassles scale (see Sarafino 1994: 95). In studies of diseases such as HIV/AIDS and cancer, measuring tools such as the Illness Perception Questionnaire, Psychosocial Adjustment to Illness Scale, the Mental Adjustment to Cancer Scale, the Coping Orientations to Problems Experienced Scale and the Profile of Mood States (see Ogden 1996: 274), have similarly been developed to take account of the various psychosocial factors involved in the disease process.

All these scales can be characterized in terms of their attempt to assess the more subjective elements of pain, stress and disease such as attitudes, meaning, emotional orientation and coping.

The rise of critical health psychology, however, as we saw in Chapter 1, has increasingly questioned whether such methodological tools are suitable for the study of psychology. In all of the previously mentioned measuring tools, the addition of subjective elements remains firmly inscribed within structured questionnaires which utilize measuring scales designed to translate into statistical techniques. The development of such measuring instruments has encouraged researchers simply to administer questionnaires, quantify the results and use these as measures of perceptions and orientations towards pain, stress and disease. From this perspective, the attempt to capture and control the complexities of experiential phenomena is solved by using increasingly sophisticated combinations of scaling techniques (e.g. Williams and Keefe 1991).

Too often, however, these results consist of simplistic and reductionist representations of complex human processes, the nature of which is 'distorted' to 'fit experimental designs which are not necessarily the most appropriate' (Bartlett 1998: 55). Implicit in the development and administration of such measuring tools is the assumption that experiences of pain, stress and disease are amenable to quantitative measurement, experimental manipulation and statistical analysis. As has previously been argued in this book, such methods are unable to provide in-depth insight into the way in which individuals actually experience, give meaning, and reflexively orient towards phenomena such as pain, stress and disease. In order to achieve such understanding, different methods and a different theoretical orientation are required. The necessity and value of adopting such an approach towards the study of pain, stress and disease will be demonstrated in the next chapter.

Reformulations of the study of pain, stress and disease: 'acute' and 'chronic'

Mainstream health psychological studies of pain, stress and disease have tended to assume that acute dimensions of these phenomena are representative of the general nature of these experiences. Horn and Munafò (1997: 51), for instance, argue that mainstream health psychology has commonly accepted that 'acute' pain constitutes the normal manifestation of pain. The same is true of mainstream health psychology's study of disease which is implicitly based on models of acute illness such as Leventhal's 'self-regulatory model of illness behaviour' (see Ogden 1996: 40). This model assumes that, given any change in the *status quo* (e.g. a change in the body, resulting in illness), an individual will be motivated to solve the problem and re-establish a state of normality. Hence, if healthiness is the individual's normal state, the individual will be motivated to re-establish their state of health. This model assumes that a 'return to normality' and a 'solution', as in the case of acute illness, is possible.

The conceptualization of stress processes and interventions to reduce stress and the possibility of illness initiation and progression, reveals a similar way of thinking. For example, one of these methods is 'cognitive restructuring' – a process by which stress-provoking thoughts or beliefs are replaced with 'more constructive or realistic ones that reduce the person's appraisal of threat or harm' (Sarafino 1994: 156). Stress, Sarafino continues, often arises from 'faulty or irrational ways of thinking', and cognitive therapy attempts to help patients see that 'their problems can be solved, and the negative events they experience are usually not catastrophes' (p. 157). Such comments, the idea that stress is caused by 'faulty', 'irrational' ways of thinking, that people can be helped to 'solve' their problems, and to see that the negative events they experience are 'not catastrophes', reveal that the stress process is conceptualized as an acute, temporary crisis. But what if the reality relating to the stress experience is that things *are* catastrophic, that there is no solution, that radical uncertainty and lack of control cannot be changed (see Chapters 5 and 6)? What if one's life circumstances, for instance, living with a chronic or terminal illness, render control and certainty unattainable? As will be argued in Chapters 5 and 6, when psychological interventions wittingly or unwittingly impose such ideals on patients, they run the risk of doing more harm than good.

These issues are important because they are central to critical health psychology's interest in exploring in greater depth the experiential dimensions of pain, stress and disease. They also point towards a shift which frequently occurs in the move towards a critical health psychological approach. This is the shift from an investigation of 'acute' to 'chronic' dimensions of such phenomena.

The main characteristics of chronic pain are that they persist over a longer period of time than acute pain (over six weeks), and that a physiological basis for the pain cannot be found. In terms of chronic illnesses, there is no cure for the condition, only various ways of managing, coping and limiting symptoms, and they tend to persist over a relatively long period of time. The most common examples include HIV/AIDS, cancer and coronary heart disease. I am unable to find a definition in the literature for 'chronic stress', but in this book, the term refers mainly to the kind of stress that accompanies conditions such as chronic illness. Accordingly, it refers to the stressful dimension of learning to live with long-term, intractable, often 'unresolvable' experiences.

It is important to note that the investigation of chronic pain, stress and disease has become increasingly pertinent in the light of the changing nature of the disease burden in contemporary Western societies. For example, the main health problems and causes of death in Britain today are chronic diseases which cannot be cured. Radley (1994) argues that an element of uncertainty pervades modern consciousness with regard to chronic diseases because of the lack of medical knowledge of what exactly causes such diseases and of how to cure them. This element of uncertainty, as will be shown in Chapter 5, is important in understanding how people have to learn to live and adapt to life in the context of chronic pain, stress and disease.

Representations of pain, stress, disease, and transformations in contemporary society

In this chapter we have been concerned to examine the way in which mainstream health psychology goes about conceptualizing, studying and analysing pain, stress and disease. In the following two chapters, we will be looking at how critical health psychology attempts to reformulate that study. At stake here, as will become increasingly apparent, is an attempt to lift pain, stress and disease 'out into the world', to invent 'objectifying' structures (such as methods of quantification or language), that will reach and accommodate these normally inaccessible areas of experience (Scarry 1985: 6). These various psychological approaches constitute nothing less than the attempt to create a language that will adequately represent experiences of pain, stress and disease. As Scarry (p. 5) argues, this is a project 'laden with practical and ethical consequences' (see also Kugelman 2000a, 2000b).

Changes in the study and experience of pain, stress and disease depicted in this chapter reflect two processes central to the transformation of modern society – objectification and rationalization (these were first discussed in Chapter 2). In the next two chapters, we will see that the critical psychological approach represents a third process – that of subjectification. The following analysis seeks to clarify this relationship further.

Early biomedical approaches to the study of pain, stress and disease reflect modernist processes of objectification. In this model, these phenomena were reduced to their physiological dimensions. In the rational world of medicine and science, under the microscope or in the controlled laboratory setting, physical or sensory stimuli came to be viewed as the main causes of pain, stress and disease.

The rise of disciplines such as health psychology is crucially related to the second, rationalizing process of modern society. Here, the development of biopsychosocial models and an emphasis on the role of psychological factors (behavioural, subjective, affective, cognitive) involved an attempt to predict and control the onset, progression and treatment of pain, stress and disease. In terms of actual application, the intent of such programmes is to develop sufficient knowledge of psychological and social processes in order that people suffering from pain, stress and disease can be informed and educated in management and control techniques to mitigate the harmful effect of such factors. Through the process of rationalization, lay people come to absorb expert knowledge and manage their experiences accordingly. Modelled on the natural scientific biomedical approach and focusing almost exclusively on acute pain, stress and disease, mainstream health psychology concertedly attempts to maintain an objective, value-free stance towards the study of pain, stress and disease.

As will become clear in the next two chapters, the rise of critical psychological approaches to the study of pain, stress and disease represents the third, subjectifying process of modern society in which 'a more complicated subjectivity comes to the fore' (Bury 1998: 12). This brings forth important questions for mainstream health psychology's study of various health- and illness-related phenomena.

Chapter summary

By the end of this chapter you should understand the following issues and concepts:

- The way early mechanical models of pain, stress and disease reduce them to physiological and biological changes in the body.
- Mainstream health psychology's introduction of psychological factors into the equation – facilitating an appreciation of a more active

role for psychological processes in the investigation of pain, stress and disease.

♦ The development of biopsychosocial models of pain, stress and disease and the theoretical problems associated with such models, e.g. limited theoretical understanding of how various factors fit together.

♦ How such theoretical limitations connect with methodological issues regarding the validity of quantitive measures and the disregard for the meaning of individual experiences of pain, stress and disease.

♦ Mainstream health psychology's predominant focus on acute dimensions of pain, stress and disease.

♦ The way in which the changing nature of investigations into pain, stress and disease reflects processes central to the transformation of contemporary society, i.e. objectification (mechanical models), rationalization (biopsychosocial models) and subjectification (critical models, see next chapter).

Discussion points

♦ Outline the ways in which investigations of pain, stress and disease have followed a similar pattern within contemporary health psychology.

♦ Critically discuss some of the limitations of the biopsychosocial model in relation to the investigations of pain, stress and disease.

Key reading

Bartlett, R. (1998) *Stress: Perspectives and Processes*. Buckingham: Open University Press.

Horn, S. and Munafò, M. (1997) *Pain: Theory, Research and Intervention*. Buckingham: Open University Press.

Ogden, J. (1996) *Health Psychology*, Chapters 10, 11, 13. Buckingham: Open University Press.

CHAPTER
5

Critically reformulating the study of pain and disease

I cannot write a conventional 'I conquered cancer' story. I read so many of them . . . By the end of the book they were always free of cancer. But what if the miracle doesn't happen? What if, like me, you are one of the many thousands of people who just have to learn to live with the disease. We have a much more restricted choice of autobiographies. Some of them approach death with such calmness. I don't. Others conclude 'I'm glad I had cancer'. I'm not.

(Dennison 1996: 1–2)

Introduction

The last chapter provided an overview of how mainstream health psychology orients towards the study of pain, stress and disease. Beginning with early mechanical models, the discipline then moved on to utilize more complex biopsychosocial models which attempted to allow a more active role for psychological and subjective interpretation. However, this has been achieved in large part through the simple addition of psychological factors which have been factored into the biopsychosocial equation and subjected to statistical analysis. In the last chapter it was argued that this approach remains theoretically and methodologically deficient to the extent that it fails to develop understanding of the way in which individuals reflexively orient and attribute meaning to experiences of pain, stress and disease.

Critical health psychology aims to re-direct the focus of study in order to take greater account of meaning and reflexivity, which, as was argued in Chapter 1, are uniquely characteristic of the 'human order of meaning'. In this chapter therefore, the main aim will be to depict some of the general experiential themes which emerge from contemporary personal accounts of people living with serious pain and illnesses. Part of the objective of such an exploration is to serve as an 'empathic witness' to such experiences. It is argued that this constitutes a crucial ethical role for the critical health psychologist. This becomes especially important when we realize that psychological ideas regarding disease causation and progression have not only infiltrated into the public imagination, but are becoming the focus of increasing resistance as a critical discourse emerges in autobiographical accounts of illness. This discourse suggests that individuals feel increasingly objectified, dehumanized and disempowered not only by medicine, but also by psychological interventions. Accordingly, the increasing proliferation of autobiographical accounts of illness and self-help groups constitutes one manifestation of the way in which a 'more complicated subjectivity' comes to the fore in the context of a rationalizing psychology which exhorts people to exercise control over their own health and illness (see Chapter 2).

From this, it will become apparent that when people live with experiences of pain, stress and disease in contemporary society, they do so in a far more complex and reflexive fashion than mainstream health psychology has even begun to depict. Such experiences cannot be limited to the neatly boxed biological, psychological and social variables depicted in dominant psychological models. Instead, as the individual is launched into the more gritty world of suffering, such categories break down and a desperate search for meaning, control, recognition and accountability ensues. Accordingly, it is to this realm, the experiential and cultural world of pain, stress and disease, that this chapter directs its attention.

Critical health psychology's reformulation of the study of pain, stress and disease

Numerous researchers such as Kleinman (1988: 9) have critically argued that approaches such as mainstream health psychology constitute a 'radically materialist pursuit' of the biological and cognitive structures and mechanisms of pain, stress and disease which can potentially be very harmful. This is because they serve to reduce these experiences to narrowly defined measurable data which are amenable to 'technical mastery and instrumental rationality' (Kleinman *et al.* 1992: 7). In so doing, they direct attention away from the way in which people actually live with and attribute meaning to their experiences, trivializing and at times 'expunging altogether' questions of suffering (p. 14). As Frank (1991: 52) similarly argues, concepts of pain and disease based on such frameworks have no interest in finding out what pain or disease 'means in a life'. Seeking 'only cure or management', such approaches fail to address a crucial, perhaps *the* crucial psychological dimension of pain, stress and disease: how humans experience, interpret and live with them. This is the dimension towards which critical psychological approaches re-direct their investigations.

As we have already discussed in previous chapters, one of the central aims of a critical health psychology is to explore in depth the meanings and experiences of individuals undergoing various health-related phenomena. This can probably be best achieved by using qualitative methods which potentiate a more detailed and rigorous exploration of the structure and meanings of individual experiences. Accordingly, a number of critical health psychologists, medical sociologists and cultural anthropologists have attempted to redirect the study of pain and disease away from the dominant natural science and predictive based biopsychosocial model, towards a more hermeneutically structured approach which looks at how people themselves experience pain, stress and disease (see Scarry 1985; Brody 1987; Kleinman 1988; Frank 1991; Good *et al.* 1992; Jackson 1994; Radley 1994, 1997; Smith 1996; Crossley 1997a, 1998a, 1999a, 2000a; Davies 1997; Williams and Bendelow 1998; Kugelman 2000a). From this perspective, a central aim is to recapture the voices and experiences of people who have themselves suffered pain and disease – to listen to how their experiences have affected their lives, ideas, feelings and relationships – in Kleinman's terms, to provide an 'empathic witnessing of the existential experience of suffering' (Kleinman 1988: 10).

Pain, illness and narrative

One central theme intrinsic to many critical approaches studying pain and disease is the importance of stories and narrative (see Murray 1999; Crossley 2000a). Brody (1987: 5) argued that suffering is produced and alleviated primarily by the meaning people attach to their experiences. As one of the primary mechanisms for attaching meaning to experiences is through storytelling, such activities assume a central role in the critical study of pain and disease. As Broyard (1992) writes:

> Always in emergencies we invent narratives. We describe what is happening as if to confine the catastrophe. When people heard that I was ill, they inundated me with stories of their own illnesses, as well as the cases of friends. Storytelling seems to be a natural reaction to illness. People bleed stories and I've become a bloodbank of them.
>
> (p. 21)

In recent years numerous studies have looked at how people cope with the disruptive effects of pain, disease and traumatizing events through storytelling and processes of 'narrative reconfiguration' (Early 1982; Brody 1987; Kleinman 1988; Robinson 1990; Viney and Bousfield 1991; Frank 1993; Del-Vecchio Good *et al.* 1994; Farmer 1994; Garro 1994; Good and Del-Vecchio Good 1994; Radley 1994; Davies 1997; Crossley 1998a, 1998c). By narrative reconfiguration, we mean the use of different forms of story which function to re-establish a moderate degree of 'ontological security', a renewed sense of meaning, order and connection in the individual's life (Taylor 1983; Radley 1994: 146; Davies 1997). Indeed, recent research has suggested that the construction of a narrative which brings meaning and order to the chaotic experience of pain and disease is intrinsic to the effectiveness of most complementary therapies (Scott 1998, see Chapter 7 for more detailed discussion). Most of these studies, however, have been conducted from sociological and anthropological perspectives rather than from within psychology. My own narrative work with HIV-positive individuals (Crossley 2000a), Taylor's work with breast cancer patients (1983) and Radley's (1994) research with people adapting to coronary heart disease, constitute notable exceptions. As Smith *et al.* (1997: 73) argue, it seems somewhat ironic that in order to explore the phenomenology of pain and disease it is necessary to turn to sociological rather than psychological studies.

Because the interpretation and meaning attributed to pain and disease contribute to how it is experienced, it is vitally important for psychologists to take the stories people tell about pain and illness ('lay stories') as a critical focus for investigation. This can be achieved through in-depth interviewing and an analysis of written autobiographies in which people describe their experiences of pain and disease. In recent years, the production of such autobiographies, especially in relation to diseases such as cancer and HIV/AIDS, has proliferated.[1] In this chapter I will draw mainly on published autobiographical accounts of cancer to depict some of the important themes related to the experience of living with serious illness. I focus on accounts of cancer mainly because I have already examined experiences of living with HIV/AIDS in previous publications. Two of the best known recently published autobiographical accounts are John Diamond's (1998) *C: Because Cowards Get Cancer Too* (1998) and Elisa Seagrave's (1995) *Diary of a Breast*.

It should be noted that in re-directing attention towards lay voices, many researchers draw a contrast between the terms 'disease' and 'illness'. This distinction is intended to distinguish between mainstream health psychology approaches which remain locked within the scientific attempt to quantify and measure subjective dimensions of adaptation to 'diseases' such as HIV/AIDS and cancer. By contrast, the word 'illness' is used to characterize more critical and hermeneutic approaches which aim to explore experiences and meanings. In Frank's terms:

> Illness is the experience of living through the disease. If disease talk measures the body, illness talk tells of the fear and frustration of being inside a body that is breaking down. Illness begins where medicine leaves off, where I recognise that what is happening to my body is not some set of measures. What happens to my body happens to my life. My life consists of temperature and circulation, but also of hopes and disappointments, joys and sorrows, none of which can be measured.
>
> (Frank 1991: 13)

From this point onwards, this chapter will use the words 'disease' and 'illness' in accordance with the above characterization.

Kleinman (1988: xiv) argues that the ability to listen to and interpret people's experiences of illness remains a core skill for doctors which has regrettably 'atrophied in biomedical training' in recent years. In this chapter, I take Kleinman's comments as equally, if not more, pertinent to health psychology. Our training in psychology is too often conceptualized as a

narrowly based science. This diverts attention away from issues of interpretation and meaning which are of central importance in the study of pain
and illness. 'Illness has meaning; and to understand how it obtains meaning
is to understand something fundamental about illness, about care, and
perhaps about life generally' (p. xiv). This chapter is written in the firm
belief that contemporary health psychology is in desperate need of a more
sustained attempt to address and understand such meanings.

Achieving recognition: the moral function of patient voices in the context of contemporary healthcare

It is important to note, however, as we have already seen in Chapters 2 and
3, that the critical project of exploring personal meanings connected with
various health- and illness-related issues, should not be mistaken for an
uncritical validation or transparent representation of the reality of such experiences. If this were so, such approaches would fail to capture the social and
cultural structuring of stories of pain and illness (Crossley 1999b, 2000b).
As Kleinman (1988: 49) argues, 'the personal narrative does not merely
reflect illness experience, but rather contributes to the experience of symptoms and suffering'. Of particular relevance is the way in which contemporary stories of pain and illness are used to perform various practical and
moral functions such as the presentation of self and the allocation of blame
and responsibility (Early 1982; Williams 1984; Kohler-Riessman 1990; Garro
1994; Davies 1995a; Radley 1997; Crossley and Crossley 1998; Crossley
1998b, 1999a).

In order to understand the general moral function performed by personal
stories of pain and illness, it is important to appreciate the social and political context in which they have become increasingly significant. This is
one in which, since the 1970s, there has been an emerging critique of 'medicalization' and the power of medicine to define experiences of illness in
narrow disease terms (see Chapters 2 and 6). An important element of this
process has been the changing nature of the disease burden in contemporary
Britain towards chronic illnesses which cannot be cured. As will be shown
in this chapter, such illnesses create a high degree of uncertainty and call into
question the necessity and value of relying too heavily on scientifically
defined reality. They highlight the importance of appreciating the reality of
illness from the patient's point of view, in Conrad's (1987) terms, moving
us from 'outsider' towards 'insider' perspectives on illness. The development of such 'insider views' is linked to the widespread growth of self-help
groups and alternative/complementary approaches (see Chapter 7), both of
which question whether people should rely on the supposed authoritative
knowledge and expertise of doctors to prevent and cure disease (see
Gouldner 1971; Johnson 1972; Morgan et al. 1985).

In this context, it is perhaps not surprising that experiential accounts of pain and illness often appropriate a hostile tone towards medicine and doctors (see Crossley 1997b, 1998b; Chapter 7). For example, many people living with chronic illnesses express concern over the way in which their contact with health professionals, especially doctors, has led them to feel objectified and unrecognized. Accordingly, part of the social function of writing or talking about illness experiences is to personalize the deperson-alizing processes of healthcare and professional interventions, to affirm one's subjectivity and identity, and to highlight the fact that there is 'a person in the patient'.

Frank, for instance, writes that:

> I always assumed that if I became seriously ill, physicians no matter how overworked, would somehow recognise what I was living through. I did not know what form this recognition would take, but I assumed it would happen. What I experienced was the opposite. The more critical my diagnosis became, the more reluctant physicians were to talk to me. I had trouble getting them to make eye contact; most came only to see my disease. This 'it' was their field of investigation; 'I' seemed to exist beyond the horizon of their interest.
>
> (Frank 1991: 54)

Dennison similarly identifies her need for recogntion when she claims that:

> What I want from my doctor more than anything else is the recogni-tion that I have a mind. The mind is the basis of identity, of individu-ality. It distinguishes the patient from the person.
>
> (Dennison 1996: 103)

And Mayer similarly:

> I wanted these doctors and nurses and technicians to know who they were dealing with, but that was really impossible. In this stripped down, stream-lined hospital world, they didn't have time for that sort of thing. I was simply another cancer patient.
>
> (Mayer 1994: 24)

In the light of such experiences of non-recognition, the process of sharing stories about illness experiences in autobiographical accounts and self-help groups performs an inherently 'moral function' (Brody 1987: 15). This is because such storytelling 'presumes both a teller and a community of lis-teners, such that the act of telling a story and responding to it is a reci-procal exercise designed in part to strengthen community bonds'. Such 'narrative reasoning', according to Brody, is 'inherently democratic' because it is widely shared by lay persons and cannot be claimed as the exclusive province of experts (p. 15). Through telling stories and raising conscious-ness, people can claim the authority of experiential reality and thus attempt to empower both themselves and others. It is in this sense that self-help groups have been characterized as forming part of wider protest movements in contemporary societies, promoting empowerment and collective action to influence decisions about biomedical research and practice (Herzlich and Pierret 1987; Wilkinson and Kitzinger 1993).

Recognizing the existential devastation caused by illness

A central theme in autobiographical and personal accounts of illness experiences is the existential devastation caused by chronic pain and illness. This relates to the sense of devastation imposed by something which is perceived as beyond the control of the individual, beyond fairness and beyond logic. 'Why me?', cries Dennison, diagnosed with ovarian cancer at the age of 31:

> I knew it was ridiculous but all I could think over and over was that I'd never hurt anybody deliberately in my life. What had I done to deserve this? It was so unfair. If there was a God he couldn't do this, not to me. It wasn't FAIR . . . Why had I been singled out? Why was it going to end just for me. It wasn't fair. Why me? Why? Why? Why?
>
> (Dennison 1996: 5)

As is apparent here, 'adapting' to such illness involves considerable 'bodily, mental, emotional and spiritual distress' (Leder 1984–5; Jackson 1994: 203). People living with such experiences feel the strong need to find meaning for their suffering. Indeed, Mayer (1994: 105) argues that the 'more catastrophic' the pain and illness is, the more the 'urgent need to mine it for meaning and life-changing potential'. In the context of such life-changing experiences, it is not difficult to see that any attempt to reduce them to narrowly defined, measurable data amenable to 'technical mastery and instrumental rationality' may not only be invalid, but also unethical. The overview that follows therefore attempts to depict some of the central, essentially immeasurable, existential themes emerging from autobiographical accounts of illness.

The 'totality' of chronic pain and illness: becoming a different person

Many studies of chronic pain and illness illustrate the potentially devastating impact they can have on a person's life. This has been characterized as an 'ontological assault' in which some of the most basic, underlying existential assumptions that people hold about themselves and the world are thrown into disarray (Taylor 1983, 1989; Kleinman 1988; Janoff Bulman 1992). Other approaches speak of 'biographical disruption' to characterize the potentially overwhelming impact that physical pain and illness can have on an individual (Bury 1982; Brody 1987; Yardley 1997). These studies all share the assumption that the onslaught of physical illness brings with it a whole range of challenges regarding the individual's interconnected conceptions of body, self and world. In his study of chronic pain Good characterizes the experience as one involving a dissolution of the 'building blocks of the perceived world' (Good 1992: 41), including a basic sense of space, time and language, all of which become overwhelmed and disintegrated by pain. In other words, chronic pain and illness 'threaten to unmake the world' (p. 42).

This 'unmaking of the world' becomes apparent in autobiographical accounts of illness in which people describe the way in which being informed about and living with their illness shakes their taken-for-granted sense of identity at its very roots. For example, Frank (1991: 9) describes the moment when his doctor called to tell him that his cardiogram showed he had a heart-attack: 'He seemed uncertain of the medical details but I hardly heard him; I was lost in a sense of sudden and profound change. In the moments of that call I became a different person' (Frank 1991: 9). This notion of becoming 'a different person' refers to the way in which chronic illness totally changes a person's life. This theme is repeated again and again in the autobiographical literature related to all kinds of chronic illnesses.

Mayer (1994), for instance, similarly writes of the way in which breast cancer 'has changed my life'. It is, she argues, 'more than a disease of the body, far more than the sum of errant cells run wild. Like any life-threatening illness, cancer invades the entire context of a life, disturbing its balance, heightening its struggles' (p. 6). Frank similarly argues that illness 'leaves no aspect of life untouched . . . your relationships, your work, your sense of who you are and who you might become, your sense of what life is and ought to be – these all change, and the change is terrifying' (Frank 1991: 6). These changes make Mayer feel 'like an émigré to another, darker country, trying to sort out what my new identity means'. In one moment of discovery, she explains, her life was totally transformed as she 'entered another world' and was 'forced to survive in a hostile new landscape, fraught with dangers'. This world was one in which 'the ordinary events of my life had abruptly become irrelevant. None of the ingredients of my former identity counted here' (Mayer 1994: 23). 'Slowly', Skloot writes, 'the banks of my old self eroded, each lush growth that fed there turning sere' (Skloot 1996: xiv).

Scarry further captures this sense of the totality of pain and illness when she argues that, from no matter what perspective pain is approached, its 'totality is again and again faced'. Pain, she argues:

> begins by being 'not oneself' and ends by having eliminated all that is 'not itself'. At first occurring as an appalling but limited internal fact, it eventually occupies the entire body and spills out into the realm

beyond the body, takes over all that is inside and outside, makes the two obscenely indistinguishable, and systematically destroys anything like language or world extension that is alien to itself and threatening to its claims. Terrifying in its narrowness, it nevertheless exhausts and displaces all else until it seems to become the single broad and omnipresent fact of existence.

(Scarry 1985: 55)

Shattering assumptions about time and the future

One of the most fundamental 'building blocks of the perceived world' (Good 1992: 41) to be destroyed in the experience of chronic pain and illness is one's basic sense of time. Many phenomenologically and existentially oriented writers have highlighted that time is basic and fundamental to an understanding of contemporary human existence in so far as our normal, routine temporal orientation is one of projecting into the future. It is important to make clear, however, that we are not necessarily consciously aware of the fact that we project into the future in this way. Our assumptions about and towards time, are only made visible when a shock or a disruption occurs, throwing them into sharp relief (see Schutz 1962; Garfinkel 1984). The experience of chronic pain or illness constitutes such a disruption. When a person receives a serious illness diagnosis, they are immediately shocked out of the complacency of the assumed futurity of their existence and their whole conception of themselves, their life and their world is likely to undergo radical changes. As the phenomenologist Van den Berg argues:

The horizon of time is narrowed. The plans of yesterday lose their meaning and importance. They seem more complicated, more exhausting, more foolish and ambitious than I saw them the day before . . . the past seems saturated with trivialities. It seems to me that I hardly ever tackled my real tasks . . .

(Van den Berg 1972: 28)

Frank (1995) uses the metaphor of 'narrative wreckage' to characterize such experiences.

In previous research, I have shown how much of the traumatic psychological impact of living with an HIV-positive diagnosis can be traced back to the disturbance and disruption of this fundamentally experienced sense of 'lived time' (Davies 1997). Autobiographical accounts of other pain and illness experiences illustrate the same theme. Having, at the age of 31, being diagnosed with advanced ovarian cancer, Anne Dennison writes that 'Suddenly, I felt the axe had fallen. Gone forever' (Dennison 1996: 1). 'Everything', she continues, was 'gone all at once'. 'I was obsessed by the waste of it all . . . I regretted all the effort, all the sacrifices directed towards a future which wasn't going to happen' (p. 4–5). Mayer similarly writes that the 'twin illusions of safety and time had been early casualties of my cancer':

> Without even realising it, before my diagnosis I had been living in an open, expansive, interior space. Now the walls and ceilings had moved uncomfortably close. Limits were everywhere I looked . . . Gone was my sense of feeling protected or secure. Gone, too, was any feeling of certainty about the future. As my treatment progressed, these invisible losses were to become more painful, in some ways, than the outward, physical losses and privations of the disease and its remedies.
>
> (Mayer 1994: 59)

Shattering assumptions about the body

According to phenomenological accounts of human experience, in our normal everyday lives neither the body nor the self is manifested as an object for consciousness, thoughts or attention. We act in the world *through* our bodies, our bodies constituting the subject of our action, 'that through which we experience, comprehend and act upon the world' (Good 1992: 39). From this perspective, our 'body-self' is experienced as the author of our activities, the originator of our ongoing actions, and thus as an 'undivided total self', a seamless whole within individual experience. Hence, our normal, taken-for-granted relationship to our body-self is one of 'bodily disappearance' (Leder 1990). In Jean-Paul Sartre's (1956) terms, the body is *le passé sous silence*, 'passed over in silence'.

All of this changes when the individual is afflicted with chronic pain and illness. Interviews with people suffering from chronic pain, and autobiographies written by people suffering pain and illness, have shown that pain directs attention away from this implicit sense of experienced whole and converts the body into an alien object (Kleinman 1988; Leder 1990). When the individual is in pain, the body, contrary to normal experience, becomes a central aspect of experience. It *dys*-appears (i.e. appears in a *dys*-functional state) and 'suddenly we feel *dys*-embodied, alienated and betrayed by our bodies' (Williams and Bendelow 1998: 135). Accordingly, pain and suffering represent something that is foreign and that threatens and invades the individual's subjectivity by fragmenting his/her lifeworld.

This sense of threat is apparent in Good's (1992) work on chronic pain, particularly in relation to his discussion of an in-depth case-study of a chronic pain patient called Brian. Good argues that Brian's body comes to take on 'special primacy' as it 'absorbs the world into itself' and 'dominates consciousness', threatening to 'unmake the everyday world'. Rather than acting in the world *through* his body, Brian's body becomes an 'object distinct from his experiencing and acting self' (p. 39). His body, taken over by pain, comes to have agency. 'It is a demon, a monster . . . Pain is an "it"' (p. 39). In this way, severe pain and illness leads the individual to lose their 'normal occupancy of everyday reality' (Jackson 1994: 215), producing 'alienation' and an 'existential vacuum' in which s/he feels 'cut off from the outer world', isolated and disintegrating (Vrancken 1989: 442).

Such feelings of alienation are commonly represented in autobiographical accounts of illness. For instance, Lucy Grealy (1994), in her account of her experience of leukemia as a child, explains how she vaguely became aware that she was 'experiencing my body, and the world, differently from other people' (p. 66). Mayer writes of how 'All my life, without even realising it, I'd retained an innocent trust in my physical being. Now, that was lost, replaced by the feeling of having been betrayed by the runaway cells of my own body' (Mayer 1994: 77). Dennison similarly writes of how 'My body had let me down, it wasn't reliable. Nothing could be trusted. Least of all myself' (Dennison 1996: 5). 'Life threatening illness,' explains Frank (1991: 50), 'gave my body a new sense of importance. I had never been so sensitive to its shortcomings, nor had I realised how much I could expect of it.'

Shattering assumptions about relationships with others

Our experience of chronic pain and illness is 'fundamentally intersubjective' (Kleinman et al. 1992: 9). Basically, this means that it is not just the individual living with pain and illness who is affected, but also the lives of his/her family, intimate friends, co-workers and care-givers. To regard pain as the experience of an individual, as it is regarded in standard biomedical practice, is 'so inadequate as to virtually assure inaccurate diagnosis and unsuccessful treatment' (Kleinman et al. 1992: 9). As Frank similarly argues, pain is about incoherence and the disruption of relations with other people and things; it is about 'losing one's sense of place and finding another' (Frank 1991: 52).

One of the most fundamental assumptions of everyday life is that we live in the same world as other people around us, and accordingly, the world we experience is also shared by others (Schutz 1962: 218–22). For people living with chronic pain and illness, however, this assumption is often thrown into doubt. Shattered assumptions regarding the future and one's body mean that the person living with pain and illness feels profoundly alienated from the world of other people. It may be very difficult for significant others to understand these feelings and, even if they do, too painful for them to confront and cope with.

Such experiences are commonly depicted in autobiographical accounts. Mayer, for instance, describes her 'crushing loneliness' that came 'from the certain knowledge that the people you love most do not – cannot – understand' (Mayer 1994: 4). Dennison poignantly describes the impact that her cancer diagnosis had on the dynamics of her relationship with her husband in terms of shattered assumptions about their future together:

> Fatigue has worn him down. This constant uncertainty, the ever present threat that I am going to die, has turned him away from me a little. It is so hard to remain committed to someone, not knowing whether they will be there in a few months or a few years time . . . It would have been easier if I had either died or been cured quickly but it just isn't like that . . . It's like the thoughts that were too terrible for Paul to share had become a barrier. I don't really want to talk in depth about his fears about how he will live without me. We joke about his predilection for long-legged dumb blondes but that is as far as it goes. There are limits to what I want to share. I genuinely don't want him to mourn me forever but I can't talk seriously about the new family I hope he will find . . .
>
> (Dennison 1996: 86)

Relationships with friends and acquaintances may also become increasingly strained and bitter as the person living with illness struggles with the unpleasant uncertainties forced on him/her. Mayer, for instance, comments on how disconcerting it was to realize how close she was to responding to people's polite 'How are you?' with the truth. She admits the anger and bitterness in her desire to respond in this way, almost as if she wanted to assault people, to rub their faces in it, in the same way that she felt she had been assaulted (Mayer 1994: 30). While she still spoke with her friends when they called to inquire how she was, she found herself becoming more and more distant from them. Her troubles outweighed theirs, she felt, and she 'envied them their unblemished lives, their unscarred bodies, their certain futures' (p. 75).

Being forced to live with uncertainty

Shattered assumptions. *Who am I? My future? My body? Our future?* All of these accounts demonstrate that the overriding theme of living with chronic pain and illness is the radical sense of uncertainty and unsafety it forces on the individual. 'When will life resume its normalcy, its safety?' asks Mayer (1994: 4). The more she found out about breast cancer, the clearer it became how little was known about the disease. Once you have breast cancer, she argues, you can be cured, or the cancer could return to kill you in two years, or ten, or twenty or thirty . . . And yet no one knows why. Mayer articulates the difficulty of having to live with the partial knowledge, the partial certainty, the crude treatments and painful side-effects, 'with no sure expectation of anything' (p. 20). 'I didn't even know', she poignantly writes, 'if

I should be using the present tense, or the past, when I talked about my illness. I didn't know whether to say I *have* cancer, or I've *had* cancer' (p. 148). 'My problem was, I didn't know if the war was over' (p. 147). The hardest thing about living with cancer, Mayer concludes, is that, over time, it 'mounts a frontal assault against the very fabric of hope' (p. 129).

This assault 'on the fabric of hope' is made very clear in Dennison's diary-like account in which she charts her experience of coming to live with this uncertainty. In the early stages of coming to terms with the disease, she begins to realize that 'nothing was ever going to be the same again'. Her cancer diagnosis shatters her expectations, her vision of herself, her 'previously charmed existence'. She felt as if she had lost her innocence and been 'forced to face grim reality' for the first time in her life. She began to see that she was going to have to live with the reality of uncertainty forever (Dennison 1996: 26).

A year or so after the diagnosis, however, Dennison writes that she feels increasingly able to cope with this sense of uncertainty as she realizes that much of her anxiety and stress has been caused by the 'constant shifting of focus between the possibility of a normal lifespan and an imminent end'. By learning how to just 'enjoy the moment' and focus completely on it, however, a lot of her pain 'suddenly vanishes'. She had finally learned to accept that the 'only reality was what was happening here and now' (Dennison 1996: 41). But then, a few months later, after having been on a relaxing holiday, one night in the bath, as she fingered the scar from her operation, her 'heart skipped' as she realized there was a large lump under her finger: 'Further up. In my armpit. Oh God. It's not moved. It's a new lump' (p. 78). As the lumps were biopsied, she starkly realized that:

All the uncertainties were back again and it was just as hard as it had ever been. Harder . . . This was all wrong. I wasn't ready. It felt like a very nasty black joke. And I didn't have a sense of humour anymore.

(p. 78)

As Dennison comes towards the end of her autobiographical account, she tells the reader that:

I really wanted to write one of those happy ever after books after all. I had planned to end with the last chapter, taking off to New Zealand, long before I wrote it. Not exactly cured but having outlived my prognosis by some years with an indefinite future ahead. It had a clarity that seemed appropriate for a book. Beginning with diagnosis, ending exactly three years later with a new beginning. But for most of us living with cancer just isn't like that. It's about living with uncertainty. Not knowing from week to week, from month to month what the future holds; whether the disease will get worse, develop quickly or slowly, respond or not respond to treatment . . .

(p. 89)

Appreciating life

The devastating impact of being forced into an awareness of uncertainty and unsafety cannot be over-emphasized. Nevertheless, it is important to note that a common theme in many autobiographical accounts of chronic illness is its ability to create an enhanced appreciation of life's basics. 'For the first time in my life, under the pressure of my disease and the heightened awareness of mortality that accompanied it', Mayer argues, 'I felt a sort of permission – no, an imperative – to pay attention to what was important to me' (Mayer 1994: 130). Diamond makes a similar point in the following anecdote:

A couple of nights ago I was sitting with Nigella in bed.

'What are you smiling at?' she said.

I didn't realise that I was, but what I was thinking about was Nigella and the children. I was holding a soft toy which Bruno had brought into the bed when Cosima had fetched him in that morning.

'It's such a strange time, isn't it?' I said.

'How so strange?'

'Oh, you know. Strange that I've never felt more love for you than I have in the past year, that I've never appreciated you as much, nor the children. In a way I feel guilty that it should have taken this to do it, I suppose. But it is strange, isn't it?'

For the first time, I found myself talking like this without resenting that it had taken cancer to teach me the basics, without resenting that there was a part of me capable of talking like a 50s magazine article without blushing.

I still don't believe that there is any sense in which the cancer has been a good thing ['I cling to the belief that anything which stops you kissing your children goodnight or telling them a story . . . has to be, on balance, a bad thing' – p. 82], but well, it is strange, isn't it?

(Diamond 1998: 240)

Such comments indicate, as Frank argues, that illness restores the sense of proportion that is lost when we take life for granted. To learn about value and proportion, 'we need to honour illness, and ultimately, to honour death' (Frank 1991: 120). The value of remaining a person with cancer, Frank argues, is that it enables one to 'hold onto that question – how did you spend today?' (p. 134). Holding onto that question reminds him 'to feel and see and hear':

It is too easy to become distracted. When the ordinary becomes frustrating, I have to remember those times when the ordinary was forbidden to me. When I was ill, all I wanted was to get back into the ordinary flux of activity. Now that I am back in the ordinary, I have to retain a sense of wonder at being here.

(p. 134)

That is why when Frank feels he has 'no time to walk out and watch the sunlight on the river', he realizes that his 'recovery has gone too far' (p. 134).

Resisting professional colonization: the need to be recognized

The above overview of emotional and existential themes relating to illness experiences illustrates that developing an understanding of how people learn to live with such experiences necessitates taking a step back from the scientific and professional requirement to impose order and control. This relates to the strong need, emerging loud and clear from experiential accounts of illness, for people simply to have their experiences listened to. Frank characterizes this as the need for people to 'bear witness' to his experience. 'The help I want,' he argues, 'is not a matter of answering questions but of witnessing attempts to live in certain ways. I do not want my questions answered; I want my experiences shared' (Frank 1991: 34). Similarly, Mayer, drawing on Frank's work, comments:

> The need to contain or control the ill person's experience, rather than to tolerate and simply acknowledge the grief, anger and fear of what has happened, is what drives well-meaning friends and family members to offer advice, reassurance or faulty comparisons from their own lives. What I call bearing witness is altogether different. Without realising it, it was this that I longed for. Bearing witness involves a mutual recognition of helplessness, vulnerability and respect. It says only, I am with you. I honour your experience. How simple, and yet how rare a gift this is.
>
> (Mayer 1994: 80)

It is this need to bear witness that contributes to the popularity of self-help groups. As Dennison comments in relation to her involvement with such a group:

> I learned a great deal from other patients and their partners. I was surprised that their support affected me so deeply. In the intensity and openness of that weekend a group of strangers had become intimate friends . . . In the group I could talk about death without turning a friend white faced, and about trying to be positive without someone saying 'you're so brave taking it like that'. Only other patients really understand that being positive is a completely selfish attempt to stay sane. I was relieved to find that emotions and thoughts which seemed so eccentric and irrational had been experienced by others.
>
> (Dennison 1996: 44)

For the first time, Dennison said, she had 'felt completely supported'. 'It was more than feeling totally understood, though that was part of it. My innermost thoughts had been listened to, more than that, responded

to, by people who could expand on and build on that shared experience'
(p. 45).

Jackson's ethnographic study of chronic pain patients similarly emphasized how pain sufferers in the clinic often claimed that only other pain sufferers could understand their experiences through a kind of intuitive sense
of empathy – what Jackson called a form of *communitas* (Jackson 1994: 213).
This sense of communitas came to function as the patients' own form of
unique language and experiential reality. This reality was perceived as
separate and in opposition to that created by health professionals, such as
doctors and psychologists, of whom patients were very suspicious and felt
had not worked for them. As one patient commented: 'they'll have their
own answers and solutions that don't jive with your own' (p. 219). Accordingly, contact and communication with other patients tended to create a
separate reality, an 'anti-language' resistant to professional forms of
intervention.

Resistance to psychological findings

Patient resistance to the ideas and interventions of professional psychology
is of particular interest to critical health psychology. This is because of critical health psychology's interest in the way in which people actively appropriate and reflexively orient towards the rationalizing and professionalizing
processes characteristic of contemporary societies (see Chapter 2). Mainstream health psychological ideas are important in this respect because they
have been widely publicized and popularized and have thereby infiltrated the
contemporary 'mind-set'. This is evident, for instance, in terms of a widespread belief in the potential role of psychological factors such as personality and stress in the cause, progression and treatment of pain and illness.
Such questions of disease causation and treatment are important because
they reflect on the moral issue of responsibility in relation to disease (Brandt
1997: 56). The section that follows therefore seeks to examine how people
writing their accounts of chronic illnesses, particularly those with cancer,
reflexively orient towards health psychology's ideas.

As we outlined in Chapter 4, health psychology suggests links between
stress, personality and illness, especially for illnesses such as coronary heart
disease and cancer. For example, Temoshok and Fox (1984) suggested that
people who develop cancer manifest a 'Type C' personality. Eysenck (1990)
similarly described a 'cancer prone personality'. And Shaffer *et al.* (1987), in
a prospective study attempting to examine the predictive capacity of personality in terms of cancer development, similarly found evidence for a
'cancer-prone personality type'. Although these studies provide slightly different definitions of such cancer-prone personalities, the main characteristics are described as 'passive', 'helpless', 'repressive', 'unexpressive of
emotion' and 'self-sacrificing'.

In the light of possible connections between stress, personality factors and illness progression, psychological interventions may serve as a means of enhancing people's sense of 'personal control', training them to become more 'hardy' personalities (Sarafino 1994: 148), using cognitive therapy to facilitate them becoming less passive, helpless, unexpressive of emotion, self-sacrificing and repressive.

The general notion that mental or psychological processes are involved in pain and disease processes probably also accounts in some large part for the increasing interest in alternative/complementary therapies (see Chapter 7). This is especially the case with regard to cancer care which has, in recent years, been criticized for being 'tumourcentric' and based exclusively within orthodox medicine, at the expense of complementary therapies which place more emphasis on the 'social, emotional and spiritual dimensions of life' (Kinghorn and Gamlin 1996: 100). In recent years this has resulted in increasing lobbying amongst patients and patient advocates for the provision of complementary approaches. Accordingly, the CancerLink (an organization emerging out of patient advocacy) document, 'A declaration of rights for people with cancer', now states that people have 'a right to a second medical opinion, to reject treatment, or to undertake complementary therapy without discrimination to continued medical services' (Kinghorn and Gamlin 1996: 105). Kinghorn and Gamlin argue that this document infers that the demand for complementary therapies, especially for people living with cancer, will increase in future years.

Exposure to people living with chronic illnesses in contemporary society, either through written autobiographical accounts or through social science interviews, reveals a widespread concern with, and orientation to, the role played by psychological processes. This relates to the increasing influence and application of mainstream health psychology's ideas which have led people to believe they can exercise some degree of control over their own health. Not only this, however. The concern to exercise control over psychological processes also relates to issues of morality and responsibility. As we saw in Chapter 3, the state of health has increasingly come to be seen as a key symbol for the good, moral, responsible self to the extent that the pursuit of health has actually become the pursuit of moral personhood. When people become ill, they do not become immune to such ideas. Instead, they continue to feel a sense of moral obligation (perhaps even an enhanced sense of such obligation) to pursue health and recovery by whatever means possible. In so doing, they attempt to retain a vision of self congruent with contemporary conceptions of the 'good self' – i.e. one displaying self-determination, will and moral fortitude (Crossley 1997b).

On the other hand, as was also demonstrated in Chapter 3, there is also a corollary to this attempt to engage in behaviours and ways of thinking that conform to cultural ideals of self-control, will and fortitude. For example, people in materially and socially deprived groups (such as single mothers living on welfare benefits, drug users, gay men) often feel radically alienated from such ideals. Such alienation frequently feeds into a sense of rebellion (either implict or explicit), which leads the individual to engage in risky health-related behaviours as a way of transgressing dominant social values. From the above overview of some of the common existential themes experienced in the wake of serious pain and illness, it is apparent that such experiences potentially induce an analogous sense of alienation from the dominant values of mainstream culture. What is the point in working hard, saving money, having pensions, paying a mortgage, etc. if everything can be taken away in one fell swoop? The shattering of basic assumptions about life introduces a radical sense of uncertainty and alienation from the central values of contemporary culture (see also Davies 1997). Accordingly, it is perhaps not surprising that such values may become the central focus of resistance and contestation for people living with such experiences. Health psychology's ideas, which are perceived as reinforcing and perpetuating such values and ideals, also become a central locus of resistance.

Orientation to the 'good' of health is apparent in the way in which psychologically influenced approaches and therapies are oriented to in a morally engaged fashion. For example, in his study of people living with multiple sclerosis, Pollock (1993: 61) found that the majority accepted the desirability of adopting a positive attitude of mind towards their illness as an ideal to which they approximated as best they could. In my study of people living with a long-term HIV-positive diagnosis (Crossley 1997b), I found the same sort of attitude. Similarly, autobiographical accounts of people living with various illnesses suggest not only that they are bombarded with advice on all kinds of alternative therapies, but also that they feel morally obliged to pursue as many such remedies as is reasonably possible. Dennison (1996: 16), for instance, comments on the many books, all of 'the most daunting kind' which exist on the theme 'I cured myself of cancer'. Only the methods vary: 'rejecting orthodox medicine, meditating three times a day, eating nothing but beansprouts or wheatgrass'. 'Still,' Dennison writes in a telling statement, 'if they did it maybe I *should* try' (p. 16).

Repeated reference is made in the autobiographical literature to holistic lifestyle programmes such as the Simonton and the Bristol programmes (self-help programmes devised to help people living with cancer). Mayer, for instance, stated that when she was first exposed to the Simonton method it 'seemed logical' to her that emotional well-being could lead to physical health and vice versa. 'It was heartening,' she continued, 'to think that psychological redemption could lead to actual physical survival' (Mayer 1994: 95). Similarly, Dennison described herself as 'discovering and devouring' the Simonton book *Getting Well Again* (Simonton et al. 1980). It was, she claimed, 'so hopeful, so sure that a cancer patient's own psychology could if not cure at least help them to live longer' (Dennison 1996: 16). Both women, however, gradually arrive at a more critical conclusion regarding their dealings with such methods.

Mayer, for instance, argued that 'it was only gradually that I began to realise what a double edged sword this notion could actually become, inducing guilt and feelings of failure in people already weakened by life-threatening illness' (Mayer 1994: 95). Mayer describes how:

> Frightened, operating on the idea that it was better to try everything, even if unproven, I dutifully practiced my visualisation, meditation, relaxation exercises. I worked my way through a shelf full of books with titles like *Cancer as a Turning Point . . . You Can Fight for Your Life* and *You Can't Afford the Luxury of a Negative Thought* – before coming to the conclusion that the sense of control these specific theories and techniques offered was far outweighed by the anxiety and self-blame they engendered.
>
> (p. 103)

Dennison made a similar point when she eventually allowed herself to admit that:

> I could also see a negative side to my positive thinking. If it could make me well maybe negative thoughts could make me ill? I was really scared by the possibility. I couldn't stop the negative thoughts even though I wanted to . . . I was trying to keep up the relaxation and meditation, but that was beginning to slip a little too. Visualising the cancer being eaten away by my white cells, doing all the right things in accordance to the Simonton plan, seemed to require such a lot of effort. I'd be dreamily visualising golden fish, then remember they were supposed to have teeth, then that I'd forgotten the eyes. At the end of these meditation sessions I was anything but relaxed!
>
> (Dennison 1996: 23)

Such theories, Mayer argued, encouraged her to fill her head with superstitious thoughts in which she vacillated 'from utter helplessness to omnipotent fantasies that I might destroy myself with such innocent weapons as daydreams and beliefs' (Mayer 1994: 64).

A similar resistant approach is apparent in the way in which people writing autobiographical accounts orient to categories such as the 'Type C' personality. Although mainstream health psychology may believe it is engaging in a value-free, neutral science when it uses such categories, unfortunately many cancer patients interpret such categorizations in a far from morally or emotionally neutral fashion. For instance, Mayer described how, 'looking for myself in this so-called "Type C" profile, I couldn't help but feel disheartened. These were so many of the same attributes I'd been struggling with . . . for years' (p. 95). It made her feel 'guilty for getting so sick' and that cancer was 'a personal failing' (p. 100). Citing Susan Sontag's work *Illness as Metaphor* (1979) (as do many people writing accounts of their illness experiences), Mayer argues that 'there is mostly shame attached to a disease thought to stem from the repression of emotion . . . The view of cancer as a disease of the failure of expressiveness condemns the cancer patient; it expresses pity but also conveys contempt . . . the cancer personality is regarded . . . with condescension, as one of life's losers' (p. 101).

Similarly, Dennison described how the analysis of the cancer personality worried her:

> I refused and refuse to acknowledge that I felt helpless and hopeless, or unduly stressed, in the months before the diagnosis. I had had my emotional ups and downs (who hasn't) but nothing out of the ordinary. But it worried me. Perhaps it was so deeply buried into my subconscious I was unable to recognise it and unable to recognise it was still doing me harm?
>
> (Dennison 1996: 16)

Seagrave (1995: 36) also worries whether there is 'really any reason why we five women have breast cancer? Do we have anything in common? Have we all repressed our emotions, or suffered from some terrible grief or loss . . .' And Skloot, charting his experience of Chronic Fatigue Syndrome, refuses to 'believe I made myself sick . . . This isn't something I deserved, nor is it a punishment for pushing myself too hard' (Skloot 1996: 59).

Above, I suggested that many autobiographical accounts are influenced by Sontag's book *Illness as Metaphor*. In this book, Sontag, herself having had breast cancer, argues that people living with chronic, intractable conditions such as TB, cancer and AIDS tend to be the subject of 'punitive and sentimental fantasies' concocted about them. This, she argues, is largely due to the use of metaphors when characterizing such experiences. Diamond (1998: 72) similarly notes that the battlefield metaphor encourages us to feed into the idea of illness as a war zone that has to be gloriously fought and won. Likewise, psychologically influenced approaches such as the Simonton methods encourage people to see illness, metaphorically, as a 'permission giver', something *required* because the 'emotionally unexpressive' person had never allowed him/herself to confront his/her needs before the illness. Sontag's main point, however, is that illness is *not* a metaphor. It is a physical condition and the most truthful way of being ill is one which is purified of, and resistant to, metaphoric thinking. Skloot appropriates Sontag's thinking as the basis for his autobiography on Chronic Fatigue Syndrome, as is evident in the following quote:

> I know it was nothing personal. I know I was simply a host the virus used to do the only thing it knew how to do, enact its sole pattern of growth . . . From the virus's point of view, I could have been a stone, or a broth of monkey kidneys . . . Or I could have been you . . . It was a matter of being as good as the next available body. Perhaps I was worn down at the wrong moment . . . but it was nothing more essential

about the self than that. Tired of my busy life, a war zone of forces besieging the fortress of who I am? Spare me metaphor. As Susan Sontag says on the first page of her book *Illness as Metaphor*, 'My point is that illness is *not* a metaphor, and the most truthful way of regarding illness – and the healthiest way of being ill – is one most purified of, most resistant to, metaphoric thinking.' I buy that, and the book you are about to read starts from the assumption that illness must be looked at straight-on . . .

(Skloot 1996: xiii)

In her study of chronic pain patients attending a multidisciplinary pain clinic, Jackson (1994) similarly noted a strong resistance amongst pain patients to feed into psychologically influenced theories of pain. Jackson noted that her interviews illustrated 'quite sharply that patients protest loud and clear at any hint that a given pain is "emotional" and therefore not ultimately produced by a physical cause' (Jackson 1994: 212; see also Broom 1997). Somewhat paradoxically, despite feeling profoundly misunderstood, pigeonholed and categorized by medicine, it is this world and language that they 'continue to pin their hopes on' (Jackson 1994: 222). This is evident in the fact that a characteristic of patients attending pain clinics for chronic pain is their relatively long history of seeking medical help.

This leads us finally to the question of why people living with chronic pain and illness seem to be manifesting an increasing scepticism and resistance to psychologically influenced theories of illness causation and treatment. A recapitulation and characterization of the language used by people in considering these psychological ideas provide a clue to the answer to this question. *Disheartened, personal failing, made myself sick, deserved, punishment, guilt, worry* . . . If others have tried, then *so should I, dutifully working through* the books and techniques, *fighting*, not *affording the luxury* of negative thoughts, *guilt, failure, anxiety, self-blame, psychological redemption* . . . This language is inescapably moralistic. As Diamond concluded in his response to letters which exhorted him to 'defeat' his cancer, 'the whole battlefield vocabulary suggested that the cure for cancer had a moral basis – that brave and good people defeat cancer and that cowardly and undeserving people allow it to kill them' (Diamond 1998: 72).

Accordingly, part of the reason why patients are beginning to resist these ideas relates to their struggle for social and moral legitimacy. Psychological theories and interventions are interpreted as making people responsible for their disease and its management. After going through all the books and methods on complementary therapies, finding themselves unable to retain a simple faith in their ability to cure themselves, people tend to experience a sense of guilt and moral failure. If others can cure themselves, why can't I? This feeling of failure often gives way to anger and a desire to reject totally and kick against the 'accuser' – in this case theories and ideas suggesting a role for psychology in illness (see also Chapters 6 and 7). The return to simple biomedical explanations reduces the problem of disease to something which is 'just' physical, something over which the individual has no influence and only modern technology can control. Accordingly, such explanations provide a useful exit from the sense of moral obligation inferred by psychologically influenced theories. Mainstream health psychology's unwillingness to engage with such reflexive and value-laden concerns not only represents a failure to appreciate the emotional and cultural nature of pain and illness experiences, it is also instrumental in reducing the potential of psychology to help people come to terms with the devastating nature of such experiences.

Conclusion: representations of pain, stress, disease, and transformations in contemporary society

In this chapter we have been concerned to examine the way in which critical health psychology reformulates the study of pain, stress and illness. In the last chapter, we argued that developments in mainstream health psychology's study of these phenomena reflected two processes central to the transformations of modern society – objectification and rationalization. We also indicated that critical health psychology represented the third process of subjectification. In what way does this have implications for health psychology?

The early objectification phase of biomedical approaches towards the study of pain and disease actually offered the potential of 'disconnecting disease from its historical associations with sin, moral turpitude and idleness' (Brandt 1997: 56). This, in turn, had the effect of depersonalizing and demoralizing pain and disease, and thus of reducing the sense of individual responsibility for such occurrences.

Representing the second, rationalizing process of modernization, the development of biopsychosocial models introduced a formal role for psychology in the scientific study of pain and disease. This involved an attempt to predict and control the onset, progression and treatment of pain, stress and disease. In terms of actual application, the intent of such programmes, as we saw in Chapter 4, is to develop sufficient knowledge of psychological processes in order that people suffering from pain and disease can be informed and educated in management and control techniques. Modelled on the natural scientific biomedical approach and focusing almost exclusively on acute pain and disease, mainstream health psychology concertedly attempts to maintain an objective, value-free stance, maintaining a demoralized approach towards the study of pain and disease.

The rise of critical psychological approaches to the study of pain and disease become important partly in relation to the epidemiological shift towards the predominance of chronic pain and illness. This is because an adequate understanding of chronic illness requires an exploration of suffering, of the 'complex inner language of hurt, desperation, and moral pain (and also triumph) of living an illness' (Kleinman 1988: 29) 'What is the metric,' asks Kleinman (p. 29) for understanding such 'existential qualities' within biomedical and (we should add) mainstream psychological research? Lacking such understanding, we must ask whether the professional knowledge created by medical and psychological science can be at all adequate to the needs of patients, their families and practitioners (see also Chapters 6 and 7).

In terms of the study of pain, stress and illness, critical health psychology's response is to examine the increasing proliferation of stories written by people and talked about in support groups and social science interviews. These narratives are seen as part of a more general process in which health and illness is becoming increasingly 'moralized'. Accordingly, people who are ill or in pain experience increasing pressure to make sense of themselves and justify themselves to others. From an ethical point of view, these attempts to make sense of pain and illness should be recognized. It is our duty as psychologists not to bypass carelessly such personal suffering, but to honour and learn from them. Accordingly, in this changing context, questions are raised as to how realistic and ethical it is to maintain a demoralized approach to the study of pain, stress and illness (see also Chapter 6).

Such questions become particularly pertinent when we realize that, hiding behind scientific values of neutrality and objectivity, mainstream health psychology is actually operating with an implicit agenda which points towards the remoralization of pain and disease. Labels such as 'Type C' personalities may have a profound influence on how people think about themselves, and on how significant others perceive them. If characterizing someone as a 'Type C' personality makes them feel guilty or a failure, this may create a self-fulfilling prophecy, turning them away from trying to explore and understand what is happening, 'returning' them to technically based biomedical explanations of pain and disease in which they continue to feel objectified and dehumanized. Failure to acknowledge its part in the remoralization of pain and disease points towards an ethical failure on the part of mainstream health psychology to recognize the suffering inflicted on people by the imputation of morally dubious categories (regardless of how professional psychologists perceive them).

If mainstream health psychology can be criticized for failing to appreciate this moral dimension of experiences of pain and illness, however, is it not the case that critical health psychology is equally guilty of feeding into and perpetuating such moralism? From this perspective, it could be said that critical health psychology facilitates a process of 'increasing governmentality' in which it is not just the physical or cognitive aspects of pain and illness that are brought under professional surveillance, but the whole 'lifeworld' of the individual (Kugelman 1997; Clark 1999). Rather than being empowering, as is commonly assumed, is the process of encouraging people to tell their stories of pain and illness just a more complicated form of attempting to govern, control and manage their experiences of pain, stress and illness? (see Crossley 1999b). When people became ill in the past, their only responsibility was to try and get well again. In contemporary culture, by contrast, it seems that the ill person is under a moral obligation to be reflexive, to develop an understanding of 'what illness means in his or her life' (Frank 1995: 13). By focusing its lens of investigation onto such accounts, is it not the case that critical health psychology is all too complicit in the process of encouraging people to become their own 'self-surveyors', thus increasing the depths of professional colonization?

Related to this point is the question of how appropriate the critical exploration of meaning and understanding is to an analysis of acute pain and illness? How important is it to 'empathically witness' a person's pain or to appreciate their 'existential suffering' if they have terrible toothache or have had a cardiac arrest? Surely, the only thing this person needs is some form of technical intervention to put the problem to rights? Is it not the case that the professional objectification and rationalization characteristic of biomedicine and mainstream health psychology are worth while if only the pain, stress or illness can be eliminated or alleviated? Why muddy the waters and complicate the issue by adding in fuzzy, often immeasurable existential issues and feelings? Is a mainstream, scientific psychological approach more appropriate for understanding the world of acute pain?

Perhaps. Clearly, if critical approaches are imputed wholesale, then we simply create an inverse repetition of the earlier problem of assuming acute pain and illness as the paradigm of all pain and illness experiences (see Chapter 4). Instead, chronic pain would be taken as representative of all types of pain experience. Having said that, however, the main aim of this chapter has been to demonstrate how important it is to appreciate the human and existential dimensions thrown up by the example of chronic pain and illness. I think this is justified as a means of rectifying imbalances in a culture dominated by biomedically defined 'scripts' of pain and disease (to a large extent uncritically accepted by scientific psychological approaches). Although I would ultimately argue that understanding this human dimension is important for *all* kinds of pain and illness, both acute and chronic, at the same time, it is important not to exacerbate problems of reductionism. If earlier scientific approaches towards pain and illness have made the mistake of reducing it to physical and cognitive dimensions, then the wholesale acceptance of critical approaches, inversely, runs the risk of existentializing and totalizing pain and illness to too great an extent. This is a risk which must constantly be borne in mind when adopting a critical psychological approach towards the study of pain, stress and illness.

Chapter summary

By the end of this chapter you should understand the following concepts and issues:

♦ Critical health psychology's focus on issues of individual reflexivity and how people orient and ascribe meaning to experiences of pain, stress and disease.
♦ The importance of stories and narrative as the primary means by which meaning is attached to suffering and adapting to experiences of pain, stress and disease.
♦ The need to use qualitative methods to explore patient voices, e.g. importance of in-depth interviews and autobiographical accounts.
♦ The distinction between 'disease' and 'illness'.
♦ An appreciation of the existential devastations caused by serious pain and illness.
♦ The social and cultural structuring of patient voices and their connection to practical and moral functions, e.g. achieving empowerment and recognition in the historical context of passive patient care and medicalization.
♦ The resistance of professional colonization and the development of an 'anti-language' resistant to professional forms of intervention. The need simply to be listened to, not made into an object of scientific or humanistic investigation.
♦ Resistance to mainstream health psychological ideas, e.g. links between stress, personality and disease. This is part of the struggle for social and moral legitimacy.
♦ The failure of mainstream health psychology to explore or engage with such value-laden issues may enhance suffering and exacerbate the very effects it is trying to manage and control.
♦ The problems of critical health psychology. Does it feed into the moralization of health? Is it just a more sophisticated form of control? Does it existentialize pain and illness to too great an extent?

Discussion points

♦ In a self-help group for women living with breast cancer, a 48-year-old woman talks about her hostility towards all health professionals. The rest of the group find themselves concurring with her hostility. How can these women's experiences be understood as part of the wider social and cultural context?

◆ Why might people living with serious chronic illnesses such as cancer or HIV, be resistant to mainstream health psychology's ideas and interventions?

◆ Describe some of the main ways in which critical health psychology would investigate a case of chronic pain or illness differently from mainstream health psychology.

◆ A 54-year-old man has just suffered a massive heart attack. What methods and interventions might be appropriate for a health psychologist to use?

Key reading

Crossley, M. L. (2000a) *Introducing Narrative Psychology: Self, Trauma and the Construction of Meaning*, Chapters 6–8. Buckingham: Open University Press.

Kleinman, A. (1988) *The Illness Narratives: Suffering, Healing and the Human Condition*. New York: Basic Books.

Further reading

Any of the empirical or autobiographical studies of pain and illness experiences discussed in this chapter.

Note

1 When I recently searched 'Whittaker's Bookbank' (all published books in UK, Canada and the US), 24 autobiographical works on cancer had been published between 1992 and 1998, 18 biographical and autobiographical works related to HIV/AIDS, and 1 autobiography on Chronic Fatigue Syndrome.

Approaches to mental illness

> Depression steals away whoever you were, prevents you from
> seeing who you might someday be, and replaces your life with a
> black hole ... Nothing human beings value matters any more –
> music, laughter, love, sex, children, toasted bagels and the
> *Sunday New York Times* – because nothing can reach the person
> trapped in the void ... Suicide sounds terrific, but much too
> difficult to plan and complete.
>
> (cited in Karp 1996: 24)

Introduction

So far in this book we have attempted to show that despite mainstream
health psychology's aspirations to produce a non-dualistic biopsychosocial
approach towards various health- and illness-related issues, it has, arguably,
failed in this task. In fact, as a consequence of interrelated theoretical and
methodological limitations, it has in many ways served to reproduce such
dualisms. This is nowhere more apparent than in the unquestioned split
between physical and mental health and illness. For instance, mainstream
health psychology textbooks very rarely mention mental health and illness
(except in the form of stress), confining themselves to more 'physically'
based problems. To a certain extent, this is because over the last twenty
years or so in psychology, the study of mental health and illness has been
appropriated mainly by clinical psychology, a 'field of practice and research
directed towards helping people who suffer from psychological problems
and disorders' (Gray 1999: 641). In this chapter, however, we will argue that
mainstream clinical psychological approaches reiterate many of the problems associated with positivism and reductionism already encountered
throughout this book.

Attempting to reduce the fragmentary division between physical and
mental health and illness, and to draw out analogies between the two, this
chapter demonstrates how clinical psychology appropriates a now familiar
biopsychosocial model in its attempt to produce a scientific investigation
of mental illness. As we have previously argued, from a critical health
psychological point of view, this is problematic. Accordingly, using the

example of two major mental disorders frequently encountered in the clinical psychology literature, schizophrenia and depression, this chapter charts the way in which such phenomena can be differentially understood from within the frameworks of mainstream clinical psychology and critical health psychology, respectively.

An eclectic approach towards the investigation and treatment of mental disorder?

It has become something of a cliché, analogous to its medical counterpart, psychiatry, to characterize clinical psychology's approach towards the investigation and treatment of mental disorder as eclectic. In order to understand what this means, it is necessary to outline briefly three main theoretical perspectives that have provided frameworks for the investigation of mental disorders since the 1950s. It is also important to characterize briefly the implications that these theoretical perspectives have had for the proposed 'treatment' of mental disorders. The three perspectives include: (1) the biological perspective; (2) the socio-cultural perspective and (3) the cognitive-behavioural perspective. It should not have escaped your notice that an eclectic approach involving a combination of these three perspectives is analogous to the biopsychosocial approach towards various health-related issues already depicted over the course of this book. Each of the three perspectives will now be discussed in turn.

Mental disorder and the biological perspective

From this perspective, mental disorders are fundamentally physical diseases, more specifically, diseases of the brain. Accordingly, the main aim of investigations premised on this perspective is to find measurable brain abnormalities which correlate with different mental disorders and then to develop drugs or other direct means of altering brain structure and/or functioning.

For example, the 1950s witnessed the development of the 'monoamine theory of depression' (Schildkraut 1965). This derived from the finding that many sufferers from depression could be treated successfully with drugs which acted in the brain to increase the activity of a group of neurotransmitters called monoamines. This led to the hypothesis that depression results from too little activity at brain synapses where monoamines are the neurotransmitters (the major monoamine transmitters in the brain include dopamine, norepinephrine and serotonin). This theory remains influential today despite the fact that the processes by which the biochemical reactions take place remain unclear, see Gray (1999: 616). For example, a frequently prescribed drug for depression is fluoxetine, otherwise known as Prozac. This acts specifically at synapses where serotonin is the transmitter, blocking the reuptake of serotonin back into the presynaptic terminal and thereby prolonging the action of serotonin on the postsynaptic neuron (p. 615). In a series of controlled experiments, 70 per cent of those treated with drugs recovered from major depression over a period of several weeks, compared with 30 per cent on a placebo treatment (Lickey and Gordon 1991).

Brain chemistry is also thought to be important in the mental disorder schizophrenia. For example, the 'dopamine theory of schizophrenia', developed in the 1970s, suggested that schizophrenia is caused by overactivity at brain synapses where dopamine is the neurotransmitter (Gray 1999: 634). The most compelling evidence came from studies demonstrating that the clinical effectiveness of drugs in treating schizophrenia were directly proportional to the drugs' effectiveness in blocking dopamine release at synaptic terminals (Seeman and Lee 1975). Although today few, if any, researchers accept the original, simple form of the dopamine theory, nevertheless, newer drugs such as clozapine have been developed which work in a similar way on other systems of neurotransmission. Many studies have shown that certain anti-psychotic drugs reduce or abolish the hallucinations, delusions and bizarre actions that characterize the active phase of schizophrenia and prevent or forestall the recurrence of such symptoms when they are taken continuously (Ashton 1987).

Heredity is another biological factor considered important in predisposing individuals to mental disorders such as schizophrenia and depression. Schizophrenia was one of the first mental disorders to be studied by behaviour geneticists and some argue that evidence is now 'overwhelming that genes play a role in predisposing some people to the disorder' (Gottesman 1991). Similarly with depression. A number of studies have demonstrated that the more closely related two people are, the more similar they are, on average, in their history of depression or lack of it, and also in terms of the depressive symptoms they exhibit (Kendler *et al.* 1996; McGuffin *et al.* 1996).

Brain structure is also considered important in the investigation of schizophrenia. For example, studies using brain imaging techniques have shown subtle, structural differences between the brains of people with schizophrenia and those without schizophrenia. The most common finding is enlargement of cerebral ventricles and reduced amount of neural tissue surrounding the ventricles (Weinberger 1995). There does not, however, seem to be any single brain difference and no reliable relationships have been established between types of brain abnormalities and different symptoms (Gray 1999: 635).

Numerous researchers have argued that there are major flaws in the biological perspective's assumption that mental disorders such as schizophrenia and depression are caused by physical factors (see Boyle 1990; Rowe 1994). Moreover, drug treatments for mental disorders have serious limitations. This is especially the case in relation to some anti-psychotic drugs which, although relieving schizophrenic symptoms such as hallucinations and delusions, fail to relieve others such as flattened affect (inability to feel emotion) and poor motivation – in some cases making them worse. In addition, such drugs may have undesirable side-effects such as tardive dyskinesia – an irreversible motor disturbance manifested as involuntary jerking of the face, tongue and other muscles. Although anti-depressant drugs do not have such serious side-effects, they are still a problem for most people (Gray 1999: 654).

Despite these problems, however, and despite the existence of alternative perspectives on mental disorder (see later in this chapter), many people argue that the mental health field is dominated by psychiatrically trained professionals who tend to assume that mental disorders are essentially caused by brain mechanisms and genetic predisposition (see Crow 1980; Haracz 1982; Davis *et al.* 1991; Gottesman 1991). For example, Rowe (1994: 327) argues that although some psychiatrists acknowledge that the cause of depression may be located in psychological and social factors, most argue that depression has a biological cause and is best treated by biological interventions such as drugs and electroconvulsive therapy (ECT). Karp (1996: 81) similarly argues that the prevailing cultural view is one which sees medication as the preferred way of combating depression. Indeed, some doctors are increasingly prescribing for problems which do not warrant a diagnosis of mental disorder, such as feelings of sadness and shyness (Gray 1999: 654). Similarly, Chadwick, in his autobiographical account which charts his own experience of schizophrenia and the complex way in which it was related to personal identity issues, family relationships and the more general social context, concludes that his illness was reduced to 'overactivity in dopamine pathways' (Chadwick 1997: 35).

Mental disorder and the situational/socio-cultural perspective

Despite the dominance of the biological perspective, at least since the 1960s it has co-existed with a more socially oriented perspective which looks towards the wider cultural environment to locate the essential cause of mental disorders. From this perspective, such disorders are the result of the person's interaction with the wider culture in which s/he develops. This perspective gained an important impetus from findings which suggested that the kind of mental distress experienced by people, and the way they respond to such distress, differ widely across historical periods and cultures, and among different social classes, ethnic groups and genders. Accordingly, mainstream psychiatric perspectives on mental distress have been criticized for medicalizing and individualizing problems which are essentially induced by social, as opposed to physical forces. This criticism is still in evidence today, as when Karp, a sociologist, argues that 'most psychiatric treatment is inherently conservative by implicitly supporting the systemic status quo . . . interpreting illness as a reflection of individual physical pathology and rarely as a normal response to pathological social structures' (Karp 1996: 80).

A great deal of research on depression has demonstrated the way in which it can result from changes in environmental conditions such as those induced by stressful life events. For example, numerous investigations have revealed positive correlations between onset of depression and stressful life events (such as death of spouse and job loss) reported as occurring a few months prior to the depression. It has been argued that these studies provide 'compelling evidence' that stressful events can cause depression (Kessler 1997).

Other research has focused on the impact of broader situational factors such as the role of gender in mental disorders. This is particularly significant in relation to depression, in which large sex differences are found. For example, women are twice as likely to be diagnosed with affective psychoses (like depression) as men (Gray 1999: 604). Although it is possible that such differences arise from biological differences between men and women, the socio-cultural perspective argues that it is the result of different roles and expectations for men and women. For instance, the essence of many affective disorders consists of feelings of fear, anxiety and sadness. Such feelings are not independent of gender. In our culture, these feelings are generally more permissible in women than men and form part of the stereotypic construction of female weakness and vulnerability. Hence, the categories of pathology constructed around these feelings are likely to occur more frequently in women than men because under the pressures which can lead to neurosis, men and women tend to 'exaggerate their responses to reality' – i.e. they manifest normal feelings but to excess. As a result, women who in normal circumstances show anxiety, fear and sadness are likely, under pressure, to become anxious, fearful or depressed; men, by contrast, may become excessively angry and violent. On this line of reasoning, we would expect to find more cases of neurotic disorders amongst women than men and similarly, more cases of anti-social behaviour, e.g. alcoholism and drug abuse, amongst men than women. This expectation is, in fact, borne out when we consider the over-representation of men in crime statistics in comparison with female over-representation in mental health statistics (Dachowski 1984). Although women are more likely to be diagnosed mentally ill, they are also less likely to find their way into the crime statistics (depending on the type of crime, the ratio of males to females is between three and five to one).

In the investigation of schizophrenia from this perspective, family factors are considered important in causing and perpetuating mental distress. These ideas originated in Laing's (1965) ideas and early developments in family therapy in which psychopathology was located in the family unit rather than in the individual. In particular, studies have focused on 'expressed emotion', which is defined as criticisms and negative attitudes or feelings expressed about and towards a person with schizophrenia by family members with whom the person lives. It has been suggested that the greater the expressed emotion, the greater the likelihood that the person's symptoms will worsen and require hospitalization (Gray 1999: 636). Such approaches have an important impact on interventions which are directed at changing the 'essential dynamic structure of the family' (Lidz 1963) through the process of family therapy. 'Cure' is thereby directed at the family, of which the patient is an integral part, and the therapist's job is to 'facilitate the maintenance of sub-systems that promote healing and growth' (Minuchin 1974: 256).

An important criticism of family therapy, however, has been its tendency to neglect wider structural factors such as class and race. For example, a diagnosis of schizophrenia is most likely to be given to black and working-class patients. In addition, cross-cultural approaches have attempted to investigate differences in schizophrenic incidence and recovery across different cultures. For instance, it has been found that people suffering from mental disorders in developing countries are much more likely to recover during a two-year follow-up period than people in developed countries (63 per cent versus 37 per cent, Jablensky et al. 1992). Explanations for this finding have varied. It may be that patients in developing countries are more likely to receive non-Western folk or religious treatments, less likely to be hospitalized, and less likely to receive anti-psychotic drugs over prolonged periods of time. Other explanations are that family members in developing countries are more accepting and less critical of individuals diagnosed with schizophrenia, placing less value on personal independence, more on familial interdependence, and exhibiting less expressed emotion (Jenkins and Karno 1992). In addition, people in developing countries suffering from schizophrenia continue to play an economically useful role, thereby experiencing less stigmatization and sense of being cut off from the normal course of everyday life (Gray 1999: 638). Finally, people in less developed countries are less likely to call the disorder 'schizophrenia' or to think of it as a permanent condition. They are more likely to refer to such mental disorders as a 'case of nerves' which creates a greater degree of normalization.

Mental disorder and the cognitive-behavioural perspective

Despite the expanding critique of the socio-cultural perspective, in Britain the belief that all mental illnesses are physical illnesses formed the basis of the theory and practice of psychiatry up until the early 1970s. When it was established in the 1950s in post-war Britain, clinical psychology was dominated by the psychometric perspective which aimed to measure the psychological characteristics of patients. This posed no threat to psychiatry and was in fact of value to it in contributing to the measurement of psychological characteristics of patients (Pilgrim and Treacher 1992). Clinical psychology's alliance with psychiatry and natural science was a way of lifting psychology above the level of particular interests and arbitrary prejudices, giving it an impartial and detached authority.

During the 1970s, however, clinical psychology began to professionalize, and part of this process involved an attempt to corner the market in distress (see also Chapter 2). This entailed clinical psychology developing its own professional identity and breaking away from psychiatric control. One of the ways it did this was by setting up a Register of Chartered Psychologists which effectively controlled resources by limiting the supply of psychologists trained to provide clinical psychology services. The supply of patients was also influenced by the Trethowan report (DHSS 1977), which brought in an era in which clinical psychology services increasingly became less dependent on psychiatry, as referrals were received directly from GPs. Another of the main ways in which clinical psychology professionalized was by creating a therapeutic approach distinct from that of psychiatry. This took the form of behavioural and cognitive therapy, advocated as alternatives (today more often complements) to biologically based treatments.

For instance, in providing a rationale for the provision of clinical psychology treatments for mental disorders such as depression and schizophrenia, Bradley (1994: 111) and Hemsley (1994: 309) highlight problems with drug treatments, such as their unpleasant, sometimes irreversible side-effects. In addition, although drug treatments may result in marked reductions in depressive symptomatology, they often leave patients well above normative levels for non-depressed subjects on measures of depression, and the generality of improvement across the various dimensions of depression remains unclear (Bradley 1994: 111). Likewise, many studies have shown that medication can have a beneficial effect, especially amongst people suffering the acute phase of schizophrenia. However, as Hemsley (1994) makes clear, amongst those who are discharged, serious social and occupational deficits often remain, indicating the clear need for additional therapeutic approaches (p. 309). Accordingly, although drugs may make it possible for a person to live outside hospital, they do not usually 'restore the zest or pleasure that should come from doing so'. Life may become more normal but it is not necessarily happier (Gray 1999: 652).

The cognitive-behavioural perspective assumes that mental disorders are learned, maladaptive habits of thinking and acting that have been acquired through a person's interaction with his/her environment. Its primary unit of analysis therefore, rather than biological mechanisms, or social and cultural factors, is the person's conscious thoughts and actions. In addition to recognizing the limitations of biological theories and interventions, this perspective also highlights the limitations of social and cultural approaches, for instance, the notion that stressful life events or social roles such as those attributed to women cause depression. The cognitive-behavioural perspective, recognizing that only a minority of women or people who experience stressful events actually become sufficiently depressed to be diagnosed clinically depressed, asks why this is the case. The finding that people respond very differently to the same objective experiences is the starting point for cognitive theories of depression. Stress and depression, as we have already discussed in Chapter 4, stem not so much from 'the objective events themselves' as from the way in which those events are interpreted (Gray 1999: 617).

Beck's (1976) theory of depression constitutes a classic example of cognitive-behavioural approaches towards mental disorders. Beck argues that depression is caused by negative thoughts and negatively biased perceptions. Depressed individuals are typically pessimistic in outlook and show negative distortions in their interpretations of experience. This negative outlook encompasses the individual's perception of themselves, their world and their future – sometimes characterized as a 'negative cognitive triad'. Beck's cognitive therapy (Beck et al. 1979) aims to identify and challenge negative thoughts, to develop 'alternative more accurate and adaptive thoughts', and to promote cognitive and behavioural responses based on those adaptive thoughts (Bradley 1994: 115).

Hemsley (1994: 310) describes a study in which a cognitive-behavioural therapy approach attempted to 'modify the delusional beliefs of three chronic paranoid schizophrenics'. The patients were not required to abandon their beliefs but just to consider the facts relating to, and arguments for them. Over the course of therapy as many lines of evidence as possible were raised against the beliefs. Patients were encouraged to voice arguments against the delusions and these arguments were endorsed and expanded by the therapists (p. 311). After six sessions, significant reductions in the strength of delusional beliefs were indicated, although the beliefs were not completely abandoned (p. 311). Another study by Liberman et al. (1973) entailed four chronic paranoid patients who were treated with four daily sessions which continued only as long as the patient spoke 'rationally'. An evening chat was used to serve as a 'reinforcer' and its length was determined by the amount of rational speech produced in daily sessions (Hemsley 1994: 312).

As is clear from these brief examples, cognitive therapy focuses on conscious mental experiences, is problem-centred, and zooms into specific problems with a 'let's get down to business attitude' (Gray 1999: 667). The approach contains a significant educational component in which patients are encouraged to identify the way in which their negative thoughts are influencing their depressive feelings. Accordingly, most cognitive therapists are 'directive' and their relationship to their clients is similar to that of 'teacher to student' (p. 667), for example, homework assignments are frequently set. Many proponents of cognitive-behavioural approaches have, however, argued that it is a radical approach because it can be explained simply to clients and 'given away' to them, thus rendering patients less dependent on experts. To this extent, it is user-friendly and draws on individual capacities for self-help and self-management.

Contemporary 'eclectic' clinical psychology

The above depiction of the main three perspectives on mental disorder is largely artificial because it is commonly accepted in contemporary clinical psychology that any given mental disorder is likely to have multiple causes (Gray 1999: 607). Accordingly, most psychological therapies for mental disorder can be characterized as eclectic in orientation (p. 657). For example, Pilgrim and Treacher (1992) quote from a 1990 survey in which clinical psychologists described themselves as using a variety of therapeutic traditions including: eclectic (31.6 per cent), behaviour/learning (22.2 per cent), psychodynamic (21 per cent), cognitive (13.5 per cent) and systemic (6.2 per cent). It is, however, important to understand that British clinical psychology, despite this alleged eclecticism, is located within a positivistic framework dominated by a cognitive-behavioural paradigm. Further elaboration of this point is required before its implications for the investigation of mental disorder can be discussed in more detail. This will be achieved by using Lindsay and Powell's (1994) *Handbook of Clinical Adult Psychology* as a typical example of the dominant characteristic style of clinical psychology.

Like most health psychology textbooks, Lindsay and Powell's book draws heavily on a 'discourse of scientific progress' which presents investigation as a strictly objective enterprise in which findings are added to a gradually increasing body of knowledge (see Chapter 1). For instance, Lindsay and Powell characterize their book as one which outlines 'scientific approaches to the investigation, treatment and management of psychological problems' (p. 35). Clinical psychology, they argue, has developed out of a tradition of 'careful and painstaking investigation' of the problems and characteristics presented by clients (p. 1). Accordingly, mirroring developments in psychiatric and neurological treatments of patients, over the last twenty years, 'there has been an enormous increase in the development of effective psychological treatment which has transformed clinical psychology' (p. 1). In this book, an image of the 'scientist-as-practitioner' reigns supreme. This involves a belief in the 'straightforward application of psychological knowledge to mental distress' (Parker *et al.* 1995: 51).

The *Handbook of Clinical Adult Psychology* strongly reflects one of the basic assumptions of positivism, namely that observations can be made objectively and that measures can be defined operationally and applied in a precise, replicable fashion. In this way, the 'scientific' clinical psychologist aims to collect data, observations about her clients, in the 'same rigorous and detached way as the astronomer observing stars' (Ingleby 1981: 29). As Lindsay and Powell make clear, their book is written from a broadly scientific or experimental approach to problems and treatment (Lindsay and Powell 1994: 37). This means that treatment strategies and specific techniques are defined as accurately as possible and 'preferably in operational terms . . . to allow as exact a replication as possible' (p. 38). The 'tight definition' of clinical psychology methods, they continue:

> helps to keep sources of unknown variance to a minimum (say, from idiosyncratic interpretation and behaviour of the therapist); it allows a more or less uniform technique to be used across individuals in group research studies . . . it aids the process whereby techniques are experimentally broken down into constituent elements to find the 'active ingredients'.
>
> (p. 38)

In accordance with such scientific principles, various psychological problems are broken down, classified and addressed in separate chapters. Each problem has two chapters devoted to it, one dealing with 'investigation', incorporating specific 'symptoms' and 'syndromes', the other with 'treatment'. Hence, 28 chapters address 14 separate psychological problems including: obsessions and compulsions, depression, fears and anxiety, sexual dysfunction, interpersonal problems, marital conflict, schizophrenia, problems related to sexual variation, drug and alcohol problems, problems in the elderly, disorders of eating and weight, cardiovascular and respiratory disease, disorders of sleep and chronic pain.

The precise diagnosis of mental disorder is regarded as 'essential to the identification of effective remedies' for clients' difficulties (p. 1). This process of diagnosis is characterized as involving two main stages in the gathering of clinical information: (1) comprehensive information gathering from which the clinician develops hypotheses (the formulation) about the causes and maintenance of problems; (2) a more selective collection of data with greater precision and hypothesis-testing. The clinical psychologist's early consultation with the client consists of an open-ended information-gathering process in which the psychologist attempts to collect as much information as possible about the client's life circumstances pertaining to his/her problem. Unfortunately, however, as Lindsay and Powell argue (p. 1), there have been few attempts to determine the validity and reliability of such open-ended methods. Accordingly, identification of the client's main difficulties and how they are maintained is often unreliable, there is poor agreement amongst psychologists when they are confronted with the same data about clients, and agreement about treatments is also poor (p. 1). For this reason, clinical psychology tends to rely heavily on questionnaires which include 'objective', psychometric tests, offering a degree of standardization useful for clinical research and potentiating more reliable and

valid diagnoses. Many of these questionnaires, in their original development, are quite lengthy, but the use of cluster analysis and other statistical
techniques has facilitated the development of shortened versions which can
be administered more quickly and efficiently.

Typical examples of questionnaires used in the process of diagnosing
mental disorder include the General Health Questionnaire (GHQ), widely
used to screen samples of adults for the presence of psychiatric distress. In
its original version it contained 60 items, but the use of cluster analysis has
enabled it to be shortened to 12 items. The GHQ uses a cut-off point for
the number of complaints acknowledged by respondents in order to determine whether they are suffering psychological distress. The Symptom
Check-List-90-Revised (SCL-90-R) is one of the most widely used screen-
ing questionnaires and is designed to measure nine dimensions of psychopathology as determined by factor analysis. These include: somatization,
obsessive compulsive difficulties, interpersonal sensitivity, depression,
anxiety, anger, hostility, phobic anxiety, paranoid ideation and psychoti-
cism. The SCL-90-R is intended to provide a 'profile of psychopathology'
for each respondent (Lindsay and Powell 1994: 10). Again, there is a shortened form of the inventory.

For more specific conditions such as depression, a range of inventories
is available. The most widely used is probably the Hamilton Rating Scale
which covers 21 items measuring various aspects of functioning. This is not
a diagnostic instrument but a measure of severity. Also common are the
MMPI, Beck Depression Inventory, Zung Self Depression Scale, Psychiatrist's Global Rating and Weschsler Depression Scale (Rippere 1994: 95).

For the diagnosis of schizophrenia, numerous questionnaires have been
developed to measure 'predisposition to psychotic symptoms'. These
include, for instance, the Perceptual Aberration Scale, Magical Ideation
Scale and the Schedule of Affective Disorders (Hemsley 1994: 297). Questionnaires such as the Present State Examination (PSE) have been designed
to establish the presence or absence of categories of schizophrenic symptomatology and thereby to determine diagnosis (p. 299). The PSE lists more
than 500 questions and is designed to elicit information which allows the
interviewer to rate 107 symptoms based on the patient's self-report.

In its concern with the classification, diagnosis and treatment of specific
mental disorders, the *Handbook of Clinical Adult Psychology* (representing the
dominant theoretical and practical framework within clinical psychology)
reflects and is modelled on the American Psychiatric Association's official
guide for diagnosing mental disorder, the *Diagnostic and Statistical Manual of
Mental Disorders IV* (DSM-IV) (1994). This manual, like the clinical psychology handbook, treats mental disorders as analogous to medical diseases,
borrowing from medicine the terms symptom, syndrome, diagnosis and
treatment (Gray 1999: 599). Following the lead of psychiatric systems of
classification, clinical psychology's ultimate goal is to 'define mental disorders as objectively as possible' in order to 'remove as much guesswork as

possible from the task of diagnosis and thereby create diagnostic reliability' (p. 601).

Critical reformulations of the study of mental disorder: diagnostic classification as a construction of reality

From a critical health psychological point of view, clinical psychology's predominant concern with diagnosis and classification, especially as established through psychometric tests, is problematic. This is because the over-use and reliance on such quantitative methods tend to create greater interest in categorizing whether a person's behaviour and thoughts are 'normal' or 'abnormal', as opposed to developing an understanding of the person *per se*. As Lindsay and Powell (1994: 19) clearly state, the severity of a person's psychological problem, and the consideration of whether or not treatment is required, should be established mainly by 'comparing measures of the variable of interest with data obtained from other subjects of similar age and other characteristics – a normative comparison'. Accordingly, it would, these researchers argue, 'be comforting . . . if the clinician could consult a table of norms for a given variable and decide upon implementing a treatment if it appeared that the client was exceptionally troubled on the target variable' (p. 19). The problem with such a table of norms is that it not only creates a state of normality, but also a state of abnormality, and an impression that both of these states exist in isolation from each other. In fact, as becomes apparent in Lindsay and Powell's above comments, such conditions of normality and abnormality are relative, and partly a product of the researcher and practitioner's attempt to make sense of the individual through a process of analytic or clinical construction.

Such observations form the core of contemporary social constructionist critiques of mainstream clinical psychology and psychiatric approaches to the study of mental disorder (Parker *et al.* 1995: 2). For instance, Parker *et al.*, drawing on the philosophical insight that words do not just describe, but *construct* reality (see Chapters 1 and 2), argue that diagnostic classification systems (such as those found in DSM-IV and the *Handbook of Clinical Adult Psychology*) do not 'study and classify what is out there . . . in a neutral and objective way' (p. 93). They do not represent a neutral and transparent means of observing reality as is implied in their style of presentation. Instead, the psychiatric language embedded in research and clinical practices, constitutes the very 'pathological phenomena' it seeks to explain (p. 93). As Boyle (1990) similarly argues, writers in the mental health field are all too often united in the assumption of the existence of mental disorder as a starting point for theory and practice, when, in fact, this existence is partly a result of such practices.

One of the main concerns of social constructionists is the way in which conditions of mental disorder are 'reified' by diagnostic classification systems and clinical practice in the mental health field. That is, such processes create the illusion that mental disorder exists as 'a real thing out there', independent of professional categories and practices (Parker *et al.* 1995: 116). For instance, Parker *et al.* argue that the images of madness that are relayed in clinical texts *construct* a reality for the clinician that is 'fantastic and frightening'. It is therefore no surprise that psychiatrists who write and read such accounts should be so frightened of being in the presence of someone who is 'mad' (p. 116). This discourse and the practice that follows from it, 'demonizes' psychotic experience, 'increasing the gap' and making the experience of those it talks about all the more 'other' (p. 116). It constitutes a powerful means of constructing and maintaining realities which involve the 'pathologisation, silencing and marginalisation of the groups of individuals who fall under its authority' (p. 93).

This concern with the way in which mental health classification systems actually construct abnormal forms of reality and in some cases intensify the distress of certain individuals and groups, echoes the earlier work of the anti-psychiatry movement which emerged during the 1960s. One of the most prominent anti-psychiatrists was R. D. Laing, who was actually a psychiatrist criticizing psychiatry from the inside. The most serious objection to the technical vocabulary used to describe the psychiatric patient, Laing argued (1965: 19), is that it 'splits' man up into discrete categories. Accordingly, by the time the mental health professional gets to see the patient, s/he is an 'already shattered Humpty-Dumpty who cannot be put together again by any number of hyphenated or compound words: psycho-physical, psycho-somatic, psycho-biological, psycho-pathological, psycho-social, etc., etc.' (Laing 1965: 20). In succinct terms, Laing describes his dilemma as follows:

> As a psychiatrist, I run into major difficulty at the outset: How can I go straight to the patients if the psychiatric words at my disposal keep the patient at a distance from me? How can one demonstrate the general human relevance and significance of the patient's condition if the words one has to use are specifically designed to isolate and circumscribe the meaning of the patient's life in a particular clinical entity?
>
> (Laing 1965: 18)

Laing's articulation of the problems of psychiatry bear an important resonance in terms of the way in which contemporary clinical psychology attempts to identify and treat discrete clinical entities. As we saw earlier in this chapter, the *Handbook of Clinical Adult Psychology* places a great deal of emphasis on information gathering and the identification and diagnosis of single problems and specific clinical disorders. In this way, it splits a person from their environment in exactly the same way as Laing described. Lindsay and Powell (1994: 2) pay lip service to this problem when they admit that many studies of depression 'describe clients in terms of their scores on the

Beck Depression Inventory, but omit any evaluation of other problems, such as marital difficulties, which might be contributing to the central problem'.

Related to this problem of identifying single disorders is the way in which such identification feeds into interventions and treatments. Most published studies of cognitive-behaviour therapy describe a target behaviour or cognition that they attempt to modify. In recent years it has also become fashionable for cognitive-behavioural therapists to target 'single-symptoms' rather than 'disease entities' (related to the social constructionist critique of diagnoses such as schizophrenia). However, an exclusive focus on symptoms has its dangers. For instance, many such studies describe target behaviours but fail to identify other behavioural difficulties or life factors that may be important (Lindsay and Powell 1994: 2). For this reason, Hemsley cautions against 'single-symptom-based' approaches to treatment because of the need to be alert to the 'possible occurrence of new aberrant behaviours' (Hemsley 1994: 313). In practice, because most problems are 'so complex and corresponding formulations so uncertain', 'large batteries' of treatments are often applied 'in shot-gun fashion', to make sure that 'all possible difficulties are tackled' (Powell and Lindsay 1994: 35). This is itself problematic, however, because there is evidence that if 'too many behaviours are identified as targets, any improvement in certain areas may be accompanied by a deterioration in other behaviours' (Hemsley 1994: 320). This may be attributable, Hemsley continues, to 'some patients' inability to attend to more than a few targets at once'.

On the other hand, it is quite reasonable to suggest that such deterioration in behaviour occurs because we are dealing with *people*, not a 'bundle of behaviours'. Perhaps people object to being treated as a 'target' onto which clinical psychologists are 'shooting in the dark' (Lindsay and Powell 1994: 35). Perhaps, in order to get better, people need to be seen and heard (see below) in a radically different fashion.

Challenging the construction of 'disorder': listening to the patient's voice and understanding

'It is just possible', Laing argued:

> to know, in fact, just about everything that can be known about the psychopathology of schizophrenia or schizophrenia as a disease without being able to understand one single schizophrenic. Such data are all ways of *not* understanding him. To look and listen to a patient and to see 'signs' of schizophrenia (as a 'disease') and to look and listen to him simply as a human being are to see and hear in radically different ways . . .
>
> (Laing 1965: 33)

In her study of depression, Rowe (1994) similarly argues that psychiatrists actually spend very little time talking to their patients. Indeed, when they did talk to their patients, or about patients, they were 'busy turning what the patient said into what the psychiatrists called the symptoms of depressive illness' (p. xxi). Hence, if the patient said, 'I no longer enjoy love making', the psychiatrist marked this down as 'loss of libido'. Or if a patient said 'I feel I'm trapped in a sea of mud and the more I try to get out the more I get sucked down', the psychiatrist marked this down as 'lowered mood'. Very little attempt was made on behalf of the psychiatrist to actually 'understand what the person was experiencing' (p. xxii). This, as does the cognitive-behavioural approach described in the previous section, constitutes a good example of Laing's notion that seeing the patient as signs of disease or as a bundle of behaviours or cognitions, and seeing him/her as a human being, constitute radically different ways of 'seeing'.

One of Laing's main objectives was to develop a new perspective that would enable an appreciation of the 'lived experience and reality' of the individual suffering mental disorder. This required a very different approach to the diagnostic oriented approach of clinical psychiatry (and clinical psychology) which can tell us very little about the *meaning* of actual experiences of mental disorder. As Chadwick (1997: 2) similarly argues, 'the science of schizophrenia . . . echoes the characterisation of a church via analysis of its bricks. The experience and its referent are simply ignored.' At the beginning of *The Divided Self* (1965: 17), Laing describes his 'existential phenomenological' approach which is 'not so much an attempt to describe particular objects of (the individual's) experience as to set all particular experiences within the context of his whole being-in-his-world'. 'The mad things said and done by the schizophrenic,' Laing continues, 'will remain essentially a closed book if one does not understand their existential context.' It is in search of such 'normalized' understanding that Laing goes 'as directly as possible to the patients themselves' (p. 18).

Laing's focus on the importance of understanding the mentally ill individual as a person, not as a psychiatric or clinical psychology category, is crucial to contemporary interest in the 'patient voice' (see also Chapter 5 in relation to physical illness). Increasingly, people suffering from various mental disorders are beginning to talk and write about their experiences (see Karp 1996; Read and Reynolds 1996; Chadwick 1997). Part of the rationale for doing so, as Karp (p. 11) argues in relation to depression, is that 'we hear the voices of a battalion of mental health experts . . . and never the voices of the depressed people themselves' (p. 11). Rowe (1994: xxi) likewise argues that the scientific literature on depression describes it almost exclusively 'from the point of view of the onlooker' (see Chapters 5 and 7 on the insider and outsider perspectives of illness). Accordingly, despite all the studies attempting to elucidate psychological and social factors predicting depression 'something crucial is missing'. 'Underneath the rates, correlations, and presumed causes of behaviour are real human beings who are trying to make sense of their lives' (Karp 1996: 11). Karp argues that in order to really understand human experience, it must be appreciated from 'the subjective point of view of the person undergoing it' (p. 11). Similarly, in relation to the experience of schizophrenia, Chadwick (a psychologist who has himself been diagnosed schizophrenic), argues that we must begin with 'stories from the inside' (Chadwick 1997: 168).

This move towards appreciating and empathizing with the voice of the user (a more commonly used term in mental health than patient) is interpreted as part of a radical and empowering shift on the part of some critical psychological approaches towards mental health. For example, Parker *et al.* (1995: 5) argue that seeing things from the standpoint of those who 'suffer psychiatry' (and clinical psychology) involves developing an understanding of the 'irrationality that is shut out of over-rational clinical knowledge' (p. 5). It requires breaking away from narrowly defined scientific and reductionist 'truths' and enabling 'alternative truths' which empower instead of marginalizing 'individuals whose speech, experience and behaviour falls outside what has come to be defined as "the norm"' (p. 93). Likewise, the increasing popularity of alternative mental health movements (as with the popularity of self-help groups in relation to physical illness, see Chapter 5) is related to a commitment to transforming current clinical work by prioritizing areas previously silenced in psychiatric practice (p. 112). Accordingly, people with serious mental and physical illness are today more likely to be viewed by professionals as 'consumers' of health services rather than as patients on the passive receiving-end of the work and ministrations of experts (Chadwick 1997: xii). Their views and needs are increasingly seen as essential to the process of treatment (Lord *et al.* 1987; Coursey *et al.* 1995).

The existential reality of mental disorder

Many of the accounts based on subjective experiences of mental disorders such as depression and schizophrenia are concerned, as we have already suggested, to describe such experiences from the inside, to characterize what it is really like to live with such illnesses. This is evident in autobiographical accounts which emphasize the horrendous reality of everyday life with depression. 'It is not just that being depressed means feeling despairing, frightened, guilty, bitter, helpless, tired and ill', Rowe argues. It is, rather, 'the most terrible sense of being trapped and alone in some horror-filled prison' (Rowe 1994: xiii). One woman describes it as 'the worst feeling in the world', 'right where my heart is . . . Like there's a black hole there' (cited in Karp 1996: 41). And another woman describes it as like 'drowning, suffocating, descending into a bottomless pit, being in a lightless tunnel' (p. 28). Karp describes his own experience of depression as akin to death and dying: 'I was dead . . . you could actually say I was dead at that point'.

Attempting to characterize the essence of the experience of depression, Karp elaborates that two central feelings were 'frantic anxiety and a sense of grief' (p. 6). During his time of depression, he felt 'deeply alone'. Each sleepless night his head was filled with 'disturbing ruminations' and during the day he felt a sense of 'intolerable grief' as though somebody close to him had died (p. 4). The essence of the depressive experience brings together themes of disconnection, isolation and withdrawal. And the 'pain of depression', Karp argues, arises in part because of separation from others, from the inability to connect, even as one desperately yearns for such connection (p. 27).

As with experiences of chronic pain and illness (see Chapter 5), first-person accounts of depressive experiences illustrate how its onslaught threatens to 'unmake the world' by dissolving the 'building blocks of the perceived world', including the individual's basic sense of space, time, language and relationships with others (Good 1992: 42). Depression, Rowe (1994: 109) argues, is a defence we use when we see that there is a 'major discrepancy between what we thought reality is and what it shows itself to be'. As we realize this discrepancy, 'the solid certainties of our life turn to matchwood, breaking and splintering round our head, as a bottomless chasm yawns beneath our feet'. Karp similarly writes of the way in which depression made 'the world lose its very dimensionality, appearing flat, lifeless and colourless' (Karp 1996: 27). The sense of hope and security normally framing his image of the future was destroyed. When our sense of life streams out to our past and future we experience 'our life story as being a proper story which has a beginning, a middle and an end' (Rowe 1994: 86). But 'when we cut ourselves off from our past or from our future, our story is incomplete, and incomplete stories always make us feel uncomfortable and dissatisfied' (p. 86). This results, as another woman describes, in depression 'stealing away whoever you were', preventing you from 'seeing who you might someday be'; it 'replaces your life with a black hole' (cited in Karp 1996: 23).

Mental disorders, empowerment, and the resistance of professional colonization

Co-existing alongside attempts to describe the negative reality of living with various mental disorders, however, is another dimension of contemporary first-person accounts of such experiences. This can be characterized as their 'empowerment agenda'. As we have already discussed in Chapter 5, part of the contemporary interest in personal stories of chronic pain and illness stems from a critique of medicalization in which illness is defined in narrow disease terms and treatment is characterized as a 'quick-fit' solution. Because chronic pain and illness do not fit easily into this model (they cannot be cured), they tend to bring forth questions regarding the necessity and value of relying too heavily on scientifically defined reality, frequently requiring the individual to develop a broader, less certain, and more existential view of life and their place within the world. The experience of mental disorders such as depression and schizophrenia is similar in this respect. As Karp (1996: 14) argues, the case of depression almost demands reflection on questions of identity and self-transformation and brings forth issues of how people make sense of 'intrinsically ambiguous' and seemingly 'intractable life conditions'.

As is the case with chronic physical pain and illness, many people when diagnosed with a mental disorder search frantically for a 'cure', whether that be in the form of medicine or more psychologically oriented approaches. Again analogously to those suffering chronic physical pain and illness, many soon become disillusioned. Karp, for instance, describes how he tried every available therapeutic avenue for his depression, but became 'fundamentally dubious' as every new therapeutic venture began with hope yet ended with disillusionment (p. 7). Writing about his experience of schizophrenia, Chadwick similarly describes how, although medication did have the power to wipe out some of his symptoms, his inner feelings of down-heartedness and guilt still remained (Chadwick 1997: 48). One of the problems here is the way in which psychiatry and clinical psychology set themselves up as technical remedies to problems which are, fundamentally, in Laing's terms, 'problems in living'. Such approaches may be 'too narrow and tight' for people who need a 'broader framework to find meaning in their lives' (Parker et al. 1995: 145). This probably explains why reviews of cognitive and behavioural approaches have found that long-term and/or generalized changes are conspicuous by their absence, raising serious doubts about the ability of such approaches to go 'beyond management' (Keeley et al. 1976, cited in Hemsley 1994: 320).

So what is the 'solution'? According to researchers examining depression from the experiential point of view, what is required are not people who tell us to 'look on the bright side', but people who can 'acknowledge and share our pain' (Rowe 1994: xviii). An ex-depressive cited in Rowe's book explains how reality, however terrible, is 'bearable if others allow its reality'. When professionals deny that reality, 'skipping around you, pretending you've got it wrong, that's rock-bottom time' (p. xxviii). It is only when people realize that various treatments are unlikely to cure them that their thinking turns away from the medical language of cure towards a more spiritual language of transformation. This reveals a paradoxical connection between depression, creativity, meaning and insight (Karp 1996: 192).

Both Karp and Rowe quote people in their studies who came to the conclusion that depression enabled them to grow spiritually. Typical examples include the following quote by a woman:

> I believe that depression is actually a gift. That if we can befriend it, if we can travel with it, that it is showing us things. Somewhere along

the line we've got to integrate it into our lives. All of us are depressed in some way, somewhere, at some time. If we don't allow it in, it can be destructive. If we allow it in, it is a teacher. I'm saying embrace it. Be in it.

(cited in Karp 1996: 104)

A psychiatrist who had suffered from depression similarly said that:

Depression is not – as I have eventually and painfully learned – something to sweep under the carpet: to deny, to forget. It is an experience that brings great misery and causes a great waste of time, but it can be, if one is fortunate, a source of personal wisdom and worth more than a hundred philosophies.

(cited in Rowe 1994: xxx)

It is in the light of such experiences that Rowe bases her book on the notion that *'depression is not an illness. It is an experience out of which we can gain greater understanding of ourselves and other people'* (p. xxx, emphasis in original).

The same attempt to reframe positively the experience of schizophrenia is evident in Chadwick's experiential account. Chadwick argues that the dominant researcher and practitioner view of schizophrenia has been one of deficit, dysfunction and disorder. Such 'deficit obsessed research', however, can only produce theories and attitudes which are 'disrespectful of clients' and which induce 'behaviour in clinicians such that service users are not properly listened to' (Chadwick 1997: xiii). The main purpose of his book therefore, is to 'redress the balance', 'to turn the coin over' and seek what has become known as the 'schizophrenic credit' – the positive dimensions of life with schizophrenia. Accordingly, Chadwick asks whether schizophrenic people have 'areas of *enhanced* functioning' and can 'access states of mental clarity and profundity' inaccessible to 'people of the middle ground' (p. xii). He characterizes the 'schizophrenic credit' as having a number of dimensions – affective, cognitive, interpersonal and spiritual (p. 3) – and sees it as a 'real manifestation of the benevolent, the positive and the uncanny – often buried beneath the rubble of apparent pathology' (p. 2).

Of particular interest for the purposes of this chapter is Chadwick's idea that the 'schizophrenic credit', like the 'depressive credit', is related to creativity, spirituality and meaning. Chadwick argues that schizophrenia is often a 'creative illness' and has the positive effect that crises sometimes have in confronting a person with their 'life in full perspective' and perhaps 'giving clarity' to their 'purpose' (p. 16). Indeed, sufferers of delusion tend to be preoccupied with 'issues of meaning and purpose' (Roberts 1991; Bentall 1994: 349) and it may be that psychosis can 'enhance a person's apprehension of their wider context and of their place in the cosmic scheme of things' (Chadwick 1997: 16). When Chadwick, in the concluding section of his book, discusses the implications and possible lessons to be learned from his and other patients' experiences, he writes about the importance of cultivating a certain attitude towards life. This is one in which one adopts a 'broad metaphysical perspective' rather than 'grasping at mechanistic answers', one which cultivates 'the quality of *being* with one's ignorance' and 'facing the fact that one does not know'. This, he argues, is 'strengthening rather than weakening' (p. 145). He points also to the therapeutic value of writing, arguing that 'the pen is undoubtedly a tool through which to realize one's own intrinsic validity and with which to define and express the Self as secure in its own terms' (p. 146). As with the experience of depression, then, schizophrenia 'almost demands reflection on questions of identity and self transformation'. Elaborating on the form that such reflections take, Chadwick argues that they are not concerned with 'the truth of the professor in the institute'. Instead, such reflection is related to one's 'own truth' – 'the truth of the dream' (p. 104). Perhaps in the world of the dream, he suggests, we can 'find a truth deeper and more meaningful than all the steel-grey essays on biocognitive engineering could ever provide' (p. 105).

Chadwick concludes by highlighting that his book is centrally about 'confidence raising' and about the empowerment of people prone to schizophrenia and of those trying to recover from it (p. 171). His book aims to provide a chance and an incentive for people 'to come above ground and start talking' and to 'gain strength . . . in their own intrinsic validity' (p. 172). 'It is time,' Chadwick continues, 'to reassess our attitudes to psychosis-prone people and to start seeing them as total human beings with dignity and with capacities of choice and discernment rather than as malfunctioning organic entities to be plied with pills and bus passes' (p. 7). It may be that 'within the sordid quagmire of disease there are genuine flowers to be preserved'. These will be totally missed 'if we focus on disease and on disease as the true and inevitable efflorescence of the evolving schizophrenic mental structure' (p. 2). Accordingly, 'it is vital that schizophrenic people . . . adopt a more "healthgenic" orientation rather than the negative staying-out-of-hospital orientation' which pervades the thinking of so many recovering psychiatric patients and their families (p. 171).

Another good example of attempts to highlight the 'schizophrenic credit' is a self-help group called the Hearing Voices Network (HVN), founded by Marius Romme, a Dutch professor of social psychiatry. Auditory hallucinations ('hearing voices') are often interpreted as one of the main 'symptoms' of schizophrenia. However, the HVN calls for partnership between 'voice hearers' as a means of combating the status of victim and subverting the concept of psychopathology. By listening to the *content* of these voices, and understanding them in the context of the individual's life as a whole, they can be reconstrued as part of a pattern of personal growth and an important creative facet of human experience (Parker *et al.* 1995: 123). The HVN is important because it indicates the emergence of a vocal group of people who are learning to cope with their voices without recourse to psychiatry. Their activities suggest it is 'possible to accept and live with voices, and that it could be of positive value in coping with life events' (p. 125).

Resistance to 'anti-psychiatry' and social constructionism

Chadwick's attempt to highlight the 'schizophrenic credit' as a means of empowering individuals is very reminiscent of Laing's earlier anti-psychiatric work. 'The cracked mind of the schizophrenic', Laing argued, 'may *let in* the light which does not enter the intact minds of many sane people whose minds are closed' (Laing 1965: 27). Note the similarity between this statement and Chadwick's idea that schizophrenic people may be able to 'access states of mental clarity and profundity' inaccessible to 'people of the middle ground' (Chadwick 1997: xii). In addition, the suggestion that depression and schizophrenia constitute 'creative illnesses', illnesses which enable the individual to question the expectations and cultural values they have taken for granted, often come close to the anti-psychiatric notion of mental 'illness' as a form of protest and rebellion against the dominant capitalist system. This is the idea of the 'schizophrenic as culture-hero', perpetuating earlier anti-psychiatric ideas that 'all delusions are political declarations and all madmen are political dissidents'.

The notion of mental illness as a form of political protest, and psychiatry as a form of social control attempting to quell such protest, was related to the anti-psychiatric attempt to declare mental illness as a 'myth'. This argument was related to the way in which the labelling, categorization and diagnosis of mental illness was not an objective, value-free act of scientific decision-making, as was commonly assumed, but instead, a value-laden and political act which served to reconstitute problems of living or acts of protest, as illness. Accordingly, it was argued, such arbitrary and destructive labels should be dropped. However, this anti-psychiatric perspective soon came under fire from critics. For instance, it was argued that the 'symptom as protest' school of thought romanticized the reality of many people suffering mental illness, tending to gloss over the difference between the kinds of behaviour that mental health professionals dealt with, and more 'normal' forms of behaviour (Ingleby 1981: 56). In attempting to remove the concept of mental illness, Sedgwick (1982: 41) argued that such theories made it all the more difficult for a powerful reform in the mental health services to get off the ground.

As we have already seen in this chapter, resonances of the 'anti-psychiatric' school of thought are still around today in the form of critical social constructionist approaches (see Parker *et al.* 1995). This is apparent in the way in which Parker *et al.* (p. 134) proleptically orient to criticism that their deconstructionist book 'denies the reality of mental illness'. 'Yes', they argue, 'this is exactly what the book does':

It denies the reality of mental illness, in the sense that it claims that mental illness is not something in people's heads but which is constructed by psychiatric theories and practices. On the other hand it does not deny the reality of mental illness, since the psychiatric construction of 'mental illness' has real effects on the people who fall into this category and it becomes their reality. Parallel to this, the book does not deny the reality of suffering of the 'mentally ill', but it argues that a considerable part of this suffering is the effect of psychiatry.

(p. 135)

Chadwick is aware, when arguing in favour of the 'schizophrenic credit', that he runs the risk of being slotted within the 'anti-psychiatric' or 'social constructionist' school of thought. It is interesting therefore, to see how he very clearly attempts to distance himself from this perspective. Despite highlighting the positive dimensions of schizophrenia, Chadwick is very concerned to preserve the *experiential* dimension of what he clearly describes as an illness. 'Having suffered from what was diagnosed as a "schizoaffective illness"', he says, 'there was no doubt I was *suffering* to a degree far beyond anything I previously had ever known . . . and . . . that I was suffering from *something*' (Chadwick 1997: 21). 'It is impossible', he continues, 'for any sane person even to begin to imagine how I felt':

It is also obvious to anyone with a shred of common sense that I was *ill*. Any characterisation of my behaviour as merely 'bizarre', such that an 'illness' attribution would then be an act of social control (to empower the medical profession), is clearly utterly absurd.

(p. 44)

Reflecting on his experience, Chadwick argues that it was helpful for him to regard himself as having had an *illness* (p. 147). This made him respectful of his need to maintain his medication which he had been on since 1981 and continues taking today. He believes that his medication has helped him to make more, not less use, of his psychological insight and thus genuinely to gain ground (p. 147). The removal of the schizophrenia label, Chadwick argues, will not make suffering go away (p. 22).

Similarly, describing his experience of depression, Karp also admits that the phrase 'I'm depressed' has now become so routine that one might presume depression to be a normal rather than a pathological condition (Karp 1996: 54). At what point does the 'discomfort inevitably a part of living become acute enough to call it a disease' (p. 54)? Karp admits, in accordance with the anti-psychiatric perspective, that this is as much a cultural and political question as it is a medical one. Nevertheless, this does not take away the fact that huge numbers of people are 'indeed in mental misery' (p. 11). On the basis of his own experience, for instance, Karp argues that he was forced to conclude that something was 'really wrong' with him (p. 3). At the age of 51, he has 'surrendered' himself to having a depressive illness in the sense that he does not believe he will ever be 'fully free of it' (p. 10). 'For me', Karp argues, 'depression has a chronicity that makes it like a kind of mental arthritis; something you just have to live with' (p. 10). To claim that 'mental illness does not exist seems nonsensical when people are catatonic, visibly psychotic, or otherwise unable to understand or carry out the most rudimentary behaviours necessary to function in society' (p. 55). The anti-psychiatry theorists, he argues, 'undercut their credibility by taking their argument too far' (p. 55).

The comments of both Chadwick and Karp demonstrate the way in which the experience of mental illness, like that of physical illness, is inextricably bound up with the individual's reflexive orientation to issues of cause, meaning, and the inevitably moral implications of such questions. Like everyone with depression, Karp argues, he has spent a lot of time considering its causes (p. 5). He believes it is impossible to live with depression without doing so. Theorizing about the cause of depression illustrates important processes of 'meaning-making' as people themselves speak about the intersection of illness, identity and society (p. 15). For example, when Karp asked interviewees with depression whether they considered themselves as having 'an illness in the medical sense', their answers, like his own, were characterized largely by 'ambivalence and confusion' (p. 53). Most people wanted to embrace a definition of the problem as biochemical in nature while simultaneously rejecting the notion that they suffered from a 'mental illness' (p. 72). The following is a typical comment:

> I don't see it like an illness. To me, it seems like part of myself that evolved, part of my personality . . . I mean biologically, I would have to say, 'yeah, I have a permanent illness or whatever'. But I don't like to look at it like that. I would prefer not to think of it in that way. I mean, if there's another word, I wouldn't use illness. I guess, disorder.
>
> (p. 72)

The ambiguity of people's orientation to the illness label is nowhere more sharply illustrated than when people first receive an official diagnosis of mental disorder. As Karp (p. 65) argues 'it is difficult to overstate the critical importance of this . . . double edged sword'. Despite the potential negative and stigmatizing implications of such diagnosis, many people welcome it. For instance, one woman described 'great relief' on her diagnosis of depression. She said to the psychiatrist:

> you mean there is something wrong with me? It's not some sort of weird complex mental thing? It's like 'No, you're sick!' (sigh). There was an enormous relief.
>
> (p. 65)

Another man described his experience as follows:

They gave me a blood test that measures the level of something in the blood, in the brain . . . they said 'Mr. Smith, you're depressed'. And I said, 'Thank God', you know. I wasn't as batty as I thought. It was like the cat was out of the bag. You know? It was a breakthrough . . . It was a chance for a new beginning.

(p. 65)

Karp argues that at the end of the day nearly everyone comes to favour biochemically deterministic theories of depression's cause (p. 31). This is partly a result of their gradual socialization into a 'medical version of reality' which predominates in psychiatry and clinical psychology, but also because of 'the intrinsic nature of depression itself' (p. 31).

The increasing acceptance of biochemically deterministic theories of mental disorder amongst users is also apparent in the schizophrenia field. A good example of this is the work of the Schizophrenia Association of Great Britain (SAGB) – an organization of lay people, many of whom are relatives of people diagnosed schizophrenic. This association lobbies to raise funds to build an institute in order to discover the biological basis of schizophrenia. Promotional campaigns suggest that a biochemical breakthrough is imminent and newsletters argue against social constructionist explanations of schizophrenic illness. As one poster argues: 'Schizophrenia is not all in the mind. It affects the body and the brain. It is a physical disease' (cited in Parker et al. 1995: 10). Another organization, The National Schizophrenia Fellowship (NSF) encourages a similarly optimistic view of biological research.

This leads us to the question of why people living with mental disorders such as depression and schizophrenia express ambiguity and resistance to critical psychological approaches such as social constructionism, and why there seems to be a return to biologically based explanations of causation. This question bears interesting resemblance to the one addressed at the end of the last chapter: why are people living with chronic physical pain and illness reluctant to endorse mainstream health psychological ideas which connect personality structure with illness causation and treatment? As we discussed in Chapter 5, such reluctance relates to the individual's struggle for social and moral legitimacy. Psychological theories and interventions are interpreted as making people responsible for their illness and its management.

In many senses, mental illness is analogous to chronic physical pain and illness because none of them possess a clear locus, and medicine, psychiatry and clinical psychology alike, are unable to produce the 'functional equivalent of an X-Ray' to affirm material causation (Karp 1996: 106). For this reason, the search for credibility, for affirmation that one is suffering from something specific and concrete, is intensified. As Rowe argues, the investment in believing that mental disorder has, at bottom, a physical basis, is high because it allows people 'to ignore . . . suffering . . . and the complexities of life' (Rowe 1994: xx). And in Chadwick's own words, recognizing that one has an illness can be therapeutically beneficial for many people because it removes feelings that 'that they are a morally "bad" person' (Chadwick 1997: 22). Karp succinctly sums up the dilemma as follows:

> Adopting the view that one is victimised by a biochemically sick self constitutes a comfortable 'account' for a history of difficulties and failures and absolves one of responsibility. On the negative side, however, acceptance of a victim role, while diminishing a sense of personal responsibility, is also enfeebling. To be a victim of biochemical forces beyond one's control gives force to others' definitions of oneself as a helpless, passive object of inquiry . . . The interpretive dilemma for respondents was to navigate between rhetorics of biochemical determinism and a sense of personal efficacy.
>
> (Karp 1996: 73)

Conclusion

In this chapter we have seen, as in previous chapters, how the identification, theorization, measurement and treatment of mental health and illness have taken on various forms over the last fifty years or so. These different forms reflect the tripartite processes of objectification, rationalization and subjectification involved in the transformation from a modern to a post-modern society (see Chapter 2). For instance, early biological approaches reflect the modernist process of objectification which attempts to reduce the investigation of mental disease to its basic physiological and chemical factors. Likewise, reflecting the modernist process of rationalization, psychological approaches became increasingly influential as clinical psychology professionalized and committed itself to a scientific biopsychosocial framework which involved quantitative measurement, categorization and an implicit assumption of the abnormality of mental disorder. Finally, reflecting the postmodern process of subjectification, critical health psychology redirects the investigation of mental disorder by deconstructing assumptions of abnormality, and listening to the 'more complicated subjectivity' of individuals who have actually been diagnosed mentally disordered.

As in previous patient or user voices depicted throughout this book, there is substantial ambiguity in the accounts portrayed in this chapter. Such ambiguity relates, for instance, to questions of the reality of mental disorder and of biological causation and treatments. This ambiguity alerts us to the importance of not viewing such accounts as an uncritical validation or transparent representation of the reality of such experiences. Personal stories of illness, both mental and physical, are inextricably related to practical and moral tasks such as the need for recognition and the search for social and moral legitimacy (see also Chapter 5).

Over the course of this book we have demonstrated how patients, users and recipients of health promotion messages, tend to resist professional processes of colonization and intervention, frequently expressing ideas that such interventions are unable to appreciate the complexity of their problems, reducing them to objects of scientific or humanistic investigation. In this chapter we have found that mental health users tend to express similar reservations with regard to the ideas of critical health psychology, for instance, in relation to issues regarding the social construction of mental illness. They feel, for instance, that such perspectives remain unable to appreciate the experiential reality of what it is like to live with mental illness, and, as such, constitute a block to witnessing and legitimating their position in the social world.

From the perspective advanced throughout this book, this is a serious problem. In the last chapter, for instance, we argued that mainstream health psychological ideas connecting personality, stress and disease, may actually prove detrimental to individuals attempting to live with serious illnesses such as cancer, because they make them feel responsible and subsequently guilty, when they find themselves unable to control the progression of their illness through various means. We criticized mainstream health psychology in this regard, arguing that its failure to address such issues constitutes an important ethical failure. If, however, mental health users are expressing similar reservations about critical approaches, then it is time for us 'to put our money where our mouth is', so to speak, and address similar issues on our own turf. Are some versions of critical health psychology exacerbating users' problems because they are failing to understand their nature adequately, thus throwing individuals into further turmoil because they do not know where to turn to next?

For instance, in typical social constructionist style, critical psychologists such as Parker et al. (1995) have argued that many users internalize the label of specific mental health categories such as 'schizophrenic' or 'depressive' because they actively participate in contemporary Western discourses which increasingly operate to conceptualize people's life problems in medical or psychological terms, thus 'constraining and "regulating" their lived reality' (p. 91). Taking mental illness as a reality, Parker et al. argue (p. 112) is a 'bad way' of building dialogue in this area because we need to be aware of 'the way in which psychiatric power insinuates itself into practices that promise, at first sight, to empower "users"' (p. 112). Many of the user accounts discussed in this chapter, however, remain unconvinced, even when aware of the social constructionist argument, that acceptance of the label 'mental illness' is a 'bad' thing. If critical health psychology is all about questioning professional forms of authority and discourse, and opening out to alternative visions and definitions of reality, then is it not somewhat hypocritical and naïve to simply conclude, as Parker et al. attempt to do, that critical health psychology's viewpoint constitutes a 'better' understanding than the views of users themselves (or indeed, of psychiatry, clinical psychology or mainstream health psychology)?

Chapter summary

By the end of this chapter you should understand the following concepts and issues:

◆ How mainstream health psychology focuses mainly on physical, as opposed to mental, health and illness.
◆ The study of mental health and illness remains largely the preserve of clinical psychology which is predominantly framed by a similar scientific framework to that found in mainstream health psychology.
◆ Clinical psychology investigates mental disorder from an eclectic, biopsychosocial framework. You should appreciate the theoretical and methodological problems associated with this framework.
◆ Critical health psychology's reformulation of the investigation of mental health and illness, e.g. an understanding of the way in which diagnostic classification operates to construct the norms and reality of mental disorder.
◆ Critical health psychology's focus on the voice of users, understanding meaning, and challenging the construction of disorder and abnormality.
◆ The existential devastation caused by mental illnesses such as depression and schizophrenia.
◆ Issues of empowerment, the importance of recognition and resistance to professional colonization.
◆ User resistance to some of the ideas of critical health psychology, e.g. anti-psychiatry and social constructionism. The importance of critical health psychology's ability to address such issues.

Discussion points

◆ From a critical health psychology point of view, the attempt to investigate mental disorders such as schizophrenia and depression from within a biopsychosocial framework is inadequate. Why?
◆ Listening to the voice of mental health users, we frequently find resistance to various professional theories and practices. How, as a critical health psychologist, can we account for this fact?
◆ Some forms of critical health psychology are as guilty as mainstream health psychological approaches of objectifying the patient or user. Discuss critically in the context of mental health and illness.

Key reading

Chadwick, P. (1997) *Schizophrenia: The Positive Perspective. In Search of Dignity for Schizophrenic People*. London: Routledge.

Karp, D. (1996) *Speaking of Sadness: Depression, Disconnection and the Meanings of Illness*. New York: Oxford University Press.

Lindsay, S. and Powell, G. (eds) (1994) *Handbook of Clinical Adult Psychology*. London: Routledge.

Parker, I., Georgaca, E., Harper, D., McLaughlin, T. and Stowell-Smith, M. (1995) *Deconstructing Psychopathology*. London: Sage.

Rowe, D. (1994) *Breaking the Bonds: Understanding Depression, Finding Freedom*. London: HarperCollins.

'Managing' illness: relationships between doctors and patients

His erection startled me. At first, it seemed merely to point me out, acknowledging my part in the simple and various human desires present in our encounter: the desire to be loved and to be healed, the desire to be naked before another and thus to be utterly understood and to be wordlessly explained, the desire for a life beyond this one, the desire to represent what is the truth. What could be more natural than that I was there, a witness to another man's ailing body? For a fleeting moment, I too wished to be naked, to be as available to him in his suffering as he had made himself to me. [But] gradually . . . I watched as if from behind a surveillance camera of my years of medical training . . . I mutated into an alien space scientist, studying and cataloguing a curious life form on a forbidding planet . . . I excused myself abruptly, saying in an oddly flat voice that I needed to get more liquid nitrogen to finish burning off the warts. I let the door slam shut loudly, definitively, behind me.

(Campo 1997: 14)

Medicine must be at the heart a moral enterprise . . . to care for humans is to be *human* and to see the limits and failures and also successes of our small humanity writ large in the struggle to help someone who hurts and fears and just plain is in need. The moral lesson is that this is what our life is about, too, what we must prepare for. I think at heart it's about the simple realities in life that all of life covers over because they are precisely that: too simple, too real.

(a doctor, cited in Kleinman 1988: 215)

Introduction

Patients come into contact with healthcare professionals in a whole variety of different healthcare settings. These include, for instance, interactions with a district nurse in the home, a consultant surgeon in the hospital, a GP at the local practice, a pharmacist in the pharmacy, a psychologist in the hospital. Despite this diversity, however, psychological studies of encounters between healthcare professionals and patients tend to focus largely on those between doctor and patient. Because of the vast amount of literature in this area, this chapter will similarly focus mainly on doctor–patient interactions. However, many of the themes which arise are also of relevance to patient encounters with other health professionals. Of particular importance in this chapter is the way in which encounters between patients and health professionals are increasingly dominated by instrumental and technical concerns which, as Habermas (1971) predicted, results in a diminished ability to engage with questions regarding the moral worth of ends and goals (see Chapter 1). As with other chapters in this book, it will be argued that health psychology feeds into this process of technical reductionism, actively preventing and exacerbating the failure to achieve a greater appreciation of values such as caring, compassion and simply witnessing the experience of the other, all of which are central to medical care.

Mainstream psychological accounts of the doctor–patient encounter

Mainstream health psychology studies of doctor–patient communication tend to focus very heavily on matters of compliance or adherence. In other words, they are largely concerned with investigating whether the patient complies with or adheres to the doctor's advice in relation to a particular illness or condition. Compliance is defined as 'the extent to which the patient's behaviour (in terms of taking medications, following diets or other life-style changes) coincides with medical or health advice' (Ogden 1996: 60). If the patient does not comply (rates of non-compliance are about 50 per cent for patients with chronic illnesses (p. 60) and 40 per cent for those with acute illness (Sarafino 1994: 300)), the health psychologist is interested in finding out why this is so.

Such non-adherence is routinely accounted for in a number of ways. Firstly, it may be explained by reference to the patient. For instance, according to the 'cognitive hypothesis model' of compliance (Ley 1981, 1989), a patient's compliance can be predicted on the basis of a number of factors. These include the patient's satisfaction with the consultation, their knowledge of the disease conditions (based on what they are told in the consultation) and their memory, or ability to recall such information from the consultations (see Ogden 1996: 60–3). Other approaches have suggested that compliance can be predicted on the basis of the Health Belief Model which involves a rational weighing-up of the costs and benefits of complying with the doctor's advice.

An alternative way of accounting for non-adherence is by locating it in the context of poor doctor–patient communication. Different communication styles such as doctor-centred and patient-centred have been identified (see Sarafino 1994: 2). The doctor-centred style, for instance, involves the doctor in a simple information-gathering technique in which she asks closed questions requiring brief 'yes' and 'no' answers, focuses narrowly on the presenting complaint, ignores attempts to widen out the discussion and, finally, demonstrates limited sensitivity to the problems, needs, views and beliefs of the patient. By contrast, the patient-centred style involves more open-ended questions, allowing the patient to relate more information and emotionally relevant material, shows greater awareness and empathy for the patient's feelings, which are considered an essential aspect of patient care, and allows the patient to participate in decisions to a greater extent. Perhaps not surprisingly, research has shown that people generally prefer medical care that involves a patient-centred style and individuals who have good relationships with their doctors are more likely to adhere to medical advice (see Sarafino 1994: 304).

Identification of the reasons for medical non-adherence leads to the next goal of mainstream health psychology: the development of interventions which improve the possibility of achieving patient adherence. Such interventions would include, for instance, improving information provision (e.g. providing written rather than just oral information), behavioural methods (e.g. providing prompts and reminders), self-monitoring, contingency contracting (whereby doctor and patient negotiate a series of treatment activities as goals and specify rewards the patients will receive for succeeding), and improving the communicative style of health professionals (e.g. training in how to be more patient-centred, how to ask open-ended questions and be more 'empathically aware').

Critical health psychology and the doctor–patient encounter

From the point of view of the critical health psychologist, there are a number of major interrelated problems with this mainstream research programme. These problems reiterate some of the themes already charted throughout this book. The first relates to a failure to locate doctor–patient interactions within the rapidly changing social context of health-care structure and delivery. The second problem refers to a failure to take account of the emotional, frequently non-rational and morally infused nature of doctor–patient interactions.

Part of mainstream health psychology's failure to locate the doctor–patient encounter within the contemporary social context of medical care, is its implicit, uncritical acceptance of the aims of a biomedical agenda – namely, to improve patient adherence to medical advice. Within this acceptance are the tacit assumptions that the doctor's judgement is correct, that the patient's knowledge, experience and beliefs are largely irrelevant to treatment considerations, and that the doctor is acting benevolently, in the best interests of the client. Such assumptions are succinctly summed up in Sarafino's (non-rhetorical) question 'How can nonadherence to medical advice be rational?' (1994: 302). This question leaves one wondering where health psychology has been for the last twenty years in which there has been a very influential patient (user) movement concerned to overturn such simplistic, naïve, medical-serving beliefs. This movement has been associated with the rise in consumerist health and currently constitutes a forceful challenge which lies at the heart of the rapidly changing nature of healthcare service and delivery. In this chapter, we will be concerned to chart the way in which such changes have a radical impact on the doctor–patient encounter.

The second problem, reducing the question of compliance/adherence to one of rational decision-making, substantially underplays the highly emotionally laden nature of encounters between doctors and patients. This, in turn, relates to their psychodynamic and socio-structural dimensions. In a recent study, for instance, Lupton (1997a, 1998) conducted a project which examined the perceptions and attitudes of doctors and patients towards each other. She found that emotional aspects played a particularly important feature, with patients and doctors frequently mentioning feelings of love, caring, gratitude, dependency, respect and trust, as well as anxiety, hatred, anger, frustration, hostility and fear. Above all, she found a high degree of emotional ambivalence towards doctors (Lupton 1998: 545). Such research supports explorations into the emotional aspect of the doctor–patient relationship initiated over forty years ago by Balint (1957) who was convinced that, 'psychologically, much more happens in general practice between patient and doctor than is discussed in the traditional textbooks' (p. 3). It seems, however, that mainstream health psychology textbooks are content to remain oblivious to such dimensions of the doctor–patient encounter.

In this chapter it will be argued that a psychology which fails to take on board such considerations remains both inadequately psychological and inadequately social. Accordingly, such a psychology fails to address some of the central problems of contemporary medical and health-related practice. This becomes apparent if we actually look at some of the research on doctor–patient relationships emerging out of the discipline of medicine over the last decade or so.

Here, increasingly, individual practitioners are taking on board criticisms that have emerged out of the critique of dominant biomedicine. Indeed, Kleinman (1988: 210), himself a medical practitioner, argued over a decade ago that we have little idea of the doctor's point of view, of the 'internal, felt experience of doctoring, the story of what it is like to be a healer'. In this respect, he argued, the 'ethnography of the physician's care lags far behind the phenomenological description of the experience of illness' (p. 211). In response to such limitations, there is a gradual sense of increasing reflexivity as doctors open themselves up to thinking critically about their professional practices, their emotions, their subjectivity and the work of doctoring more generally.

At present, this process is probably most developed in the US. with the publication of autobiographical accounts of their work by doctors such as Campo (1997), Hilfiker (1985) and Verghese (1994). In Britain, such published accounts are few, although a number of accounts criticizing the dominance of biomedical approaches and advocating more awareness of psychodynamic and experiential factors in the doctor–patient encounter have recently begun to emerge (see Holland 1995; Broom 1997; Smith and Norton 1999).[1] Empirical research on the experience of doctors (especially in general practice) in Britian is also increasing (May et al. 1996; Weiss and Fitzpatrick 1997; May and Sirur 1998).

Manifest in this process of increasing reflexivity is the emergence of a critical discourse. This discourse is characterized by a strong sense of hostility towards the increasing bureacratization and technologization which is increasingly sweeping through the medical profession. Such processes are perceived as serving to dehumanize and demoralize the work of the doctor. Accordingly, doctors are expressing concern with a social process which increasingly forces a shift away from doctor–patient relationships (concerned with moral and ethical issues such as continuity of care, treatment, trust and beneficence) towards a more limited concern with rationalized, effective consultation techniques (characterized by a focus on communication skills whose aim is to maximize the content of the interaction and enable a quicker diagnosis) (see May and Sirur 1998: 173).

The General Medical Council (GMC) corroborates this concern in contemporary documents for medical education and training, in which it significantly emphasizes the importance of communication, ethical behaviour, treating patients with dignity and serving as a 'team player' – what Smith (1998: 1623) characterizes as the 'softer' side of medicine. This 'softer side' involves developing doctors' abilities to tackle important emotional and psychological issues such as 'facing anxiety, enhancing self–other awareness and modifying interpersonal behaviour', none of which are easily achieved (Smith and Norton 1999: 123). In the context of this increasingly reflexive and critical literature, it becomes clear that mainstream health psychology's limited focus on rational and effective consultation techniques is rather outdated. Indeed, it is significant that recent books such as Smith and Norton's *Counselling Skills for Doctors* (1999) do not draw on mainstream health psychological research at all, relying instead on the sociological and psychoanalytic literature. Not only is this indicative of the limitations of mainstream health psychology, it also points to the way in which such limitations remain complicit in the perpetuation of a dehumanizing medical practice.

In this chapter, as part of the move towards a critical health psychology, it will be argued that not only does health psychology need to locate doctor–patient and other health encounters in terms of social and cultural changes, but it also needs to locate itself as part of those changes. Implicit in this argument is the suggestion that, as health psychologists, we need to take on some of the questions and issues that many doctors have begun to address, not only in their application to medical practice, but also in relation to the profession of health psychology. Rather than teaching narrowly circumscribed communication skills to health-related professions, mainstream health psychologists have important lessons to learn from critical medicine (and also from patients, see Chapters 5 and 6). These lessons relate to the dangers and limitations of an overly-rationalized and bureacratized practice and profession, which ultimately reduce both human and communicative potential.

The medicalization critique

As has previously been outlined in Chapter 2, the 1970s witnessed a challenge to biomedicine from writers such as Zola (1972) and Freidson (1970) who articulated fundamental critiques of the way that society is structured, calling into question the social roles played by members of powerful and high status occupational groups such as the medical profession. It was argued that social life and social problems have become increasingly medicalized or viewed through the lens of scientific medicine as diseases. Illich (1975) suggested that, rather than improving people's health, contemporary scientific medicine undermined it, through the side-effects (iatrogenic effects) of medical treatment. Moreover, it diminishes people's capacity for autonomy in dealing with their life problems and healthcare by encouraging dependency on medicine and allowing doctors to dictate to others how they should behave (Lupton 1997b: 96). From this perspective, mainstream health psychology approaches, which focus narrowly on improving doctor–patient communication, uncritically accept the medical standpoint, are inherently conservative, and serve merely to buttress the harmful process of medicalization.

The medicalization critique has been one of the most dominant perspectives in the sociology of health and illness since the 1970s, and remains dominant today, particularly for feminist writers. In a sociolinguistic study of doctor–patient communications, for instance, Mishler (1984) characterized the medical encounter as a dialogue between the voice of medicine and the voice of the life-world. He argued that the voice of medicine drowns out the voice of the life-world in a way that is disrespectful and intolerant of the patient's perspective. In a similar vein, Marxist sociologist Waitzkin (1991) examined the way in which doctor–patient interactions served to medicalize and depoliticize the social structural dimensions of health and highlighted how doctors implicitly exercised social control as they acted on moral ideologies relating to family, work, etc. Feminist critics of medicine have likewise viewed the medical profession as a largely patriarchal institution which uses definitions of disease and illness to maintain the relative inequality of women, taking over areas of their lives such as pregnancy and childbirth that were previously the domain of female lay practitioners and midwives (Ehrenreich and English 1974; Graham and Oakley 1986; Martin 1993; Doyal 1998).

Advocates of the medicalization critique have argued that medicalization should be resisted in favour of some degree of demedicalization. The right of medicine to make claims about its powers to define and treat disease and illness should be challenged. For example, the state should be encouraged to exert greater control over the actions of the medical profession to limit its expansion and deprofessionalize it. As we saw in Chapter 2, this is actually happening in today's healthcare system (the restructuring of the NHS). It is reaching its height as I write this chapter (April 1999), with a great deal of media coverage pillorying the medical profession in the light of various inquiries into alleged cases of medical incompetence. This has led, as an article in *The Guardian* (19/1/99: 15) discussed, to increasing pressure by the government on the ancient bastions of medical privilege, the Royal Colleges. 'Veiled threats from ministers' have made it increasingly clear that if the Royal Colleges do not 'put their house in order', then the 'state will do it for them'. One senior college figure is quoted as seeing a 'doomsday scenario': 'If a big scandal broke . . . we might see a Cabinet meeting decide that self-regulation had finally failed. They could decide to sort doctors out – scrap the GMC, create a new body in its place and . . . make regulation bite.' The article concludes that 'at the heart of what is happening is a public scrutiny of competence'. Accordingly, doctors may 'no longer be in charge of their own destiny'.

Research in British general practice suggests doctors are undergoing adverse changes in work experience (Weiss and Fitzpatrick 1997) and experiencing a decrease in job satisfaction, high levels of stress, anxiety and depression (Sutherland and Cooper 1992; Chambers and Belcher 1993; Caplan 1994). Young doctors are also reporting increasing disillusionment with medical practice and there is concern about the declining popularity of general practice as a career (Grey 1990; Dillner 1994). This, arguably, is partly a consequence of the deprofessionalizing process.

Another component of the deprofessionalization process has been the transformation of patients into healthcare users, as the user movement has encouraged them to exercise choice, become empowered, and act as discriminating 'consumers'. As we saw in Chapter 5 an important element in this process has been the changing nature of the disease burden in contemporary Britain towards chronic illnesses. This has led to increased interest in insider views of illness such as those presented in autobiographies and self-help groups. Not surprisingly, such changes have had a significant impact on the patient's relationship with his/her physician because the relevant knowledge or competence required may not be the kind of technical or biomedical knowledge that the physician is trained to provide. The practical and emotional problems experienced by the person with chronic illness may be better understood by other people in the same situation. Accordingly, the nature of the relationship between patients and doctors has changed radically over the last twenty years or so. Whereas the professional–patient relationship used to be characterized as a meeting between knowledgeable expert and ignorant lay person, it can now, arguably, be characterized as a 'meeting between experts' (Tuckett et al. 1985).

This insider view celebrates the authority of the individual in living or dealing with his/her illness, challenging the authority of medical knowledge and competence assumed in mainstream health psychology's concern with issues of compliance/adherence. It also highlights how such models are based largely on a conception of acute illness which is largely inappropriate to contemporary medicine's clientele. It is in accordance with such insider perspectives that the increasing popularity of autobiographical accounts, self-help groups (see Chapters 5 and 6) and alternative/complementary therapeutic approaches can be understood. It is to the latter that we now turn.

Alternative/complementary approaches and the treatment of illness

As was touched upon in Chapters 5 and 6, an important feature of the process of patient empowerment is a resistance to biomedicine's objectivity, its rationality and depersonalization. This is achieved by a renewed focus on subjectivity, meaning, and the importance of relationships, empathic witnessing, and humane recognition. In this chapter it will be argued that these resistant elements of the empowerment ethos play an important part in the increasing popularity of alternative/complementary approaches towards the treatment of illness.

A wide range of health practices are referred to as alternative/ complementary, including herbal medicine, aromatherapy, reflexology, osteopathy, homeopathy, acupuncture, chiropractic, spiritual healing, hypnotherapy, faith healing, prayer, yoga, T'ai Chi, Reiki, Alexander technique, etc. Numerous surveys conducted over the last twenty years suggest that alternative/complementary medicine is becoming increasingly popular in Britain, Europe and the United States (West 1992; Sharma 1995). The few studies that have been conducted regarding the user's motivation to seek alternative/complementary therapy, however, have been largely of a quantitative nature (Vincent and Furnham 1996). Such studies are useful for extrapolating some of the major factors affecting people's decisions to seek alternative/complementary treatment but, as these authors themselves point out, they fail to provide a deeper understanding of the 'strong appeal . . . of some aspects of complementary therapies'. In some way, they hypothesize, this appeal may be tied into the 'emotional aspects of illness' and the complementary practitioner's alleged willingness to engage with such issues (p. 47).

This points towards a number of general themes that seem to character-ize the attraction of alternative/complementary approaches. The first per-tains to popular notions of 'holistic' and 'psychosomatic' healing (Csordas 1994: 39). Alternative/complementary approaches are frequently perceived as working with a holistic philosophy, by which is meant, 'an emphasis on stimulating the life force of the individual in his/her total social environment with the aim of promoting health and preventing illness' (Saks 1992: 4). Such a holistic philosophy places social and emotional issues at centre stage in the cause and treatment of illness. For instance, in homeopathy, illness is viewed as being caused by the 'vital force's reaction to social or environ-mental stresses' (Scott 1998: 200). While these forces remain in place there is little possibility of effecting a cure. A prominent Indian theoretician (Sankaran 1991, 1994) argues that each remedy represents a bodily/emotional 'posture' which is the best possible response to some social or environmental situation. Accordingly, homeopathic constitutional treat-ment can be used to identify the body/mind posture, match it with an appro-priate remedy, and release the body/mind to move more freely between postures.

The holistic emphasis and the related importance of social and emotional issues characteristic of such approaches are frequently espoused in con-tradistinction to the mind–body dualism characteristic of orthodox medi-cine. The latter is perceived as wedded to a biomedical approach in which the body is viewed as a machine atomistically separated from its environ-ment. In this sense, as Scott argues (1998: 197), there are strong overlaps between alternative/complementary approaches such as homeopathy and feminist critiques of the biomedical model.

The orientation towards possible connections between illness and per-sonal and social context leads to another important theme: the importance of appreciating the patient's subjective experience in order to understand their illness adequately. This, in turn, means that subjective experience remains central to the diagnostic procedures of many alternative/complementary approaches. For instance, the homeopathic consultation is characterized as time-consuming because it needs to explore the patient as a whole individual. As one doctor training in homeopathy claimed, this means that 'the absolutely essential thing is to hear what the patient wants to tell you' in contrast to the way in which doctors are normally taught to 'pare down what we want to know' (p. 205). It is in this sense that some researchers have argued that the 'contrast between clinical biomedicine and most complementary and alternative therapies is stark' (p. 205).

The focus on subjective experience and listening to the patient introduces another characteristic of alternative/complementary approaches. This is the emphasis on *care* rather than an exclusive focus on *cure*. The few empirical studies of users of alternative/complementary medicine have found that the majority first used such approaches as an attempt to cure a condition for which orthodox medicine had been unable to offer them relief or cure to their satisfaction (Sharma 1995; Vincent and Furnham 1996). Sharma found that patient dissatisfaction tended to revolve around a number of themes including: complaints that orthodox medicine treats symptoms rather than causes; the iatrogenic effects of orthodox medicine such as drug side-effects and invasive treatments; and the lack of time and attention provided within the conventional medical doctor–patient encounter. Overall, these factors tend to diminish the individual's sense of control and led to Sharma's suggestion that orthodox medicine, becoming ever more technological in its approach, is increasingly providing medical services in which cure is detached from care. By contrast, alternative/complementary medicine allegedly enables individuals to experience an increased sense of control over their illness and its management, thus serving to reinstate a sense of care.

This renewed concern with care as well as cure serves to re-cast the patient–practitioner relationship in alternative/complementary approaches. The word 'healing' enjoys enormous vogue in holistic medicine and alternative/complementary therapists frequently advertise themselves as healers and make claims to their healing capacities. In order to be successful, alternative/complementary therapies of various kinds frequently necessitate the individual retreating from 'explicit or linear forms of thought', and beginning to 'rely on the unconscious', 'intuitive senses' and the 'spiritual dimension' of human experience (Frohock 1992: 104). This kind of healing is similar to that depicted in the Gospels, when Jesus allegedly healed through the transference of some kind of psychic power. As Frohock argues (p. 107), these healing stories constitute powerful influences on contemporary Christian societies, forming the basis for ideas regarding the power of a spiritual world to enter human experience and reverse material causality. Given the 'spiritual', for which (in the contemporary mind-set) read 'non-scientific', dimensions of such ideas, it is not at all surprising that orthodox medical practitioners very rarely use the word 'healing'. Instead, they are far more comfortable with the notion of cure, which rids medical practice of the subjective connotations associated with the word 'healing' (Spiro 1986: 149).

The focus on personal experience and the psychic and spiritual dimensions associated with the orientation towards healing, suggests that the contemporary popularity of alternative/complementary approaches is, as Csordas (1994: viii) argues, 'all about self'. As we have argued in previous chapters, the pursuit of health has become a moral ideal in contemporary Western societies. It is one of the ways in which individuals convince themselves of their 'goodness' and 'moral worthiness' (or, by 'rebelling', demonstrating that they don't have any truck with such values). Likewise, studies of a wide spectrum of middle-class American healing groups have suggested that, for many of them, health represents an 'idealisation of a kind of self' and healing is 'part of the process by which growth toward that ideal is achieved' (McGuire, cited in Csordas 1994: 20). From this perspective, the 'healing' vogue draws its strength from an increasing discontent with the objectifying and rationalizing processes manifest in contemporary society (in this case, orthodox medicine), and the need to move beyond such limits. In other words, the increasing popularity of alternative/complementary approaches is related to the remoralization of issues of health and illness.

The remoralization of medicine from within?

This explanation for the increasing popularity of alternative/complementary approaches, however, is not entirely satisfactory for a number of reasons. Firstly, as Saks (1992) makes clear, many heterogeneous practices are categorized under the generalized label of alternative/complementary approaches. In fact, this category hides a whole variety of practices and philosophies, some of which are more holistic than others. For example, osteopathic practice should not really be characterized as holistic as it is based on a mechanistic conception of the human organism. By contrast, another reason why the explanation is not satisfactory is because it does not take account of some of the critical transformations and discourses that have been emerging in the context of orthodox medicine over the last decade or so. As will be shown in the following overview, the negative characterization of orthodox medicine from both the medicalization critique and, relatedly, the alternative/complementary agenda, is overly simplistic. This is because the holistic discourse characteristically associated with alternative/complementary approaches (including the themes depicted above, such as the importance of emotional and social issues, listening to the patient's subjective experience, care, healing and the irrational dimension of the patient–practitioner encounter, and the remoralization of medical care), also pervades contemporary orthodox medical and health-related practice.

This is partly the result of the work of medical reformers such as Balint (1957), Kleinman (1988) and Spiro (1986), who have attempted to democratize and humanize medicine by taking on board many of the themes highlighted by the anti-medical critique. All of these medical writers are critical of scientific medicine and training because of its narrow focus on disease to the exclusion of illness (see also Chapters 5 and 6). Kleinman, for instance, argues that there are two sets of long-term problems associated with chronic illnesses: medical complications of the disease and the 'life trajectory' that the illness marked and 'inexorably shaped'. He argues further that his medical training 'systematically educated' him about the former 'but tended to discount and in certain ways even blinded' him to the latter (Kleinman 1988: xii). Spiro (1986: 4) similarly claims the same distinction between disease and illness, fearing that 'modern medical culture has somehow mistaken the means – science – for the end – caring for patients'. This 'pernicious value transformation', Kleinman (1988: 9) continues, constitutes 'a serious failing of modern medicine'. This is because it 'disables the healer' and 'disempowers the chronically ill'. Accordingly, biomedicine 'must be indicted for this failure in order to provoke serious interest in reform'.

As can be seen from the above comments, central to the renewed focus on illness (as opposed to disease) is the rise in chronic illnesses and the recognition that these are related in a complex way to the individual's personal and social environment. These ideas are related to Balint's (1957: 2) notion that social changes such as industrialization and geographical mobility have led us to lose our sense of roots and connections, thus becoming more solitary and lonely. The people to whom we can turn when we become emotionally or mentally stressed are few and far between. Hence, such stress 'is either accompanied by, or tantamount to, various bodily sensations' (p. 2). A frequent outlet is to visit the doctor and seek help. Balint's work constituted a strong influence on the 'discourse of holism', important because of its potential to 'liberate sufferers and practitioners from the oppressive iron cage imposed by a too intensely morbid preoccupation with painful bodily processes' (Kleinman 1988: 9). Instead, the practitioner's attention is redirected towards possible connections between the individual's illness and his/her familial and social environment.

In accordance with this objective, Kleinman emphasizes the importance of the doctor's ability to interpret the patient's and family's perspective on illness. 'The interpretation of narratives of illness experience' he argues, 'is a core task in the work of doctoring' (p. xiii; see also Broom 1997). Accordingly, one of Kleinman's main aims is to develop a rationale for a practical clinical methodology which involves the 'sensitive solicitation of stories of illness', a kind of 'mini-ethnography' which 'amounts to a brief medical psychotherapy for the multiple, ongoing threats and losses that make chronic illness so profoundly disruptive' (Kleinman 1988: 10). At the heart of this endeavour is *empathic listening, translation and interpretation* – 'the craft of the clinician who treats illness, not just disease' (p. 228). 'When the empowerment of patients and families becomes an objective of care', Kleinman continues, 'the empathic auditing of their stories of the illness must be one of the clinician's chief therapeutic tasks' (p. 130).

These considerations have led reformers such as Kleinman and Spiro to criticize the way in which the heavy focus on science which characterizes the contemporary era, results in a split between care and cure. Spiro, for instance, argues that physicians in hospital training learn the virtues of cure but seldom of care (Spiro 1986: 2). Likewise, Kleinman argues that empathic care, incorporating an appreciation of illness meaning and the handling of deeply felt emotions within intimate personal relationships, cannot be dismissed as peripheral tasks. Rather, they consitute 'the point' of medicine. The failure to address these issues constitutes a fundamental flaw in the work of doctoring. It is in this very particular sense, Kleinman argues, that in spite of remarkable progress in the control of disease, contemporary biomedicine has 'turned its back on the purpose of medicine' (Kleinman 1988: 254).

Related to these concerns with care is a renewed emphasis on the importance of a sustained and meaningful relationship between the doctor and patient. This, in turn, is related, especially in Spiro's work, to the placebo effect – the non-specific therapeutic effect of the doctor–patient relationship. Spiro argues that the placebo effect is despised in medical research because it confounds a clear-cut understanding of the specificity of succesful treatment. However, it is, in fact, the essence of effective clinical care, helping physicians 'recover a sense of the person in the patient' (Spiro 1986: 3). Kleinman similarly argues that clinicians 'should work assiduously' to cultivate the highest possible placebo effect rates in their routine medical care. In order to achieve this, they must 'establish relationships that resonate empathy and genuine concern for the well-being of their patients' (Kleinman 1988: 245).

'Lying as it does at the border of the known and the unknown, the measurable and the unmeasurable, the rational and the mystical', Spiro argues, the placebo effect reminds him, at 'a time when technology is triumphant', that much of what physicians do '*is still not grounded on reason and may never need to be*' (Spiro 1986: 7, emphasis in original). In contemporary medicine, physicians are embarrassed to 'consider themselves as healers' and 'relegate any such notion to a fictitious charisma'. The reason for this, Spiro argues, is that physicians are taught to cure disease not to heal and care for persons (p. 28). Accordingly, physicians need to find ways of reclaiming the 'art of medicine' (p. 28), of seeing themselves as 'poets rather than as physicists' (p. 4).

All of this amounts to what can generally be characterized as a remoralization of medical education and practice. Towards the end of his book, Kleinman asks his reader to consider what seems like an 'absurd question' in the context of the immense healthcare enterprise of Western industrialized nations:'What is the purpose of medicine?', 'Why medicine?' (Kleinman 1988: 253). It is, he argues, a question that must be asked if we are to avoid acquiescing with the 'dominant economic clichés of our day' which reduce the doctor–patient relationship to a 'commercial relationship between a purveyor of services and a customer' (p. 253). Although medicine *is* intimately involved with economics, it *must* not be reduced to that. 'There is a moral core to healing', Kleinman continues, 'that I take to be the central purpose of medicine'. The doctor–patient relationship is a 'deeply moral relationship' from which both doctor and patient 'change and learn' (p. 246). Other researchers, using the philosopher Emmanual Levinas's work, have similarly argued that the 'deep meaning' of doctoring (or nursing) can be found 'outside the self', in an 'ethical experience' of simply 'being there' to help and care for the 'vulnerable other' (van Manen 1998: 21).

The social structure of the orthodox doctor–patient relationship

Given that similar critical themes related to the discourse of holism are manifest in both alternative/complementary approaches and from within the medical profession itself, how can we account for the seeming increasing popularity of the former, in contrast to the rising tide of criticism against orthodox medicine and doctors? Hilfiker, an orthodox practitioner writing about his experience of being a doctor (1985: 13) succinctly characterizes this situation when he comments on the:

> rising tide of criticism against physicians as a group, criticism of our attitudes towards patients and of our general behaviour. We are accused of being unavailable, of no longer making house calls, of being scheduled weeks in advance . . . We are too preoccupied with disease and not concerned about the whole person. We don't listen to our patients, won't communicate with them. We are authoritarian, dictatorial. We are told that we place too much reliance on science and technology, that we don't put enough energy into personal, caring contact with our patients. And we're too interested in money . . . our incomes extravagant. 'Doctors don't really care any more. It's just a job to them.'
>
> (p. 13)

Although there is obviously some truth in these allegations, in order to fully understand the hostility of patients towards orthodox medicine (and the associated increased interest and value attached to alternative/complementary approaches) it is necessary to connect these to the social and political context of contemporary healthcare.

In this respect, it is useful to return to the work of sociological critics such as Talcott Parsons (1975) who criticized the anti-medical position for its failure to locate the orthodox doctor–patient relationship adequately within the wider social structure. In particular, he criticized the anti-medical perspective for its assumption that an equal, more humanitarian and caring relationship between doctor and patient (as advocated by alternative/complementary approaches and the medical reformist position) could be achieved. Parsons's point was that the frequently emotionally laden nature of the encounter which, in part, relates to the social structure of orthodox medicine, militates against this possibility.

Parsons argued that regardless of the type of illness suffered by the patient, and regardless of the degree of active participation and responsibility assumed by the patient for his/her own health, dealings between patients and physicians are inevitably characterized by asymmetry because they take place within a social structure where hierarchical positions of power, authority and prestige are involved. Moreover, this asymmetrical structure is functional in so far as a particular profession is involved with the responsibility for maintaining the state of health of the general population.

According to Parsons, there are two major features of the doctor–patient relationship which consistently serve to reinforce its asymmetry. These are professional competence and professional concern. Professional competence is characterized by a level of knowledge and skill capacity independent of personal experience or exposure to a particular disease, and founded on formal training and experience. This is complemented by professional concern, by which the physician is trained to perform a function of social control by operating as a 'general trustee' of the health interests of the general population. The physician's medical training socializes her into this way of thinking through instilling ethical values such as trust, fairness, discipline, and reputation (see Beauchamp and Childress 1994). Orientation to these values constitutes an important part of professional training and is significant in the creation and maintenance of medical dominance and the promotion of medical authority. As Daniels (1998: 208) argues, without the concession of trust a practitioner cannot practise, and without a generalized trust a profession loses its authority (p. 208).

Many researchers have challenged this functionalist approach to doctor–patient relationships, arguing that it reinforces orthodox medical dominance and fails to take account of lay and alternative competencies (e.g. alternative/complementary approaches) in the wake of increasing public access to medical professional expertise and an increasingly educated consumerist public. This is especially so with the changing nature of the disease burden towards chronic illnesses in which it is claimed that the subjective experience of the patient is of more relevance than the technical knowledge of biomedicine (Pilnick 1998). The problem with these arguments, however, is that they focus very narrowly on the technical knowledge component of professional training, and fail to consider the professional concern dimension of the doctor–patient relationship.

Even if it is possible for the patient (and/or alternative/complementary practitioners) to reach the same level of technical knowledge as the doctor, the same cannot be said of the professional concern dimension because this relates to the doctor's social role and function. This is to serve as a general trustee of the health interests of both the individual patient and that of society more generally. This role demands a degree of professional objectivity and rationality which means, in effect, that the doctor should be able to stand back from the immediate personal and emotional dynamics of the situation, in order to assess the most effective, fair and appropriate course of action in the circumstances. This is necessary for the pursuit of professional and competent practice.

Although the possibility of achieving such objectivity may be somewhat idealized, it is arguably more likely to be achieved than if the patient serves as his own trustee. This is because the patient frequently has a great deal of emotional investment in the situation and, as we saw in Chapters 5 and 6, is often frightened, uncertain, and desperate to gain relief from symptoms or illness. This state of mind is not necessarily conducive to a solution that is in the best interests of the patient. As Spiro argues, 'the old adage has it that the doctor who treats himself has a fool for a patient and a fool for a physician . . . the patient is less likely to make adequate choices unless guided by a physician' (Spiro 1986: 116).

The issue of trusteeship is becoming more relevant as patients are transformed into consumers who demand their rights to certain kinds of healthcare. A number of doctors have written about the problems faced in the medical encounter because patient and doctor operate with different priorities. For instance, Hilfiker gives the example of a 44-year-old female patient who demands treatment that he does not believe is in her best interests. This patient visits his surgery with the express intent of gaining a prescription for Valium. He is reluctant. On the basis of his personal experience with other patients, he does not believe Valium will do her any good in the long term. Hilfiker believes his patient's stress and depression will lift only when she can confront the source of her loneliness, alienation and anxiety. Accordingly, he has referred her to a counsellor but she has failed to turn up to appointments.

Hilfiker uses this anecdote as a means of highlighting the way in which he frequently becomes locked in a 'value struggle' with his patients, whereby he acts in accordance with contemporary professional values regarding the health and good of his patient. Unfortunately, these values may be at odds with the patient who simply wants immediate relief from symptoms. The main point to appreciate about such conflicts is that they remain fundamentally unequal because the doctor has the ultimate power, in this case, the power to refuse to write the prescription. The patient cannot do a lot about this.

Accordingly, it is important to understand that part of the reason why patients so often perceive physicians in a hostile fashion, is related to the physician's legal and social responsibilities (and the power to pursue those responsibilities) which are often in conflict with the patient's goals and desires (Hilfiker 1984: 148). In accordance with Parsons's functionalist argument, it could be argued that, to a certain extent, such conflicts are inevitable. This is because part of the doctor's job (her social function) is to serve as a 'general trustee' of the health interests of the general population, which sometimes involves acting as an agent of society against the wishes and needs of the individual patient.

By contrast, the alternative/complementary practitioner, working largely in private practice, does not perform the same social function as the orthodox doctor. Although the GMC permits GPs to refer patients to non-orthodox practitioners, not only do GPs retain legal and moral responsibility for the patient, the NHS is also unlikely to pay for such treatments. As Sharma (1995: 211) argues, to some extent this transforms the practitioner–client (as opposed to doctor–patient) relationship, not least because the client is paying for treatment. Working for the paying client, rather than in the interests of the health and well-being of society as a whole, the alternative practitioner does not have to act against the needs and desires of the former. It is in this sense that the popularity of alternative/complementary approaches remains dependent on their occupation of a socio-politically defined marginal standing in the healthcare system. In fact, from the findings presented in Chapter 5, we may tentatively hypothesize that when alternative/complementary approaches become increasingly institutionalized (i.e. available on the NHS), as in the case of psychological therapies for cancer care, they become the object of greater resistance from patients who resent the intrusion of ever expanding professional interventions into their lives.

The psycho-social dynamics of the orthodox doctor–patient encounter

Ambivalence, dependency and projection

The failure of the anti-medical perspective to appreciate that the inequality of the doctor–patient relationship is related to the social and political structure of contemporary healthcare, also relates to a failure to appreciate the ambivalent nature of the feelings and attitudes people have in relation to orthodox medicine – the ways in which they willingly participate and feed into medical dominance, and yet resist it at the same time (Lupton 1997b: 98). Such ambivalence is related to the complex psychological and emotional feelings released by illness. As has been illustrated in Chapters 5 and 6, the experience of illness often constitutes a severe shock to the system and involves a shattering of trust in one's body, self, future and relationships with others. Not surprisingly, this leaves the individual feeling very vulnerable. In psychoanalytic terms, such vulnerability encourages a process of regression, i.e. the adult's return to more primitive, childish behaviour. As Mayer (1994: 6) wrote in relation to her experience of cancer: 'Disease holds all of us hostage to our childhood terrors. A critical illness catapults us back there, to that primitive, emotional state, reminding us that life is circular, that where we are going is where we came from.'

In contemporary Western societies, if we are ill, our first inclination is to turn to doctors or medical interventions (e.g. pills, potions) to relieve our suffering. Medicine comprises the central locus of cure. Indeed, a major part of the impetus for the medicalization critique, the promotion of insider views of illness and the increasing popularity of alternative/complementary approaches, stems from the inability of medicine to provide effective forms of intervention or cure. It is notable in this respect that empirical studies of users of alternative/complementary approaches have found that the majority first used such approaches as an attempt to cure a condition for which orthodox medicine had been unable to offer them relief or cure to their satisfaction (Sharma 1995; Vincent and Furnham 1996). But even in these cases, dissatisfaction with orthodox medicine is seldom total and users of alternative medicine will generally combine such approaches with orthodox medicine (Thomas *et al.* 1991; Sharma 1995; Vincent and Furnham 1996). As we saw in Chapters 5 and 6, despite being disillusioned with orthodox medicine, people suffering from chronic physical and mental conditions still continue to pin their hopes on it (Jackson 1994: 222).

Such findings shed a slightly different light on patient empowerment perspectives which frequently involve a repudiation of medical and health-related professionals' authority, and the associated dependence imposed on the patient. For example, in previous research (Crossley 1997b; 1998b) with people living with a long-term HIV-positive diagnosis, I have demonstrated that the independent stance of the patient and frequently associated demonization of doctors and medicine, are not quite so straightforward as they seem. To understand this process it is necessary to take account of the emotional vulnerability of the person who is ill. The concept of 'projection' is useful in this respect (see Balint 1957; Holland 1995; Crossley 1997b, 1998b; Lupton 1997b). In very simple terms, this refers to a psychological process through which we resolve our personal worries, fears and vulnerabilities (in this case about illness), by mentally passing them on to another person or group external to the self. Rather than facing up to these strong emotions and fears, the ill person projects them onto the doctor, or a more general sense of medicine. The doctor can then be used as an object onto which the patient transfers her bad feelings of fear and vulnerability. Doctors and orthodox medicine are the obvious targets in this respect because they represent most strongly the patient's hopes, desires and fears – the possibility of life, cure and relief from symptoms.

This process of projection is manifest in some of the autobiographical accounts of illness encountered in Chapter 5. As Mayer comments, throughout her treatment for cancer, 'I had to continuously try to contain my anger about what had happened to me and keep it from contaminating my relationships with the medical people who took care of me, since I was so dependent upon them' (Mayer 1994: 46). The worst thing, she claims, was the 'blind irrational anger I felt at the monstrous unfairness of it all, a black fury that could be drawn like lightning to any unsuspecting target – a lab technician . . . my therapist . . . the oncologist' (p. 76). 'I was so petrified', Mayer continues, 'about the prospect of chemotherapy that I might have taken an active dislike to anyone who represented the treatment I so dreaded' (p. 46). Her anger is characterized as 'a targetless, helpless rage' running around and around inside her, 'building up a charge, seeking an outlet' (p. 76). Similarly, Seagrave, in her autobiographical account of cancer, claims that the worst part of being a patient, worse than the pain and tiredness, is the 'sense of the loss of power' (Seagrave 1995: 13). She admits to having become 'like a retired colonel', firing off letters of complaint against the medical profession, 'hitting out to get rid of my aggression' (p. 63). These accounts add weight to Balint's notion that 'any privation imposed on the individual by his illness may be felt as coming from the doctor' leading to 'resentful fantasies' and feelings of 'anger and hatred against the doctor' (Balint 1957: 241).

Similar feelings are evident in experiential accounts written by people living with mental disorders such as depression and schizophrenia (see Chapter 6). In his interviews with people with depression, for instance, Karp (1996: 89) describes how he was 'surprised by the virulence of the animosity expressed toward psychiatrists'. The following interview is recalled as illustrative of one individual's 'clear edge of anger in his feelings about psychiatrists':

> I don't think very highly of psychiatrists. You can tell. I tolerate them because I have to take this medicine. [But] everything can be cured with a drug, everything. They've got a drug for everything . . . They like to tinker with the body through these drugs rather than trying to have people express what they're feeling. They just took one look at me and pronounced me depressed and put me on a battery of antidepressants . . . They're not very human. They don't look at the humanistic side.
>
> (p. 85)

Note how the psychiatrist has become 'other': '*they*'ve got a drug for everything'; '*they* like to tinker'; '*they're* not very human'. And yet, as we found in Chapter 6, people living with mental illness are themselves profoundly ambiguous about the biochemical genesis of their difficulties and the value of taking drugs. Karp, for instance, speaks of his own attitude towards drugs and psychiatrists as a 'mixture of hostility and dependence' (p. 79). Although he remains ambivalent about their value, he reluctantly 'sticks with medications because I am afraid that things could be much worse if I were to stop' (p. 79). This feeling of dependence on drugs is, of course, also transferred onto the psychiatrist who prescribes them.

It is important to note that projective dynamics can also work to produce a good, loving object in the figure of the doctor, rather than one of badness and hatred. In this situation, the patient similarly deals with her feelings of vulnerability by passing them onto the doctor, but in a dependent and trusting fashion (the 'good doctor will take care of me', 'everything will be all right') rather than in the independent, resistant fashion characteristic of the contemporary empowerment position. This kind of response was probably more likely before the rise and popularization of the medicalization critique. In his personal account of his sister's experience of cancer, Shapiro (1997) provides a good example of such positive projective dynamics, claiming that his sister's moods, hopes and her view of the world increasingly came to depend on the doctor's tone of voice and his every gesture. 'Reduced by her disease to almost infantile helplessness', Shapiro writes, 'she came to see her doctor as an all-knowing and all-powerful parent. Since her survival depended on his expertise, it was almost impossible for her not to invest that experience with almost magical potency' (p. 53)

Responding to patient projections: repression, objectification and control

Processes of projection may be adaptive for the patient to the extent that they help minimize feelings of vulnerability, but it is not difficult to imagine that they create a great deal of anxiety and conflict for the doctor, a 'dumping ground' for intense feelings of anger, hatred and hope. How do doctors cope with being the object of such strong emotions?

Hilfiker claims that the only way he could cope with the constant emotional turbulence induced by his work as a doctor, was 'to harden myself to it, to shield myself from it' (Hilfiker 1985: 27). As many doctors report, this skill of emotional detachment is taught, both implicitly and explicitly, from the early days of medical school. One example cited by Hilfiker concerns learning the technical skills of examination. He and his colleagues had to practise, initially on each other, breast, genital and rectal examinations. This 'quite naturally caused some embarrassment'. When Hilfiker asked the instructor how they were supposed to deal with feelings of sexual arousal when examining someone of the opposite sex, his answer was essentially that those feelings should not arise and they should be suppressed as completely as possible. Even as a student, Hilfiker claims he knew *that* would not be possible. He sensed a deep unwillingness to allow medical students to look at their own feelings (p. 28).

A classic study of nursing practice conducted by Menzies-Lyth (1960), similarly illustrates the way in which nurses are routinely institutionalized in the hospital setting to detach themselves emotionally from patients and their families. The intimate bodily and emotional contact that nurses have with patients on a daily basis, and their confrontation with the realities of pain, suffering and death, mean that their work arouses strong emotions and mixed feelings such as pity, compassion, love, hatred, guilt, anxiety and resentment. In addition, as with doctors, patients and families tend to project onto nurses their own emotional demands and feelings of anxiety, depression and disgust. One of the main ways in which nurses cope with such demands is by detaching themselves from their emotions and getting on with more physical and routine nursing tasks.

Contemporary nursing is strongly influenced by the notion of holistic care, sometimes referred to as 'new nursing' or the 'nursing process', terms which suggest an alternative to the medical model and a simple equating of patients with physical conditions (Fulton 1996: 37). The nursing process is related to the increasing professionalization of nursing which has involved a preoccupation with improving the quality of nursing. Despite these changes, however, recent studies suggest that a tension exists between the ideals of practice as taught in nurse education and the clinical reality of implementing them (Fulton 1996: 36; Henderson 1998). There is a widespread dislike amongst nurses of the nursing process. Many argue that there is not the time nor the resources to provide the personalized care implied in the holistic model. However, according to Fulton, this is not the whole story. Instead, the failure of nurses to provide such care can be accounted for in terms of their 'understandable reluctance to connect themselves to care that entails difficult or painful relationships' and their fear of becoming 'overinvolved' with patients (Fulton 1996: 36). Nurses find it easier simply to provide physical care because they are then able to 'place boundaries' around the patient.

Clinical detachment and the suppression of emotion obviously constitute a basic requirement of a great deal of medical work. For example, they are necessary in routine examinations, emergency situations and when diagnosing disease. However, as Hilfiker argues, there is a great tendency for the physician, when under constant pressure, to begin to use the tool of clinical detachment as 'personal protection' and a 'generalised defensive response' (Hilfiker 1985: 127). When this happens, 'the unintended consequence is that the person tends to disappear and the patient becomes an object, a thing upon which the physician acts' (p. 127). Emotional detachment and repression bear the cost of losing the possibility of achieving intimate connection with others. Accordingly, 'it is no accident that the talk of medical personnel is filled with references to people as if they were diseases or parts of the body' (p. 127).

Contemporary changes in healthcare and the exacerbation of objectification

Contemporary changes in the structure and delivery of healthcare, the increasing rationalization or bureaucratization of healthcare (see Chapter 2), tend to exacerbate the tendency for doctors and patients to use destructive and defensive ways of coping such as projection, detachment and objectification. Of particular importance in this respect are pressures towards increased efficiency and productivity and increased use and reliance on technology. In the analysis that follows, we will discuss some of the ways in which these social and economic changes impact on the doctor's and patient's perception of each other.

Pressures for increased efficiency and productivity

Like many practicing physicians I entered medicine out of a desire to be of service to people. Whatever other motives I may have had, my root ambition was to help, to respond to others' needs. What I failed to realize, however, was that the very nature of my work as a doctor would push me continually into the position of limiting the help I would give, of ignoring the needs of others. One of the pressing realities of my job was that I repeatedly found myself contradicting my own inner desire to be of service, a conflict that created in me a deep sense of guilt. At the heart of this conflict lay the simple fact that there were too many patients' needs for the time and energy I had available ... It is, in fact, one of the basic dilemmas of the physician – to be caught between a desire to be of service and a need for respite.

(Hilfiker 1985: 32)

In this comment, Hilfiker pre-empts May and Sirur's (1998) articulation of contradictions inherent in the recent history of British general practice. This history, they argue, has been marked by an 'expansive professional rhetoric' on 'the discourse of holism' which stresses the central place of the interpersonal relationship between doctor and patient. However, this creates a problem for GPs because it sets up a massive disparity between professional aspirations and what it is structurally possible to achieve in the context of an encounter that is profoundly limited by competing demands on the doctor's time (p. 172). In addition, in recent years, the number of patients registered with individual GPs has declined by about 20 per cent. There has also been a decline in the extent to which patients attribute responsibility for their care to a specific doctor in the practice they attend (Dowrick 1997).

Such problems are, in part, related to the increasing rationalization of health-care. Time management has become big business in medicine as doctors are increasingly pressurized to become maximally efficient and to modernize or streamline patient care (Hilfiker 1985: 135; see also Beardwood et al. 1999). Hilfiker gives the example of how, to encourage the smooth flow of patients in and out of his office in surgery hours, he found it more efficient for the practice nurse to prepare the patient by getting them to undress before their appointment with him, 'practically convincing' himself that the state of undress helped patients 'get to the point' more quickly (Hilfiker 1985: 136). He readily admits that in his medical training 'the surgeon who could perform an appendectomy in twenty minutes rather than forty, became, in our minds, the better surgeon' (p. 138). Under pressure to create an efficient service, the values of 'efficiency and productivity seem to acquire an independent life of their own, becoming a yardstick by which the physician measures herself as competent physician' (p. 137).

Increasing pressures for productivity and efficiency also compromise the possibility of achieving an encounter between patient and doctor which will elucidate potential connections between the individual's presenting symptoms and his/her wider social environment (as advocated by the holistic discourse). Although medically trained to perform a thorough systems review in dealing with each patient problem (including how psychological well-being and social adjustment might impinge on biological functioning), because of constant time pressures, doctors increasingly find themselves evading such issues. And although in medical school doctors are taught the importance of open-ended interviewing techniques as a means of encouraging people to expand on their needs, unfortunately, engaging with psychosocial problems is not conducive to productivity and efficiency. Accordingly, doctors are increasingly likely to find themselves relying on direct questions which call for specific information and do not allow other problems to surface (Hilfiker 1985; Weiss and Fitzpatrick 1997).

The tendency to objectify the patient in this most fundamental sense, by restricting attention to physical needs in the service of efficient production, is not confined to doctors dealings with patients. For example, in her study of nursing aides in an American nursing home setting, Foner (1994) demonstrates some of the ways in which the bureaucratic demands of state regulation, pressures for administrative efficiency, and the sheer difficulty of formally regulating and measuring emotional care have conspired to create a situation in which aides are judged primarily in terms of their performance of physical tasks which can be easily quantified, recorded in medical records, and used for reimbursement purposes. This creates a situation in which aides are encouraged to follow orders and finish tasks on schedule, and are castigated for spending time talking to residents and doing 'emotional work' (p. 68). Similarly, nurses at the nursing home, far from being 'ideal models of compassionate care' or 'romantic Florence Nightingales who gently minister to the sick and needy', were mainly preoccupied with 'bureaucratic requirements' in which they 'plowed ahead with paperwork and official duties' and spent very little time in direct patient care (p. 85).

Numerous doctors have argued that the pursuit of efficiency and productivity directly compromise the care offered to patients in the doctor–patient encounter. This is because the quality of work is judged by 'immediate technical results' in which the aim is to reach the 'correct diagnosis', prescribe the 'right treatment' and 'shorten' the whole process as much as possible (Hilfiker 1985: 139). The doctor's role is reduced to that of an ideal bureaucratic official who performs her job impartially and impersonally, omits emotions, and treats patients alike, meting out equal justice in treatment. Such 'virtues' create specialists who carry out their duties 'without hatred or passion, affection or enthusiasm' (Weber 1964: 340). This is somewhat problematic in relation to healthcare, especially if we accept the reformist medical line in which the doctor should be involved in a deeply emotional and moral relationship with her patient. It is in this way that the bureaucratization of medical care has the effect of devaluing the healing function of the doctor and her commitment and desire to 'be of service'.

Not only that, but in such an atmosphere of bureaucracy and efficiency, it is actually very unlikely that the doctor will be able to perceive her patients 'without hatred or passion'. In fact, patients are more likely to be viewed as obstacles to efficient production, as objects to be manipulated and moved through the clinic as quickly as possible. The question 'How can we move Mrs. Smith most efficiently through this office?', Hilfiker comments, is not so different a question from 'What kind of assembly line is best for making a Ford?' (Hilfiker 1985: 142). Such issues become even more pertinent to the physician when her income becomes proportional to productivity, as in the case of performance-related pay, common to US physicians. In Britain, the relationship is less direct but practitioners are being made increasingly aware of the cost implications of their actions and their decisions are increasingly influenced by economic considerations. Such considerations induce profound changes in doctors' perceptions of their patients who are increasingly viewed as objects of disdain and potential recalcitrance. In a recent study, one GP summed up this perception pretty succinctly when he talked about increasing workloads and the fact that the aim of the consultation is to 'get the blighter out as quickly as possible' (cited in Weiss and Fitzpatrick 1997: 314). Campo highlights a similar process of objectifying patients in the following quote:

Incapable as I was of loving my patients, I hated them instead . . . I wished that they would hurry up and finish dying, all of them in one fell swoop, and that they would take all the dying left in the world with them when they did. In time, my heart was gradually pressed out of me, and I blamed my inability to cry on the long, dehydrating hours.

(Campo 1997: 28)

Increasing technology

Another feature of contemporary medicine which exacerbates the tendency to objectify patients is the increasing use of technology. 'Each bone marrow biopsy, each rectal exam, each ECG I performed seemed only to compound the indignity of it all', argues Campo. 'I watched', he continues, 'with detachment at the end of so many lives, as unmoved and bored as if I were taking out the garbage' (p. 52). 'Feeling the power of seeing into their brains and lungs, without ever noticing their faces – that had been partly how I lost sight of my patients' (p. 3).

Increasing technology facilitates not only the objectification of the patient, however, but also the doctor's objectification of herself. Over the last twenty years, clinical knowledge has become increasingly codified. For instance, computerized systems have been developed for diagnostic purposes. Such systems assume that decisions about diagnosis and prognosis are based on the systematic application of logic to a given knowledge base, rather than on more intuitive clinical judgements (Nettleton 1996: 208). Recent new technologies combined with case-notes perpetuate such assumptions in their construction of a 'virtual patient'. This ideal of 'virtual representation' encourages the idea that diagnosis can be reduced to 'tax-onomies free of location and time' (Hardey 1998: 8). Such technologies obviously have implications for the work of doctors in so far as they encourage the belief that doctors count for little *as individuals*. As Cassell (1991: 20) argues, doctors increasingly come to feel that it is their knowledge of disease and medical science that cares for the patient.

Such developments in technology also have a profound, often destructive, effect on the patient's expectations of medicine and doctors. As numerous doctors have argued, the technical wonders and near-miraculous drugs created by modern medicine have also created an 'expectation of perfection' of the doctor – an expectation that both doctors and patients adhere to. This, in turn, has created 'wholly unrealistic expectations' that 'all disease should be treatable and no medical encounter should lead to a negative outcome' (Kleinman 1988: 241). Likewise, in a letter to *The Guardian* (21/11/98: 24) one doctor criticizes the recent 'avalanche of press interest' in 'cases where perfection has not been achieved'. 'In all this', he continues, 'there is the assumption that the job should be easy and that the ability to prevent and predict problems can be learned if only there was enough monitoring and audit.' The problem, rather, is that, more often than not, 'there is not the time or space to think or plan to anticipate better'.

Hilfiker argues that such expectations of perfection are ultimately un-realistic and unsustainable. The vast majority of illnesses patients bring to doctors are difficult to diagnose with certainty and their treatment is equally problematic. This is because, despite all the technology in the world, medicine is a highly uncertain science and, even at its best, cannot provide all the answers both practitioners and patients would like it to provide. One of the main problems of dealing with such fundamental uncertainty, however, is that it is highly stressful for both patient and physician (Hilfiker 1985: 61).

A constant danger for the doctor, in the face of vulnerability and pain, is to succumb to the pressure to create a greater sense of certainty than actu-ally exists. 'I was always tempted', Hilfiker writes, 'to be definite, to be pos-itive, to be the utterly authoritative healer of my patient's dreams: "Mrs. Smith, you *obviously* have a bad case of rhinopharyngitis. Take this magic elixir and come see me next Thursday. I'm *sure* you'll feel better!"' (p. 70). He quotes the case of a pregnant woman who developed toxaemia, a dan-gerous complication of pregnancy. When she asked her doctor if the tox-aemia could possibly hurt the baby he replied 'Not with *me* as your doctor' (p. 71).

The doctor's appropriation of such an authoritative and paternalistic stance creates problems in the long term because it encourages the patient to harbour God-like expectations of the doctor that cannot possibly be ful-filled. Moreover, such patient expectations are disempowering because they encourage the patient to remain passive, waiting to be cured by the doctor's 'magic incantations' (Hilfiker 1984: 71). Concealing uncertainty with false reassurances, and shrouding value-judgements in scientific logic, the doctor ultimately robs the patient of responsibility for her own life. At bottom, Hilfiker argues, 'life *is* uncertain' and the patient should not be led to believe otherwise (p. 71). If we consider the way in which increasing technology exacerbates illusions of progress, perfection and certainty, it is perhaps not surprising that we are witnessing an era in which doctors face an increasingly hostile and litigious climate.

Conclusion

In this chapter we have argued that mainstream health psychology's study of communication between doctors and patients remains locked within a narrowly focused approach which attempts to maintain an objective, value-free, demoralized stance. As such, it epitomizes and exacerbates the rationalizing process characteristic of modern societies (see Chapter 2), attempting to quantify, predict, control and intervene in doctor–patient interactions as a means of improving adherence to the dominant agenda of biomedicine. In so doing, these approaches fail to examine both the emotional dimensions of such encounters, and their related connection to the social and political environment. Even more problematically, they diminish the possibility of understanding such dimensions by perpetuating a very narrow and limited conception of medical practice.

The emotional elements of the doctor–patient encounter do not, however, disappear by focusing exclusively on more objective and quantifiable processes such as improving the efficiency of communicative processes. Instead, they are pushed underground and repressed, serving only to exacerbate the negative and debilitating emotions which fuel the generalized and dehumanizing ways in which doctors and patients so frequently encounter one another.

It is for this reason that adoption of a critical health psychological approach necessitates an exploration of the subjectifying processes at work in the context of contemporary healthcare. This includes taking account not only of the proliferation of patient voices in the world of medicine (and the increased interest in alternative/complementary approaches) but also of the expansion of reflexivity from within the medical profession itself. In the same way that the experience of illness is becoming increasingly moralized, so too is the practice of medicine. As part of the process of deprofessionalization, the medical profession is finding itself increasingly open to competition and accountable. As some doctors begin to respond to such calls through the resistant and democratizing act of telling their stories, it becomes clear that the objectification and dehumanization so often complained about by patients is actually related, in a complex fashion, to the emotionally laden nature of illness and the social structure of healthcare. Recent changes in this structure, such as increasing technology and increasing bureaucratization and rationalization (in which mainstream health psychology interventions are complicit), are actually serving to exacerbate such dehumanizing processes. While continuously bearing in mind the limitations imposed by this structure, a critical health psychological approach welcomes the attempts by doctors to reflect on their everyday practices and ways of thinking, as a potential means of creating more humane healthcare, both for patients and doctors. Moreover, it suggests that mainstream health psychology, both in research and practice, would benefit substantially from a similar process of critical reflexivity, rather than remaining locked within an immature stance of scientific rigidity.

Chapter summary

By the end of this chapter you should understand the following concepts and issues:

- Mainstream health psychological accounts of the doctor–patient encounter – dominant focus on issues of compliance and adherence. The way such approaches reduce the encounter to a question of technical and instrumental management.
- From a critical health psychology point of view, this is problematic. Fails to account for:
  1 The changing social context of healthcare
  2 The 'non-rational' dimensions of doctor–patient interactions
- The medicalization critique and issues of patient empowerment. The way in which increasing interest in alternative/complementary approaches connects to patient empowerment, e.g. emphasis on subjectivity, meaning, humane care and recognition – the remoralization of issues of health and illness.
- Increasing emergence of remoralization and critical discourse within medicine itself.
- The way in which patient hostility towards medicine connects to the doctor's social role and function.
- An understanding of the psychosocial dynamics of the doctor–patient encounter, e.g. ambivalence, dependency, projection and objectification.
- The way in which contemporary changes in healthcare, e.g. drives towards increased efficiency, productivity and technology, exacerbate harmful processes of objectification.
- Mainstream health psychology may participate and exacerbate such processes of objectification by reducing doctor–patient encounters to issues of technical management.

Discussion points

◆ Mainstream health psychology's approach to doctor–patient communication is inadequate to understanding the complexities of the doctor–patient encounter. Discuss.
◆ A 43-year-old man is suffering from a chronic lower back problem. Describe some of the psychosocial dynamics that may make his relationship with his 30-year-old female doctor problematic.
◆ The increasing emphasis on efficiency, productivity and technology in contemporary medical practice is harmful to patient care. Critically discuss.

Key reading

Kleinman, A. (1988) *The Illness Narratives: Suffering, Healing and the Human Condition*. New York: Basic Books.
Ogden, J. (1996) *Health Psychology*, Chapter 4. Buckingham: Open University Press.

Further reading

Balint, M. (1957) *The Doctor, the Patient and His Illness*. London Pitman and Sons.
Hilfiker, D. (1985) *Healing the Wounds: A Physician Looks at His Work*. New York: Pantheon Books.
Smith, S. and Norton, K. (1999) *Counselling Skills for Doctors*. Buckingham: Open University Press.

Note

1 It is important not to over-play this notion of medical reflexivity. As a member of the Medical Communication Education Working Party in Manchester, I am all too aware that there is a general disdain for ideas such as Balint's. At a recent meeting, such ideas were castigated as a '1960s throwback'. Medical students were reported as perceiving training in communication skills as 'not the real stuff' and thought it was all about 'sitting around in hippy groups with peepy-toe sandals'.

Living in the face of death

The distance between the finite and the infinite is still infinite,
and no amount of pinpointed and defeated causes of dying will
make death less inevitable than it was at the start. There is an
essential incommensurability between the ways and means of
disease-fighting, and the stern reality of human mortality, and
the two do not become 'more commensurate' as the ways and
means get more refined and effective; but the amount of
continuous attention and effort which the disease-fighting-and-
preventing requires helps enormously to obscure, or at least
temporarily push aside, the chilling thought that death tolerates
no cheating and allows no escape.

(Bauman 1998: 230)

Introduction

Throughout this book we have seen how mainstream health psychology,
along with biomedicine, remains caught up in a modernist, rationalizing
mind-set in which complex experiential phenomena are reduced to
quantifiable and measurable data-sets which pay no regard to the interpretive and reflexive ambiguities characteristic of human experience. These features of human experience are perhaps nowhere more important than in the
investigation of death, dying and bereavement. And yet health psychology
textbooks remain curiously silent on these issues. As has been charted over
the course of this book, mainstream health psychology holds out the
promise that by performing various rational and logical behaviours and
thoughts – having safe sex, eating healthily, not smoking, thinking positively, etc. – people can minimize their risks, managing and exercising a
degree of control over what, in a sanitized way, is referred to as their health.
It is almost as if the aspiration and progression towards this state of physical and mental health existed in isolation from issues of death and dying.
But what is this aspiration towards health and risk minimization other than
a desperate attempt to ward off death? Why are we pursuing health other
than to avoid death? Mainstream health psychology, by focusing on individual and fragmentary risk behaviours, manages to lose sight of this fact.
Diverting all of its attention towards rational strategies about which something can be done, it conveniently forgets the central, inevitable fact lying
at the heart of its existence. We are all, one day, going to die. When that

time comes there is nothing we can do about it. It is the irrationality, unpredictability and uncontrollability of this fact that renders health psychology silent in the face of death and dying. This, in turn, highlights further the essential limitations of modernist projects committed to practical interventions in the hope of managing, controlling and changing people and the world we live in. Ultimately, they are unable to address the wider, existential and inherently moral problems that are brought forth by the inevitable and uncontrollable crises of life. It is at such times that more open and reflexive ways of thinking may be most in need.

Medicine and the objectification of death

In Chapter 2, drawing on the 'anti-medical' work of Zola, we argued that three fundamental values underlay contemporary medical science: activism, instrumentalism and worldliness. More generally, such medical science has been described as a characteristically modernist enterprise in which there is an 'unacknowledged will to mastery' (Fox 1993: 122). Such forms of thought and practice declare out of order all '"metaphysical", non-empirical ruminations about *illusory* problems – that is . . . things "one can do nothing about"' (Bauman 1998: 220). Death certainly belongs to this category because it resists 'the practical measures which human reason is capable of conceiving' (p. 220).

Accordingly, one of the main ways in which contemporary medicine addresses the issue of death is by reducing it to issues of technical and practical management. This involves '*deconstructing* the intractable issue of human mortality' by dispersing it into a 'plethora of single, always individual and unique, cases of death' (p. 221, emphasis added). Contemporary medical practice is designed to effect this deconstruction, with its division into specialities and sub-specialities. As long as small puzzles can be solved, fixing this or medicating that, the threat of death is deconstructed into small, manageable portions. This ultimately enables the threat of death to be denied, the big issue of mortality evaded, and the whole mystery of life sublimated. In this way, contemporary medical practice, as representative of modernist forms of thought and practice, seeks to turn 'mysteries into puzzles'. Whereas a mystery can only be faced up to, a puzzle admits solution. The absence of solution makes mysteries a scandal to contemporary medicine (Frank 1995: 81). Only those puzzles which one can 'do something about' 'have the right to remain inside the realm of rational thought and practice' (Bauman 1998: 221).

In recent years, this technologized, solution-based approach to death and dying has been criticized by both medical professionals and patients alike. As we saw in the last chapter, more doctors are opening themselves up to thinking critically about their professional practices and the kind of relationships and communicative patterns such practices endorse and exacerbate. An important feature of such criticism relates to the way in which death and dying is managed within medicine. Numerous doctors, for instance, are critical of the over-reliance on technology and medical procedures in dealing with the process of death, especially with the terminally ill.

An influential example is Nuland (1994), a North American surgeon critical of the 'rescue credo' of high technology medicine. In his influential book *How We Die*, Nuland describes the way in which oncologists are conditioned by their training to perceive their patients as 'problems to be solved' and 'riddles to be mastered' more than 'people to be cared for'. This, he claims, is highly detrimental to the dying person and the ability s/he has to exercise personal choice over the manner of his/her death. Likewise, Kleinman (1988: 153) argues that at the end, the 'doctor's work is to assist his patient to die a good death'. This task, however, 'has been usurped by medical technology's mandate to keep the patient alive at any cost' – an ideology which encourages the doctor to see the patient as a passive object to be acted upon by medical intervention.

Campo (1997: 168) similarly provides a lucid description of one of his patients, a 28-year-old man dying with AIDS. Because of chronic pneumonia this man could no longer breathe. Admitted as an emergency case, it was the medical team's objective, after consulting with the patient as much as possible, to save his life. Accordingly, the patient was intubated, which involves passing a tube through the vocal chords to connect the respirator to the airspaces of the lungs. However, this procedure, by necessity, renders the patient unable to speak. Campo describes how he watched the patient's face change as the tube passed through his vocal chords and forced him to 'lose his language'. A few days later, the patient died. Campo remained haunted by the thought that 'I am still not sure whether what he needed more during those last few days of his life was to speak or to breathe . . . He died without his last words' (p. 168).

Similar reservations abound in autobiographical accounts written by patients and their relatives. Writing of his sister, Beth, dying from cancer, Shapiro suggests that her dependency and helplessness were encouraged by the 'chronic combination of high-tech treatments and hyperspecialized language', from the 'feeling that her body was inescapable from the plastic tubes and monitors without which she couldn't live'. 'Everything about her treatment', he continues, 'undermined her sense of agency and power' (Shapiro 1997: 54). 'Did that last treatment extend her life?' asks Shapiro. 'By how much, a day or two? In doing so, it also ravaged her mouth and throat with sores, so that she paid for those potential extra days with extra suffering' (p. 56). Noll (1989: 20), writing about his own imminent death from cancer of the bladder, is similarly sceptical about technical intervention, becoming 'hooked up to tubes' as he puts it. 'The urge to survive must never be allowed to become so absolutely overpowering that one submits to all these indignities. The will to live must oppose it' (p. 20).

Shapiro also describes a scene in which Beth is in a hospice, in the final stages of cancer. Her oncologist visits, checks her chart and tubes and says '"So". Silence. And more silence. He then said he had to go' (Shapiro 1997: 55). There was nothing left to be done, and nothing more to say. This, Frank argues (1991: 57), is the main danger of allowing physicians to 'dominate the drama of illness' – 'they leave as soon as the disease is resolved to their satisfaction or when they have done all they can'. It is only then that the ill person and those around him/her are left to deal with the consequences of 'what has not been recognized'. Likewise, if the ill person dies, those who survive must deal with 'all that was not said, the unfinished business of a life closed out in a setting where dying is a problem of management, not a continuity of experience' (p. 57).

As will be argued in this chapter, the treatment of death and dying as a problem of management is not confined to the medical profession. As with so many areas of life in contemporary Western societies, the attempt scientifically to increase control over unpredictable and irrational events and processes has involved the creation of specialized languages, practices and professions to deal with such events. In terms of death and dying, this has involved increasingly specialized forms of professional colonization which have had the effect of segregating and banishing such events from the context of everyday life and 'entrusting them to the wardenship of the specialists' (Bauman 1998: 224). It is in this sense that Obholzer (1994: 171) has argued that our entire health service 'might more accurately be called a "keep-death-at-bay" service'.

Mainstream health psychology: the rationalization of dying and bereavement

As we have already argued throughout this book, the modernist rationalizing tendency of medicine is reproduced in mainstream health psychology. This is nowhere more apparent than when we come to examine issues of death and dying. In relation to such issues, mainstream health psychology appropriates medicine's puzzle-based approach. For example, in the index of Sheridan and Radmacher's (1992: 1.13) textbook, for 'death' 'see Mortality', which is then divided into causes of death from various diseases such AIDS and coronary heart disease. Likewise, in Ogden's text (1996: 330), 'death' is indexed as 'deaths from' which are then subdivided into diseases such as AIDS, cancer, heart disease and obesity. Here we see the same deconstruction of the 'intractable issue of human mortality' by a dispersion into a 'plethora of single, always individual and unique, cases of death' (Bauman 1998: 221). Such texts suggest that psychology has nothing to add to medically defined reality in terms of the investigation of death and dying.

This conclusion is, however, somewhat unfair. As Owens and Payne (1999: 149) argue, unlike many topics in health psychology, the investigation of death and dying has, from its early days, relied less on quantitative research methods and methodologies, and branched out to more qualitative and interpretive dimensions of study. For example, it was the psychiatrist Elizabeth Kubler-Ross's research into the psychological and emotional aspects of death and dying in the late 1960s and early 1970s which first captured the public imagination. In her classic book, *On Death and Dying* (1969), for instance, Kubler-Ross adopted a 'broadly narrative approach' (Owens and Payne 1999: 149) in which she insisted that we simply 'listen to the dying patient'.

This work was bound up with the hospice and palliative care movement which emerged at the end of the 1960s, in the wake of widespread dissatisfaction with the provision of care for the terminally ill. Dame Cicely Saunders, the founder of the hospice movement, similarly argued of the need to 'listen to the dying patient' in the context of biomedical care which produced passive patients and lack of individual autonomy and decision-making during the final stages of life (Saunders and Baines 1983). As we have already seen in previous chapters, the discipline of health psychology, emerging in the early 1970s, likewise provided a critique of the dominant biomedical model which paid insufficient attention to the role of psychological factors and individual autonomy in the investigation of health and illness (see Chapter 1). It is therefore clear that the emerging health psychology and hospice/palliative care movement, shared a similar basis in the 'New Public Health' movement in which people were actively encouraged to exercise individual control over their life and death (see Chapter 3).

Although early hospice care may have begun with the intent of providing more humane care through the open-ended process of listening to dying patients, and although interpretive, qualitative research into death and dying may continue to make 'a substantial contribution' to the literature (Owens and Payne 1999: 150), it is important to understand that such methods and objectives no longer comprise the dominant focus of investigation in mainstream health psychology. This is because practices and investigations of death and dying, as in other areas depicted in this book, have become increasingly subject to the rationalizing processes of modernism. In the following section, it will be argued that one of the main implications of the rationalization of death and dying is that both hospice care and psychological investigations become similarly geared up (as in medicine) to reducing death and dying to issues of professional management and control.

This is apparent in the way in which hospice/palliative care, although traditionally regarded as marginal to mainstream medicine, has, in fact, quickly become integrated into the 'vast cultural system of biomedicine' and mainstream medical care (McNamara 1998: 171). This fact is easily obscured because hospice and palliative care continue to serve as a 'symbolic critique' of how dying people are managed in other terminal care settings (p. 171). Nevertheless, it is now widely recognized that hospices have to work in the climate of market competition partly created by the NHS and Community

Care Act (1989). The intention and implementation of this Act was to reduce distinctions between NHS, voluntary and private sector provision of health-care. As a result, health authorities now contract for palliative care services, encouraging all sectors to compete on equal terms for funding; successful bidders are likely to be those offering the most cost-effective care of the highest standard (Butler 1992; Clark 1993). It is therefore not surprising that hospices are today being forced to become much clearer about what exactly they are offering and to engage in assessments of the quality and auditing of their services. As was discussed in Chapter 7, however, the increasing rationalization of healthcare (in this case care of the dying) compromises care because increasing pressures for productivity and efficiency tend to per-petuate objectification of the patient, reducing the potential for quality emotional work. More emphasis is placed on physical tasks and procedures, such as 'aggressive medical interventions', rather than the emotional work of, say, holding a person's hand while they are dying (see Crossley and Small 1998).

In previous chapters we have also seen how the construction of biopsy-chosocial models of various aspects of health and illness constitutes a central feature of contemporary mainstream health psychology. The psychological investigation of issues related to death and dying has in no way escaped this 'modelling' culture (Cooper *et al.* 1996: 13). A good example is the way in which Kubler-Ross's initial work of 'listening to dying patients' was later transformed into the famous five-stage theory in which people 'adjust' to dying by going through a series of stages including: denial, anger, bargain-ing, depression and acceptance (Kubler-Ross 1969). Another good example can be seen in the investigation of experiences of bereavement in which early research by Lindemann (1944) suggested a typical response to bereavement including somatic symptoms, anger, guilt, preoccupation with the dead person, behavioural changes and psychosomatic illnesses. Lindemann's work subsequently served to open up experiences of bereavement to inter-disciplinary inquiry. Since then, thousands of studies have been directed towards a clearer elucidation of bereavement experiences (Hale 1996: 111). The general aim of such studies has been to identify factors influential in the nature and development of grief and to clarify the significance of these factors in order to identify those most at risk of developing complications in their response to bereavement (p. 111). Accordingly, Hale characterizes the contemporary position as one in which there is a 'pervasive adoption' of a biopsychosocial model of grief amongst researchers and practitioners (p. 110) and an attempt to 'integrate understandings of bereavement into some form of multidimensional model' (p. 111).

However, as we have argued over the course of this book, such bio-psychosocial models remain problematic in terms of their lack of theoreti-cal integration and their failure to engage with issues of central importance such as individual meaning, interpretation, reflexivity and wider existential issues which are not necessarily amenable to quantitative measurement. This is obviously of particular importance in relation to investigations of dying and bereavement. As Hale (p. 111) argues, the relationship between the various dimensions of experience (biological, psychological and social), and their relationship to grief experiences, have yet to be determined. Hence, 'even as methodological rigour increases and understandings become more complex, concern has frequently been expressed as to the plausibility and utility of grief research to date' (p. 111). Kamerman (1988: 68–9), for instance, argues that although it is clear that grief follows certain patterns, 'the room for individual variation is considerable'. This leads us to question the extent to which the 'complexity of a multidimensional approach [can] allow space for such variation to emerge' (Hale 1996: 111) and to query whether this is the best way forward in terms of increasing our understanding of bereavement experiences (and we might add, experiences of dying) and serving the interests of those who have been bereaved (p. 111).

Hale argues a very definite 'no' in response to these questions. This is because, although bereavement models claim to be holistic, in the sense of adopting a multidimensional explanatory framework, in fact, they create a tension 'between the continuing development of increasingly sophisticated models of grief and a perception that such developments serve to constrain what is in reality an extremely complex experience' (p. 111). Such constraint occurs because models of bereavement serve as ways in which norms are created for the bereaved person to compare him/herself against (p. 113). This process of normalization, in turn, sets the scene for the problematization of individual experience. The proliferation of self-help books and academic texts on bereavement, for instance, makes it easy for the bereaved person to start reading about their experiences:

> What will happen when they read about 'symptoms' of grief which they themselves have not experienced? . . . How will they feel when they read about the 'stages of grief' . . . and realise they didn't pass through one or more of these stages? Does this mean they have not really 'worked through' their grief? . . . Does this mean they did not really love the person who has died because they have not experienced the full gamut of emotions that 'normal' people experience?
>
> (p. 114)

Such normalizing properties are also frequently carried through into the counselling situation. While many practitioners argue that such bereavement models are used merely to provide guidelines for working with bereaved individuals, Hale (1996: 110) argues, on the basis of her experience as both client and counsellor, that they are 'frequently used in a prescriptive rather than a reflexive way'. There is an 'ever present danger' of the inexperienced counsellor finding it 'safer to fall back onto the familiar ground offered by a theoretical model' and failing to acknowledge and appreciate the diversity of individual experiences of bereavement (p. 114).

Brody (1987: 18) has similarly argued against Kubler-Ross's stage theory of the dying process, suggesting that health professionals who are 'seduced by such theories' are unlikely to 'listen carefully as dying patients attempt to tell us their own stories of their unique dying experiences and concerns'. Frank (1991: 46) has similarly argued that although it was not her original intent, Kubler-Ross's theory has been used to 'categorise rather than to open up people's experiences'.

What we see here, then, is a critique of mainstream health psychology's tendency to feed into the normalizing and rationalizing processes of modernity, uncritically creating norms by which people's experiences of dying and bereavement can be standardized, measured (as with all other experiences depicted in this book we have the appropriate measuring scales for 'fear of death' and 'bereavement adjustment', complete with shortened versions), and compared. In this way, although the psychological study of death and dying was originally formulated as a way of challenging biomedicine, introducing issues of individual autonomy and decision-making into the medically determined agenda, in fact it has actually served to reinforce and perpetuate the medical stance towards reality, increasingly technologizing the psychological elements of death, dying and bereavement, and reducing them to problems that can be solved through various forms of counselling and therapeutic intervention.

Resistance to the professional colonization of death, dying and bereavement: accepting the existential reality of death

Numerous autobiographical and academic accounts of death and dying have argued against the modernist tendency to categorize and manage this ultimately sacred and mysterious life process. Frank (1991: 45), for instance, has argued that medical and psychological care can be characterized as 'treatment', not 'care' based (see also Chapter 7). Treatment is not the same as care because it 'gets away with making a compromise between efficiency and care by creating an illusion of involvement' (p. 45). This illusion frequently begins with 'a recipe', made up of 'key words referring to psychological states' which tell 'treatment providers what to expect' (p. 45). Fitting people into such categories and recipes is efficient – 'each category indicates a common treatment: one size fits all' (p. 45). This is not care. Care begins only when 'difference is recognized'. But 'most people who deal with ill persons', Frank argues, 'do not want to recognise differences and particularities because sorting them out requires time. Even to learn what the differences are, you have to become involved' (p. 45).

But how is it possible to understand people's responses to dying and bereavement without reference to such recipes and models (p. 115)? With echoes of Laing (see Chapter 6), Hale argues that to adequately understand such experiences, we must attempt to appreciate them as a gestalt rather than as a collection of symptoms or stages of adjustment (p. 115). This entails a shift from pre-existent models of dying and bereavement, to the 'bereavement experience itself and however it is expressed by the individual' (p. 116). Again paraphrasing Laing, we could argue that to look and listen to a patient and see signs of adjustment (to dying or bereavement), and to look and listen to him/her simply as a human being accommodating to the inevitable losses of life, are to see and hear in radically different ways. Accordingly, Hale argues, there is an 'urgent need to *stop modelling* and to *stop tidying up* bereavement experiences' (p. 118, emphasis in original). Only then can the 'acknowledged diversity of such experiences be given full expression, and be addressed as a strength rather than an "inconvenience" to be addressed through a never-ending process of research' (p. 118).

Bauman (1992) argues that the technologization and management of dying and bereavement through the construction of various medical and psychological models involve dismantling and denying an important fact of philosophical and existential significance. This relates to the inevitable mortality of human beings. Focusing on various models, and attempting to categorize people in accordance with such models, divert our attention from this fact, removing it from the range of legitimate concerns of human reason. Discarding such models is analogous to kicking away a crutch or discarding scaffolding. It often means facing up to the fact that death is a 'complex reality' which 'cannot (and must not) be reduced to a simple answer' (Kleinman 1988: 157).

As an example of facing death in this way, Kleinman discusses the case of a doctor and his patient, Gordon, whose 'terminal period' is not allowed 'to become technologized'. On the basis of a tape-recorded interview between doctor and patient during the patient's final days, Kleinman argues that the doctor's task is to 'struggle to maintain authenticity, to avoid sentimentalizing or in other ways rendering inauthentic a relationship centred on the most existential of problems' (p. 153). The doctor has no answers to his patient's questions. Nor does the patient expect, or even want, his doctor to try and answer them. Instead, the doctor provides 'intense listening' and 'empathic witnessing', a 'moral act, not a technical procedure' (p. 154).

Inherent in this moral act of bearing witness is a simple attempt to appreciate what the dying or bereaved is going through, rather than trying to impose some kind of professional model or intervention (whether medical or psychological) on the individual (see also Chapters 5 and 6). In terms of death and dying, this often involves coming to terms with the fact that there may not be a solution to the problem. As Dennison writes in her autobiography of her experience of cancer:

I finally began to accept that maybe there wasn't a lot more medicine could do for me. I'd resisted that knowledge for so long that when I finally faced it it had lost its power. I was beginning to abandon my obsession with numbers; survival rates, response rates and percentages . . . Eventually I had to accept that there was little else to be done.

(Dennison 1996: 41)

Another example of facing up to the fact that there is 'little else to be done' comes from my research with the national long-term HIV survivors group (NLTSG) (Crossley 1997b, 1998a, 1998b, 1999a, 2000a; Davies 1997). In the following quote, Tim, a 41-year-old HIV-positive man expressed reservations about what he called 'the whole survival thing', the whole philosophy, characterizing the NLTSG:

> It's not a criticism of the Survivors Group but it is like the whole fighting thing. You know, that you have to fight and you must fight until the end, and it is that fighting that keeps you alive. But in some way I think it is actually just recognising that there is a point where there is actually no point any more in just fighting. Because in fact I would rather just relax and that for me is the big, there is a big question in my life at the moment, which is, where am I now?, sort of thing. You know, because my partner and my parents and everyone are saying, come on, take more drugs, eat more, relax more and all that and you will be fine, you will pick up your weight, you will. But my body, in a way, is telling me otherwise, you know, my body is actually just getting tired now. It's saying 'just enough already'.

Tim went on to say that he was very aware, being a white South African, of the need for political activism. He had seen what positive action could do with the political activism of the African National Congress, for instance. Also, being Jewish, he had always asked his parents why the 'Jews just walked like sheep to their deaths' and could not understand why they didn't rebel more. But now Tim felt that he had a greater understanding of their actions. This was because he felt that there is also a time when you just have to 'give up fighting', characterized in his use of the terms 'I'm alright already', 'just enough already'.

Tim talks about the big question in his life at the moment, the question that he feels a great need to feel free to address – the all-time elusive 'where am I now sort of thing?' What he makes lucidly clear here is the fact that we all eventually have to face the 'reality and responsibility of mortality, and its mystery' (Frank 1995: 84). But he also points to the problems of a culture geared up to the denial of death and the ultimate inability of 'survivor-speak' to enable him to address his big question.

His thoughts and actions, perceived as a passive acceptance of mortality, remain unpopular in a modernist culture geared up towards technical solutions and rational management (which, as we saw in Chapter 2, mainstream health psychology epitomizes). *Surely something can (and must) be done?* This kind of thinking probably accounts for the constant pressure that Tim gets from his partner and parents to 'take more drugs, eat more, relax more and all that and you will be fine, you will pick up your weight'.

These simple examples highlight the ultimate limitation of the single-minded focus and belief in cure and survival so characteristic of modernist enterprises. As Frank (1995) argues, 'the confrontation with mortality cannot be part of the story'. This is why one of the main aims of this book, depicting a critical approach towards health psychology, has been to bring such confrontation back into the equation. Exploring the crises in people's lives, such as serious pain, illness and death, shows us that these are not always problems that can be solved. Sometimes, we just have to live in their wake. And one day, we will all have to come to terms with a fact that is not at all popular. Despite our attempts to decrease our risks, each of us will die and most of our deaths will be preceded by a long or a short illness (Frank 1991: 116). Accordingly, we must learn to accept that 'disease is part of the dust of our bodies'. It is 'our humanity' to contest disease as long as we can, but it is also 'our humanity to die' (p. 111). It is only when we learn such acceptance, when we 'no longer require health, however much we may prefer it' (p. 21), that we become free. As Noll, dying from cancer, wrote:

> Premeditation of death is premeditation of liberty. He who has learned to die has unlearned servitude. There is no longer any evil in life for those who have well understood that the loss of life is no evil; to know that we have to die makes us free of all subjection and constraints.
>
> (Noll 1989: 33)

Concluding reservations: we can talk about death, but can we stand the smell?

In this chapter, we have criticized mainstream health psychology for reducing death, dying and bereavement to largely technical questions relating to stages and models, and colluding in a process of professional colonization which hands over such issues to medical and psychological interventions such as counselling and therapy. This sequestration of death and dying by professionals is reinforced by the fact that death and dying are largely removed from people's everyday lives, through establishing special places for the dying, such as hospices. This enables the reduction of death and dying to issues of sanitized and controlled management, just another problem to be dealt with as quickly and efficiently as possible.

In contrast, by looking at some of the academic and patient voices resisting such a reduction of death and dying, we have witnessed the germination of a more critical psychological approach towards such issues. This involves reflexively opening ourselves towards the inevitability of death and dying, refusing to be sucked into medicine and psychology's scheme-based approaches towards the management of death, and understanding the existential significance that death and dying has for a renewed appreciation of life itself (see also Chapter 5). This approach attempts to retrieve death and dying from professional agendas, placing it back in the hands of dying people themselves. A logical corollary of this process, occurring over the past decade or so, has been a noticeable shift away from hospitals and hospices as sites of death and dying in the UK (Lawton 1998: 121). For instance, a recent review of terminal cancer services in Britain, showed that a shift in emphasis had taken place from the establishment and support of hospice in-patient units, to the financing of home-care services (p. 122). This brings us to the question of whether such changes indicate a greater acceptance and more openness and reflexivity, towards the process of death and dying.

Perhaps to certain *types* of death and dying. On the basis of ethnographic research in a hospice in the UK, for instance, Lawton argues that hospices no longer operate to 'veil the process of dying *per se*; rather they have come to sequester a particular type of dying and a particular category of patient' (p. 139). This is the category Lawton characterizes as 'dirty deaths' and 'dirty dying'. I want to provide a brief detour describing Lawton's findings in more detail because, as will become apparent, they highlight certain prob-lems with the critical health psychological approach towards death and dying depicted so far in this chapter.

During the course of her fieldwork, Lawton found that the most common reason for a patient to be admitted to the hospice was for 'control of symp-toms'. The most common symptoms included: incontinence of urine and faeces, uncontrolled vomiting (including faecal vomit), fungating tumours (rotting away of the tumour site on the surface of the skin) and weeping limbs (due to the development of gross oedema in the patient's legs or arms, resulting in limbs swelling to such an extent that the skin bursts and lymph fluid continuously seeps out) (p. 127). Another important symptom was the uncontrolled emission of smells, which not only precipitated patients' admission to the hospice, but also resulted in 'further marginalization within the building itself' (p. 133). Lawton describes the case of one patient, Sydney, who had a fungating tumour. The smell 'proved so repellent to his wife' that she refused to go into his room from the time of his admission till his death six days later (p. 133). Another patient, Ron, was moved into a side room when he began to smell 'like dog shit'. One of the nurses reported that 'you couldn't go into his ward this morning without squirt-ing lemon aerosol in front of your nose' (p. 133).

A characteristic feature of these symptoms leading to hospice admission is that they all 'caused the surfaces of the patient's body to rupture and break down' (p. 127). Fluids, matter and smells normally contained within the patient's body leaked out, often in an uncontrolled and unpredictable fashion. Patients whose bodies could not be 're-bounded' tended to be the ones who stayed in the hospice until they died. What was striking about this group of patients, Lawton argues, was that they 'all exhibited behaviour which suggested a total loss of self and social identity once their bodies became severely and irreversibly unbounded' (p. 129), disengaging and switching off from the world.

For instance, Lawton describes the case of Dolly, a woman with colon cancer who was admitted to the hospice after becoming chronically incon-tinent. Her husband told Lawton that every time she had a severe bout of diarrhoea she begged him to help her take her own life. Her request for euthanasia continued during the first week of her stay in the hospice. The staff were unable to get her diarrhoea under control and she also went into obstruction because the tumour mass expanded, blocked her colon, and, as a consequence, digested food would reach her lower gut and then come back up as faecal vomit (p. 130). At about this same time, the staff noticed a change in Dolly's behaviour. She stopped requesting euthanasia and, in fact, stopped talking altogether. When the nurses came to turn her in bed or to attend to her she would close her eyes and totally ignore them. As one nurse observed, 'it's as if she's shut the outside world out and herself off in the process' (p. 130).

Drawing on anthropological and cross-cultural research, Lawton argues that this concern with 'bodily boundaries' is related to contemporary Western concepts of the person in which identity remains 'fundamentally dependent upon the possession of a physically bounded body' (p. 131). This, as we saw in Chapter 3, is also related to the rise of individualism in which the ideal body and self are constructed as healthy, enclosed and disciplined, reflecting and reproducing the concerns, values and preoccupations of the culture in which it is located (Crawford 1994, cited in Lawton 1998: 136). Accordingly, 'self control . . . has become mapped onto, and experienced within, the physical body as *self-containment*' (p. 136, emphasis added). Lack of bodily control is thus perceived symbolically as a locus and a source of 'dirt', as 'matter out of place' (p. 138). Dirt offends against order and this is why contemporary hospices serve to remove patient's dirt, and the patient *as dirt*, from mainstream society (p. 138).

Lawton argues that such issues of dirt, decay, disintegration and smell are rarely, if ever, written about by hospice professionals or media representations of hospice care. Instead, they are 'glossed over' as 'symptoms requiring control' (p. 139). It is in this sense that Lawton concludes that contemporary hospices 'set a particular type of bodily deterioration, demise and decay apart from mainstream society'. In doing so, they enable certain ideas about living, personhood and the 'hygienic, sanitised, somatically bounded body to be symbolically enforced and maintained' (p. 123).

I have provided this brief detour into Lawton's research because, as I suggested earlier in this section, it throws up some important problems relating to critical health psychology's approach towards death and dying. This chapter has suggested that mainstream health psychology feeds into the technical management and control of death and dying, reducing it, sanitizing it, making it more palatable. What then of critical health psychology? Does the subjectification of death and dying, its exploration of the psychological, emotional, reflexive and existential aspects of dying, sanitize things to an even greater extent? Reiterating our concerns from previous chapters, does it existentialize death and dying to too great an extent? Does it focus simply on clean deaths to the detriment of the dirty? And as such, does it just provide a deeper and more sophisticated reproduction of the ideals and values of the healthy, bounded person, the one who is able to talk and reflect until the very end? Despite claiming to provide a more detailed exploration of experiences of death and dying, does it enable us to turn our faces away further, to make our 'numbness in the face of the real thing, the death itself' even more complete (Bauman 1992: 224)? Critical health psychologists can talk about death till the cows come home. But can we stand the smell?

Chapter summary

By the end of this chapter you should understand the following concepts and issues:

- Problems with biomedicine's technologized approach to death and dying.
- Mainstream health psychology's silence in the face of death and dying.
- The way in which earlier, more qualitative psychological investigations of death and dying have been supplanted by a modelling culture which has reduced dying and bereavement experiences to stages and pathological processes.
- Resistance to the professional colonization of death and dying and the importance of appreciating/facing up to the inevitable fact of death.
- Reservations about critical health psychology's approach to death and dying. Does it existentialize death to too great an extent? Does it focus only on clean deaths?

Discussion points

- The management of death and dying should be left to professionals such as medics and psychologists. Critically discuss.
- Since its inception in the late 1960s, palliative hospice care has been increasingly institutionalized into mainstream medical care. Outline the advantages and disadvantages of this process.
- When a patient is dying it is important to bear witness to their issues and concerns. Using examples from five different patients, discuss how this might be achieved.
- Critical health psychology emphasizes the importance of opening the investigation of death and dying out to take more account of individual people's experiences of death and dying. But this just reproduces the contemporary ideal of a 'good, clean death' and denies the reality of what the dying process is like for many people. Discuss.

Key reading

Bauman, Z. (1992) *Mortality, Immortality and Other Life Strategies*. Cambridge: Polity Press.

Frank, A. (1991) *At the Will of the Body*. Boston: Houghton Mifflin.

Kubler-Ross, E. (1969) *On Death and Dying*. New York: Macmillan.

Payne, S., Horn, S. and Relf, M. (1999) *Loss and Bereavement*. Buckingham: Open University Press.

Concluding comments

When the physician finds that he is not taking the needed time for 'reflective meditation' upon the meaning of his job . . . when he finds he is using laboratory tests and X-ray studies instead of in-depth interviews . . . It is at these times, Hilfiker (1984: 144) argues, that he must ask himself whether the 'values of efficiency and productivity have not in fact gained the upper hand, submerging other important medical and human values'. Has productivity become a goal in itself (p. 145)?

I cannot think of a more pertinent issue to ask of contemporary health psychology. Are health psychologists encouraged to reflect on the meaning of their research and practice? Or are they also all too ready to reach for their battery of pre-tested measures, statistical packages and the safety of numbers (or increasingly, in social psychology, their discourses) as a way of dealing with the more messy reality of human life? I have worked with enough psychologists now to realize that, just as Hilfiker claimed the surgeon with the most kudos was the one who could perform the most operations in an allotted time (see Chapter 7), the psychologist with the most kudos (normally a man), is the one with the most sophisticated research needs (for which read the most expensive, the most laboratory-oriented, the most whizz-kid 'boy-like' of toys). It is time to question whether this obsession with science, technology, research techniques and quantification has served to submerge other important human values. These values must surely take central place in psychology, even if in no other domain? We must question whether technology has become an end in itself. Is health psychology serving simply to reinforce the potentially destructive changes occurring in the wake of the rationalization of healthcare?

Such questions may seem irrelevant to the health psychologist who is simply trying to conduct empirical research, or to provide effective healthcare, whether that be clinical care for individual patients, or more community oriented in the form of health promotion. But they are not irrelevant if the health psychologist is willing to question her actions and theories, to question whether her practices and interventions are really of use to the people she is dealing with, to ask whether she might be exacerbating the very problems she is trying to resolve. This book does not pretend to offer easy answers or solutions to any of these questions. That never was its intention. Instead, my overarching aim throughout, as stated in the opening chapter, has been to open health psychology to questioning, without necessarily reaching for the nearest solution.

To this end, I have attempted to depict the characteristic features of two very different approaches within health psychology: mainstream health psychology and critical health psychology. This has not been easy and a number of major problems have arisen during the course of this task. The book carries the traces of these problems throughout. For this reason, I would like to take this opportunity to clarify three of the main problems, all of which are interrelated. These problems relate to:

1. A characterization of mainstream health psychology which is overly simplified and provides insufficient account of the complexity and diversity of the field as a whole
2. Lack of clear definition of what actually constitutes a 'critical' health psychology and;
3. Over-stating the existence of 'critical' voices and 'over-existentializing' the nature of health and illness-related problems

Each of these problems needs to be discussed in more detail.

The first problem arose mainly due to lack of space. Mainstream health psychology obviously constitutes a vast domain of research and investigation. By necessity, I have been forced to rely on the material available in mainstream health psychology textbooks. My justification for doing so stems from the fact that most students' conception of what health psychology is derives mainly from these textbooks. This is increasingly the case with modularization and the related tendency of course leaders to base their course around a single major textbook. In addition, this book is even unable to provide a detailed rendition of the material covered in such textbooks. For this reason, it is imperative that it is read in conjunction with one or more mainstream health psychology texts. If this is not done, then this book ceases to be critical, and instead becomes dogmatic. I feel confident that most readers, reading the book in this way, will find there is at least a kernel of truth in what I have been trying to say.

The second problem relates to the need for this book. At the time of writing, no other textbook on critical health psychology exists. Numerous edited collections depicting critical approaches are beginning to emerge (see Chapter 1) but these are not textbooks. Accordingly, one of the tasks of *Rethinking Health Psychology* has been to formulate an overall picture of what such a critical approach might look like. Over the course of the book, this has emerged as one which can be broadly characterized as taking account of the way in which people themselves orient to and understand various health- and illness-related events, but at the same time maintaining a critical appreciation of the way such understandings relate to the wider social and economic structure, and the practical and moral tasks of everyday life. I am sure some people will disagree with this formulation of critical health psychology. But one of my main aims in writing this book has been to promote debate, and to lay down some basic foundations in order that further clarification can be achieved in the future.

Finally, the third problem. Throughout this book, in developing a conception of critical health psychology, I have drawn on dissenting voices, the voices of patients and professionals resistant to dominant ideas and practices prevalent in mainstream healthcare. This runs the risk of creating the impression that such dissent is more widespread than it actually is. This also relates to the problem of over-existentializing the nature of health- and illness-related problems. This issue has come up at various points throughout this book, for instance, in relation to experiences of pain, illness and death. Again, the problem is that the emotional and moral dimensions of such experiences are over-played, whereas perhaps for most people, such issues do not really figure at all. It is for this reason that it is important to bear in mind that the ideas and views expressed in many of the experiential accounts cited in this book are not necessarily representative of those of society at large. Instead, they are more adequately characterized as lone, alternative voices, working against dominant and accepted views of reality – in much the same way as this book is doing in relation to mainstream health psychology.

In this role of dissent lie both strengths and weaknesses. This book has attempted to draw on strengths, by highlighting the potential for critical thought and reformulation. In doing so, it has inevitably underplayed the weaknesses of critical health psychology (which have become increasingly apparent to me over the course of writing this book) and also over-played the potential that such a reformulation has to play in contemporary health psychology. My justification for this bias lies in the current subordination of critical health psychology, in contrast to more mainstream approaches.

One of the main aims of this book, then, has been to set out a stall for critical health psychology in a way that has not been done before. My main fear in having done so is that I have exaggerated the differences between approaches, thus exacerbating the polarization that already exists. Another related worry is that this book will be perceived as an uncritical advocacy of the critical health psychology perspective. I truly hope this is not the case. As I see it, our major task for the future is to bring about increased integration and collaboration within the field of health psychology. I not only believe this is possible but that it is the only way of achieving good quality health-related research and practice – surely one aim which, despite our differences, we all share.

References

Abraham, C. and Hampson, S. (1996) A social cognition approach to health psychology: philosophical and methodological issues. *Psychology and Health*, 11: 233–41.

Ader, R. and Cohen, N. (1985) CNS-immune system interactions: conditioning phenomena. *Behavioural and Brain Sciences*, 8: 379–95.

Aggleton, P. (1989) Evaluating health education about AIDS, in P. Aggleton, G. Hart and P. Davies (eds) *AIDS: Social Representations, Social Practices*. New York: Falmer Press.

Anderson, H. and Goolishian, H. (1992) The client is the expert: a not-knowing approach to therapy, in S. McNamee and K. Gergen (eds) *Therapy as Social Construction*. London: Sage.

Antoni, M., Schneiderman, N., Fletcher, M., Goldstein, D., Ironson, G. and Laperriere, A. (1990) Psychoneuroimmunology and HIV-1. *Journal of Consulting and Clinical Psychology*, 58: 38–49.

Antonovsky, A. (1979) *Health, Stress and Coping*. San Francisco: Jossey-Bass.

Armstrong, D. (1987) Bodies of knowledge: Foucault and the problem of human anatomy, in G. Scrambler (ed.) *Sociological Theory and Medical Sociology*. London: Tavistock.

Armstrong, D. (1994) Bodies of knowledge/knowledge of bodies, in C. Jones and R. Porter (eds) *Reassessing Foucault: Power, Medicine and the Body*. London: Routledge.

Armstrong, D. (1995) The rise of surveillance medicine. *Sociology of Health and Illness*, 17(3): 393–440.

Ashmore, M., Mulkay, M. and Pinch, T. (1989) *Health and Efficiency: A Sociology of Health Economics*. Buckingham: Open University Press.

Ashton, H. (1987) *Brain Systems, Disorders and Psychotropic Drugs*. Oxford: Oxford University Press.

Atkinson, P. (1995) *Medical Talk and Medical World*. London: Sage.

Augustinous, M. and Walker, I. (1995) *Social Cognition: An Integrated Introduction*. London: Sage.

Baker, R. and Firth-Cozens, J. (1998) Evidence, quality of care and the role of psychology. *The Psychologist*, 11(9): 430–2.

Balint, M. (1957) *The Doctor, the Patient and His Illness*. London: Pitman and Sons.

Bandura, A., Cioffi, D., Taylor, C. and Brouillard, M. (1988) Perceived self efficacy in coping with cognitive stressors and opioid activation. *Journal of Personality and Social Psychology*, 55: 479–88.

Bandura, A., Reese, L. and Adams, N. (1982) Micro-analysis of action and fear arousal as a function of differential levels of perceived self efficacy. *Journal of Personality and Social Psychology*, 43: 5–21.

Barber, B. (1983) *The Logic and Limits of Trust*. London: Longman.

Bartlett, R. (1998) *Stress: Perspectives and Processes*. Buckingham: Open University Press.

Bauman, Z. (1992) *Mortality, Immortality and Other Life Strategies*. Cambridge: Polity Press.

Bauman, Z. (1998) Postmodern adventures of life and death, pp. 216–33 in G. Scrambler and P. Higgs (eds) *Modernity, Medicine and Health*. London: Routledge.

Beardwood, B., Walters, V., Eyles, J. and French, S. (1999) Complaints against nurses: a reflection of 'the new managerialism' and consumerism in health care? *Social Science and Medicine*, 48: 363–74.

Beauchamp, T. and Childress, J. (1994) *Principles of Biomedical Ethics*, fourth edition. Oxford: Oxford University Press.

Beck, A. (1976) *Cognitive Therapy and the Emotional Disorders*. New York: International Universities Press.

Beck, A., Rush, A., Shaw, B. and Emery, G. (1979) *Cognitive Therapy of Depression*. New York: Guilford Press.

Beck, U. (1992) *Risk Society: Towards a New Modernity*. London: Sage.

Beecher, H. (1959) *Measurement of Subjective Responses*. New York: Oxford University Press.

Bellah, R., Madsen, R., Sullivan, W., Swindler, A. and Tipton, S. (1985) *Habits of the Heart: Individualism and Commitment in American Life*. New York: Perennial Library.

Bennett, P. and Murphy, S. (1997) *Psychology and Health Promotion*. Buckingham: Open University Press.

Bentall, R. (1990) The syndromes and symptoms of psychosis, or why you can't play 'twenty questions' with the concept of schizophrenia and hope to win, in R. Bentall (ed.) *Reconstructing Schizophrenia*. London: Routledge.

Bentall, R. (1994) Cognitive biases and abnormal beliefs: towards a model of persecutory delusions, in S. David and J. Cutting (eds) *The Neuropsychology of Schizophrenia*. Hove: Hillsdale.

Berger, P. and Luckman, T. (1967) *The Social Construction of Reality: A Treatise on the Sociology of Knowledge*. New York: Anchor Books.

Best, S. and Kellner, D. (1991) *Postmodern Theory: Critical Interrogations*. Basingstoke: Macmillan.

Billig, M. (1991) *Ideology and Opinions*. London: Sage.

Blair, A. (1993) Social class and the contextualisation of illness experience, in A. Radley (ed.) *Worlds of Illness: Biographical and Cultural Perspectives on Health and Disease*. London: Routledge.

Bordo, S. (1993) *Unbearable Weight: Feminism, Western Culture and the Body*. Berkeley: University of California Press.

Boulton, M., McLean, J., Fizpatrick, R. and Hart, G. (1995) Gay men's accounts of safe sex. *AIDS Care*, 7(5): 619–30.

Bourdieu, P. (1984) *Distinction: A Social Critique of Judgement and Taste*. London: Routledge.

Bourdieu, P. (1992) *The Logic of Practice*. Cambridge: Polity Press.

Bowlby, J. (1961) Processes of mourning. *International Journal of Psychoanalysis*, 42: 317–40.

Bowlby, J. (1980) *Attachment and Loss: Vol 3. Loss, Sadness and Depression*. Harmondsworth: Penguin.

Boyle, M. (1990) *Schizophrenia: A Scientific Delusion?* London: Routledge.

Bradley, B. (1994) Depression: treatment, in S. Lindsay and G. Powell (eds) *Handbook of Clinical Adult Psychology*. London: Routledge.

Brandt, A. (1997) Behaviour, disease and health in the twentieth century United States: the moral valence of individual risk, in A. Brandt and P. Rozin (eds) *Morality and Health*. London: Routledge.

Brody, H. (1987) *Stories of Sickness*. New York: Yale University Press.

Broom, B. (1997) *Somatic Illness and the Patient's Other Story: A Practical Integrative Mind/Body Approach to Disease for Doctors and Psychotherapists*. London: Free Association Books.

Broyard, A. (1992) *Intoxicated by My Illness and Other Writings on Life and Death*. New York: Clarkson Patter.

Buckman, R. and Sabbagh, K. (1993) *Magic or Medicine: An Investigation into Healing*. London: Macmillan.

Bunton, R. and Macdonald, G. (eds) (1992) *Health Promotion Disciplines and Diversity*. London: Routledge.

Bury, M. (1982) Chronic illness: a biographical disruption. *Sociology of Health and Illness*, 4(2): 167–82.

Bury, M. (1998) Postmodernity and Health, pp. 1–29 in G. Scrambler and P. Higgs (eds) *Modernity, Medicine and Health*. London: Routledge.

Butler, J. (1992) *Patients, Policies and Politics. Before and After 'Working for Patients'*. Buckingham: Open University Press.

Butler, S. and Rosenblum, B. (1994) *Cancer in Two Voices*. London: Women's Press.

Calnan, M. (1987) *Health and Illness: The Lay Perspective*. London: Tavistock.

Campo, R. (1997) *Poetry of Healing: A Doctor's Education in Empathy, Identity and Desire*. New York: W. W. Norton and Company.

Cape, J. and Hewer, P. (1998) Employment of psychology graduates in NHS clinical audit. *The Psychologist*, 11(9): 426–9.

Caplan, R. (1994) Stress, anxiety and depression in hospital consultants, GPs and senior health service managers. *British Medical Journal*, 309: 1261–3.

Cassell, E. (1991) *The Nature of Suffering and the Goals of Medicine*. Oxford: Oxford University Press.

Castel, R. (1991) From dangerousness to risk, in R. Burchell (ed.) *The Foucault Effect*. Hemel Hempstead: Harvester.

Castells, M. (1996) *The Rise of the Network Society. Vol 1*. London: Blackwell.

Chadwick, P. (1997) *Schizophrenia: The Positive Perspective. In Search of Dignity for Schizophrenic People*. London: Routledge.

Chambers, R. and Belcher, J. (1993) Work patterns of GPs before and after the introduction of the 1990 contract. *British Journal of General Practice*, 43: 410–12.

Charlton, B. (1993) Holistic medicine or the humane doctor? *British Journal of General Practice*, 43: 475–7.

Clark, D. (1993) *The Future for Palliative Care: Issues of Policy and Practice*. Buckingham: Open University Press.

Clark, D. (1999) 'Total pain': disciplinary power and the body in the work of Dame Cicely Saunders, 1958–1969. *Social Science and Medicine*, 49: 727–36.

Comaroff, J. (1976) A bitter pill to swallow: placebo therapy in general practice. *Sociological Review*, 24: 79–96.

Conrad, P. (1987) The experience of illness: recent and new directions. *Research in the Sociology of Health Care*, 6: 1–31.

Coombs, R., Chopra, S., Schenck, D. and Yutan, E. (1993) Medical slang and its functions. *Social Science and Medicine*, 36(8): 987–98.

Cooper, N., Stevenson, C. and Hale, G. (eds) (1996) *Integrating Perspectives on Health*. Buckingham: Open University Press.

Cooper, N., Stevenson, C. and Hale, G. (1996) The biopsychosocial model, pp. 1–17 in N. Cooper, C. Stevenson and G. Hale (eds) *Integrating Perspectives on Health*. Buckingham: Open University Press.

Coulter, A., McPherson, K. and Vessey, M. (1988) Do British women undergo too many or too few hysterectomies? *Social Science and Medicine*, 27(9): 987–94.

Coursey, R., Keller, A. and Farrell, E. (1995) Individual psychotherapy with persons with serious mental illness: the clients' perspective. *Schizophrenia Bulletin*, 21(2): 283–301.

Coward, R. (1989) *The Whole Truth*. London: Faber and Faber.

Coyne, J. and Lazarus, R. (1980) Cognitive style, stress, perception and coping, in L. Kutash, L. Schlesinger and associates (eds) *Handbook on Stress and Anxiety*. London: Jossey-Bass.

Craib, I. (1992) *Modern Social Theory*. New York: Harvester Wheatsheaf.

Crawford, R. (1980) Healthism and the medicalisation of everyday life. *International Journal of Health Services*, 10: 365–88.

Crawford, R. (1984) A cultural account of 'health': Control, release and the social body, in J. McKinlay (ed.) *Issues in the Political Economy of Health Care*. London: Tavistock.

Crawford, R. (1994) The boundaries of the self and the unhealthy other: reflections on health, culture and AIDS. *Social Science and Medicine*, 38(10): 1347–65.

Crossley, M. L. (1997a) The divided self: the destructive potential of an HIV positive diagnosis. *Journal of Existential Analysis*, 8(2): 72–94.

Crossley, M. L. (1997b) 'Survivors' and 'victims': long-term HIV-positive individuals and the ethos of self-empowerment. *Social Science and Medicine*, 45(12): 1863–73.

Crossley, M. L. (née Davies) (1998a) Women living with a long-term HIV-positive diagnosis: problems, concerns and ways of ascribing meaning. *Women's Studies International Forum*, 21(5): 521–33.

Crossley, M. L. (1998b) Sick role or empowerment: the ambiguities of life with an HIV-positive diagnosis. *Sociology of Health and Illness*, 20(4): 507–31.

Crossley, M. L. (1998c) A man dying with AIDS: psychoanalysis or existentialism? *Journal of Existential Analysis*, 9(2): 35–57.

Crossley, M. L. (1999a) Making sense of HIV infection; discourse and adaptation to life with an HIV-positive diagnosis. *Health*, 3(1): 95–119.

Crossley, M. L. (1999b) Stories of illness and trauma survival: liberation or repression? *Social Science and Medicine*, 48: 1685–95.

Crossley, M. L. (2000a) *Introducing Narrative Psychology: The Self and the Construction of Meaning*. Buckingham: Open University Press.

Crossley, M. L. (2000b in press) Deconstructing autobiographical accounts of childhood sexual abuse. *Feminism and Psychology*.

Crossley, M. L. (2000c in press) The 'Armistead Project': assessing a community-based health prevention programme for gay men/men who have sex with men. *International Journal of Health Promotion of Education*.

Crossley, M. L. and Chapman, T. (1999) *Evaluation of the 'Armistead Project': A Sexual Health and HIV Prevention Service for Gay Men and MWHSWM in the Sefton and Liverpool Area*. Sefton Health Authority.

Crossley, M. L. and Small, N. (1998) *Evaluation of HIV/AIDS Education Training Services Provided by London Lighthouse at St. Ann's Hospice*, Stockport Health Authority.

Crossley, N. (1996) *Intersubjectivity: The Fabric of Social Becoming*. London: Sage.

Crossley, N. and Crossley M. L. (1998) HIV, empowerment and the sick role: an investigation of a contemporary moral maze. *Health*, 2(2): 157–74.

Crow, T. (1980) Molecular pathology of schizophrenia: more than one disease process? *British Medical Journal*, 280: 66–8.

Csordas, T. (1994) *The Sacred Self: A Cultural Phenomenology of Charismatic Healing*. Berkeley: University of California Press.

Csordas, T. (ed.) (1994) *Embodiment and Experience: The Existential Ground of Culture and Self*. Cambridge: Cambridge University Press.

Cushman, P. (1990) Why the self is empty: toward a historically situated psychology. *American Psychologist*, 45: 599–611.

Dachowski, M. (1984) Sexism or social reality? *American Psychologist*, 15: 702–3.

Daniels, A. (1998) Trust and medical authority, in A. Peterson and C. Waddell (eds) *Health Matters: A Sociology of Illness, Prevention and Care*. Buckingham: Open University Press.

Danziger, K. (1990) *Constructing the Subject: Historical Origins of Psychological Research*. Cambridge: Cambridge University Press.

Davies, M. L. (1995a) *Healing Sylvia: Childhood Sexual Abuse and the Construction of Identity*. London: Falmer Press, Taylor and Francis.

Davies, M. L. (1995b) *Final Report to the Health Directorate DGIV of the European Community: An exploration of the emotional, psychological and service delivery needs of people who have been living with an HIV-positive diagnosis for five years or more*. Luxembourg: European Commission.

Davies, M. L. (1997) Shattered assumptions: time and the experience of long-term HIV positivity. *Social Science and Medicine*, 44(5): 561–71.

Davis, K., Kahn, R., Ko, S. and Davidson, M. (1991) Dopamine and schizophrenia: a review and reconceptualization. *American Journal of Psychiatry*, 148: 1474–86.

Davison, C. (1996) Predictive genetics: the cultural implications of supplying probable futures, in T. Marteau and M. Richards (eds) *The Troubled Helix: Social and Psychological Implications of the New Genetics*. Cambridge: Cambridge University Press.

Davison, C., Frankel, S. and Davey Smith, G. (1992) The limits of lifestyle: reassessing 'fatalism' in the popular culture of illness prevention. *Social Science and Medicine*, 34(6): 675–85.

De Swaan, A. (1990) *The Management of Normality: Critical Essays in Health and Welfare*. London: Routledge.

De Wit, J., Teunis, N., Godfried, N., Van Griensven, J. and Sandfort, T. (1994) Behavioural risk-reduction strategies to prevent HIV infection amongst homosexual gay men: a grounded theory approach. *AIDS Education and Prevention*, 6(6): 493–505.

Del-Vecchio Good, M., Munakata, T., Kobayashi, Y., Mattingly, C. and Good, B. (1994) Oncology and narrative time. *Social Science and Medicine*, 38: 855–62.

Dennison, A. (1996) *Uncertain Journey: A Woman's Experience of Living with Cancer*. Newmill, Cornwall: Patten Press.

Department of Health (1989a) *Working for Patients*. Cmnd 555. London: HMSO.

Department of Health (1989b) *General Practice in the NHS: The 1990 Contract*. London: HMSO.

Department of Health (1991) *The Patient's Charter*. London: HMSO.

Department of Health and Social Security (1977) *The Role of Psychologists in the Health Service (The Trethowan Report)*. London: HMSO.

Department of Health and Social Security (1983) *NHS Management Inquiry (Griffiths Report)*. London: HMSO.

Descartes, R. (1969) *Discourse on Method* and *The Meditations*. Harmondsworth: Penguin.

D'houtaud, A. and Field, M. (1984) The image of health: variations in perception by social class in a French population. *Sociology of Health and Illness*, 13: 1–19.

Diagnostic and Statistical Manual of Mental Disorders IV (1994) New York: American Psychiatric Association Press.

Diamond, J. (1998) *C: Because Cowards Get Cancer Too*. London: Random House.

Dillner, L. (1994) Doctors are more miserable than ever, says report. *British Medical Journal*, 309: 1529.

Dobson, R. (1999) Cheating the reaper. *The Guardian*, 16 February: 13.

Dobson, S., Beardworth, A., Keil, T. and Walker, K. (1994) *Diet, Choice and Poverty*. London: Family Policy Studies Centre.

Donovan, J. (1986) *We Don't Buy Sickness, It Just Comes: Health, Illness and Health Care in the Lives of People in London*. Aldershot: Gower.

Douglas, M. and Calvas, M. (1990) The self as risk-taker: a cultural theory of contagion in relation to AIDS. *Sociological Review*, 38: 445–64.

Douglas, M. and Wildavsky, A. (1982) *Risk and Culture*. Oxford: Blackwell.

Downie, R., Fyfe, C. and Tannahill, A. (1990) *Health Promotion Models and Values*. Oxford: Oxford University Press.

Dowrick, C. (1997) Rethinking the doctor–patient relationship in general practice. *Health and Social Care in the Community*, 5: 11–14.

Doyal, L. (ed.) (1998) *Women and Health Services*. Buckingham: Open University Press.

Duff, K. (1993) *The Alchemy of Illness*. New York: Bell Tower.

Dunne, J. (1995) Beyond sovereignty and deconstruction: the storied self. *Philosophy and Social Criticism*, 21: 137–57.

Early, E. (1982) The logic of well being: therapeutic narratives in Cairo, Egypt. *Social Science and Medicine*, 16: 1491–7.

Edwards, D. and Potter, J. (1992) *Discursive Psychology*. London: Sage.

Ehrenreich, B. and English, D. (1974) *Complaints and Disorders: The Sexual Politics of Sickness*. London: Compendium.

Elias, N. (1978) *The Civilising Process: The History of Manners, Vol. 1*. New York: Pantheon Books.

Elias, N. (1985) *The Loneliness of Dying*. Oxford: Blackwell.

Engel, G. (1977) The need for a new medical model: a challenge for biomedicine. *Science*, 196: 129–36.

Eysenck, H. (1990) The prediction of death by cancer by means of a personality/stress questionnaire. Too good to be true? *Perceptual Motor Skills*, 71: 216–18.

Farmer, P. (1994) AIDS talk and the constitution of cultural models. *Social Science and Medicine*, 38(6): 801–9.

Featherstone, M. (1991) The body in consumer culture, in M. Featherstone, M. Hepworth and B. Turner (eds) *The Body: Social Processes and Cultural Theory*. London: Sage.

Featherstone, M. (1992) The heroic and everyday life. *Theory, Culture and Society*, 9: 159–82.

Featherstone, M. and Hepworth, M. (1998) Ageing, the life-course and the sociology of embodiment, in G. Scrambler and P. Higgs (eds) *Modernity, Medicine and Health*. London: Routledge.

Flowers, P., Smith, J., Sheeran, P. and Beail, N. (1997) Health and romance: understanding unprotected sex in relationships between gay men. *British Journal of Health Psychology*, 2: 73–86.

Flynn, R. (1992) *Structures of Control in Health Management*. London: Routledge.

Foner, N. (1994) *The Caregiving Dilemma: Work in an American Nursing Home*. Berkeley: University of California Press.

Førde, O. (1998) Is imposing risk awareness cultural imperialism? *Social Science and Medicine*, 47(9): 1155–9.

Fox, D. and Prilleltensky, I. (eds) (1997) *Critical Psychology: An Introduction*. London: Sage.

Fox, N. (1993) *Postmodernism, Sociology and Health*. Buckingham: Open University Press.

Frank, A. (1991) *At the Will of the Body*. Boston: Houghton Mifflin.

Frank, A. (1993) The rhetoric of self-change: illness experience as narrative. *The Sociological Quarterly*, 34(1): 39–52.

Frank, A. (1995) *The Wounded Storyteller: Body, Illness and Ethics*. Chicago: University of Chicago Press.

Freidson, E. (1970) *Professional Dominance: The Social Structure of Medical Care*. Chicago: Aldine.

Freidson, E. (1994) *Professionalism Reborn: Theory, Prospect and Policy*. Cambridge: Polity Press.

Frohock, F. (1992) *Healing Powers: Alternative Medicine, Spiritual Communities and the State*. Chicago: University of Chicago Press.

Frosh, S. (1991) *Identity Crisis: Modernity, Psychoanalysis and the Self*. London: Macmillan.

Fulton, J. (1996) Nursing: biopsychosocial care? in N. Cooper, C. Stevenson and G. Hale (eds) *Integrating Perspectives on Health*. Buckingham: Open University Press.

Gaines, A. (1992) From DSM-I to III-R; voices of self, master and the other: a cultural constructivist reading of US psychiatric classification. *Social Science and Medicine*, 35: 3–24.

Garfinkel, H. (1984) *Studies in Ethnomethodology*. Cambridge: Polity Press.

Garro, L. (1994) Narrative representations of chronic illness experience: cultural models of illness, mind and body in stories concerning the temporomandibular joint (TMJ). *Social Science and Medicine*, 38(6): 775–88.

Gergen, K. (1985) The social constructionist movement in modern psychology. *American Psychologist*, 40: 266–75.

Giddens, A. (1991) *Modernity and Self Identity: Self and Society in the Late Modern Age*. Cambridge: Polity Press.

Giddens, A. (1992) *The Transformation of Intimacy*. Cambridge: Polity Press.

Giddens, A. (1994) *Beyond Left and Right*. Cambridge: Polity Press.

Goffman, E. (1961) *Asylums: Essays on the Social Situation of Mental Patients and Other Inmates*. Harmondsworth: Penguin.

Gold, R. (1995) Why we need to rethink AIDS education for gay men. *AIDS Care*, 7, Supplement 1: S11–19.

Good, B. (1992) A body in pain: the making of a world of chronic pain, in M. Good, P. Brodwin, B. Good and A. Kleinman (eds) *Pain as Human Experience: An Anthropological Perspective*. Berkeley: University of California Press.

Good, M., Brodwin, P., Good, B. and Kleinman, A. (eds) (1992) *Pain as Human Experience: An Anthropological Perspective*. Berkeley: University of California Press.

Good, B. and del-Vecchio Good, M. (1994) In the subjunctive mode: epilepsy narratives in Turkey. *Social Science and Medicine*, 38(6): 835–42.

Goodkin, K., Blaney, T., Feaster, D., Fletcher, M., Baum, M., Mantero-Atienza, E., Klimas, N., Millon, C., Szapocznik, J. and Eisdorfer, C. (1992) Active coping style is associated with natural killer cell cytotoxity in asymptomatic HIV-1 seropositive homosexual men. *Journal of Psychosomatic Research*, 36: 635–50.

Gottesman, I. (1991) *Schizophrenia Genesis: The Origins of Madness*. New York: W. H. Freeman and Co.

Gouldner, A. (1971) *The Coming Crisis of Western Sociology*. London: Heinemann.

Graham, H. (1993) *When Life's a Drag: Women, Smoking and Disadvantage*. London: HMSO.

Graham, H. (1996) Researching women's health work: a study of the lifestyles of mothers on income support, in P. Bywaters and E. MacLeod (eds) *Working for Equality in Health*. London: Routledge.

Graham, H. (1998) Health at risk: poverty and national health strategies, in L. Doyal (ed.) *Women and Health Services*. Buckingham: Open University Press.

Graham, H. and Oakley, A. (1986) Competing ideologies of reproduction: medical and maternal perspectives on pregnancy, in C. Currer and M. Stacey (eds) *Concepts of Health, Illness and Disease*. Leamington Spa: Berg.

Gray, P. (1999) *Psychology*, 3rd edition. Boston, MA: Worth.

Grealy, L. (1994) *In the Mind's Eye*. London: Century.

Greaves, L. (1996) *Smoke Screen: Women's Smoking and Social Control*. London: Scarlet Press.

Green, M. (1993) Cognitive remediation in schizophrenia: is it time yet? *American Journal of Psychiatry*, 150: 178–87.

Grey, D. (1990) Recruitment in general practice. *Practitioner*, 234: 1011.

The Guardian (21/11/98) Letters: A noble profession . . . but doctors have become a target for the media. p. 24.

The Guardian (19/1/99) Analysis: Royal Colleges of Medicine: the doctor's dilemma. p. 15.

Habermas, J. (1971) *Knowledge and Human Interests*. Boston: Beacon.

Habermas, J. (1973) *Theory and Practice*. Boston: Beacon.

Habermas, J. (1987) *The Theory of Communicative Action (Vol. 2)*. Boston: Beacon.

Habermas, J. (1991) *The Philosophical Discourse of Modernity*. Boston: MIT Press.

Hale, G. (1996) The social construction of grief, pp. 110–19 in N. Cooper, C. Stevenson and G. Hale (eds) *Integrating Perspectives on Health*. Buckingham: Open University Press.

Hall, D. (1980) Prescribing as social exchange, in R. Mapes (ed.) *Prescribing Practice and Drug Usage*. London: Croom Helm.

Hamburg, D., Elliott, G. and Parron, D. (1982) *Health and Behaviour: Frontiers of Research in the Biobehavioural Sciences*. Washington, DC: National Academy Press.

Handy, J. (1987) Psychology and the social context. *Bulletin of the British Psychological Society*, 40: 161–7.

Haracz, J. (1982) The dopamine hypothesis: an overview of studies with schizophrenic patients. *Schizophrenia Bulletin*, 8(3): 438–69.

Hardey, M. (1998) *The Social Context of Health*. Buckingham: Open University Press.

Hare-Mustin, R. and Marecek, J. (1997) Abnormal and clinical psychology: the politics of madness, in D. Fox and I. Prilleltensky (eds) *Critical Psychology: An Introduction*. London: Sage.

Harrison, S., Hunter, D. and Pollitt, C. (1990) *Just Managing: Power and Culture in the NHS*. London: Macmillan.

Haug, M. (1988) A re-examination of the hypothesis of physician deprofessionalisation. *Millbank Quarterly*, 66: 117–24.

Hearnshaw, H. and Robertson, N. (1998) Quality health care and psychologists. *The Psychologist*, 11(9): 421–5.

Heidegger, M. (1962) *Being and Time*. Oxford: Blackwell.

Hemsley, D. (1994) Schizophrenia: investigation, in S. Lindsay and G. Powell (eds) *Handbook of Clinical Adult Psychology*. London: Routledge.

Henderson, S. (1998) Nurses and the ideal of patient participation, in A. Peterson and C. Waddell (eds) *Health Matters: A Sociology of Illness, Prevention and Care*. Buckingham: Open University Press.

Henriques, J., Hollway, W., Urwin, C., Couze, V. and Walkerdine, V. (1984) *Changing the Subject: Psychology, Social Regulation and Subjectivity*. London: Methuen.

Herzlich, C. and Pierret, J. (1987) *Illness and Self in Society*. Baltimore, MD: Johns Hopkins University Press.

Higgs, P. and Scrambler, G. (1998) Explaining health inequalities. How useful are concepts of social class? in G. Scrambler and P. Higgs (eds) *Modernity, Medicine and Health*. London: Routledge.

Hildebrand, P. (1992) A patient dying with AIDS. *International Review of Psychoanalysis*, 19: 457–69.

Hilfiker, D. (1985) *Healing the Wounds: A Physician Looks at His Work*. New York: Pantheon Books.

Holifield, E. (1983) *A History of Pastoral Care in America: From Salvation to Self-Realization*. Nashville, TE: Abingdon Press.

Holland, J. (1995) *A Doctor's Dilemma: Stress and the Role of the Carer*. London: Free Association Books.

Holmes, T. and Rahe, R. (1967) The social readjustment rating scale. *Journal of Psychosomatic Research*, 11: 213–18.

Horkheimer, M. (1974) *The Eclipse of Reason*. New York: Continuum.

Horn, S. and Munafò, M. (1997) *Pain: Theory, Research and Intervention*. Buckingham: Open University Press.

Illich, I. (1975) *Medical Nemesis*. London: Calder and Boyars.

Ingleby, D. (1981) *Critical Psychiatry*. Harmondsworth: Penguin.

Jablensky, A., Sartorius, N., Ernberg, G., Anker, M., Korten, A., Cooper, J., Day, R. and Bertelsen, A. (1992) Schizophrenia: manifestations, incidence and course in different cultures. A World Health Organisation ten country study. *Psychological Medicine, Monograph Supplements*, whole volume 20.

Jackson, J. (1994) Chronic pain and the tension between the body as subject and object, in T. Csordas (ed.) *Embodiment and Experience: The Existential Ground of Culture and Self*. Cambridge: Cambridge University Press.

Jacobson, B., Smith, A. and Whitehead, M. (1991) *The Nation's Health*. London: Health Education Authority.

Janoff Bulman, R. (1992) *Shattered Assumptions: Towards a New Psychology of Trauma*. New York: Free Press.

Jenkins, J. and Karno, M. (1992) The meaning of expressed emotion: theoretical issues raised by cross-cultural research. *American Journal of Psychiatry*, 149: 9–21.

Jenkins, R. (1991) Demographic aspects of stress, in C. Cooper and R. Payne (eds) *Personality and Stress: Individual Differences in the Stress Process*. Chichester: John Wiley.

Jensen, M., Karoly, P. and Harris, P. (1991) Assessing the affective component of chronic pain: development of the Pain Discomfort Scale. *Journal of Psychosomatic Research*, 35: 149–54.

Joffe, H. (1997) Intimacy and love in late modern conditions: implications for unsafe sexual practices, in J. Ussher (ed.) *Body Talk: The Material and Discursive Regulation of Sexuality, Madness and Reproduction*. London: Routledge.

Johnson, T. (1972) *Professions and Power*. London: Macmillan.

Johnson, T. (1977) Professions and the class structure, in R. Scase (ed.) *Industrial Society: Class, Cleavage and Control*. London: Allen and Unwin.

Kamerman, J. (1988) *Death in the Midst of Life: Social and Cultural Influences on Death, Grief and Mourning*. London: Prentice Hall.

Karesek, R. and Theorell, T. (1990) *Healthy Work: Stress, Productivity and the Reconstruction of Working Life*. New York: Basic Books.

Karp, D. (1996) *Speaking of Sadness: Depression, Disconnection and the Meanings of Illness*. New York: Oxford University Press.

Kearl, M. (1989) *Endings: A Sociology of Death and Dying*. New York: Oxford University Press.

Kellehear, A. (1998) Health and the dying person, pp. 287–99 in A. Peterson and C. Waddell (eds) *Health Matters: A Sociology of Illness, Prevention and Care*. Buckingham: Open University Press.

Kelner, M. and Bourgeault, I. (1993) Patient control over dying: responses of health care professionals. *Social Science and Medicine*, 36(6): 757–65.

Kendler, K., Lindon, J., Walters, E., Neale, M., Heath, A. and Kessler, R. (1996) The identification and valuation of distinct depressive syndromes in a population-based sample of female twins. *Archives of General Psychiatry*, 53: 391–9.

Kessler, R. (1997) The effects of stressful life events on depression. *Annual Review of Psychology*, 48: 191–214.

King, L. (1982) *Medical Thinking*. Princeton, NJ: Princeton University Press.

King, S. (1993) *Treading the Maze: An Artist's Journey through Breast Cancer*. San Francisco, CA: Verve Editions.

Kinghorn, S. and Gamlin, R. (1996) Cancer care: conventional, complementary or consensus, in N. Cooper, C. Stevenson and G. Hale (eds) *Integrating Perspectives on Health*. Buckingham: Open University Press.

Kirk, S. and Kutchins, H. (1992) *The Selling of DSM: The Rhetoric of Science in Psychiatry*. New York: Aldine de Gruyter.

Kissen, D. (1966) The significance of personality in lung cancer in men. *Annals of the New York Academy of Sciences*, 125: 820–6.

Kleinman, A. (1988) *The Illness Narratives: Suffering, Healing and the Human Condition*. New York: Basic Books.

Kleinman, A., Brodwin, P., Good, B. and Del-Vecchio Good, M. (1992) Pain as human experience: an introduction, in M. Del-Vecchio Good, P. Brodwin, B. Good and A. Kleinman (eds) *Pain as Human Experience: An Anthropological Perspective*. Berkeley: University of California Press.

Kohler-Riessman, C. (1990) Strategic uses of narrative in the presentation of self and illness: a research note. *Social Science and Medicine*, 30(11): 1195–200.

Kubler-Ross, E. (1969) *On Death and Dying*. New York: Macmillan.

Kugelman, R. (1997) The psychology and management of pain: gate control as theory and symbol. *Theory and Psychology*, 7(1): 43–65.

Kugelman, R. (2000a forthcoming) Pain in the vernacular: implications for health psychology.

Kugelman, R. (2000b forthcoming) Pain, exposure and responsibility: suffering pain and suffering the Other.

Laing, R. D. (1965) *The Divided Self*. Harmondsworth: Pelican.

Lasch, C. (1980) *The Culture of Narcissism*. London: Abacus.

Lasch, C. (1984) *The Minimal Self*. London: Pan Books.

Lawrence, C. (1995) *Medicine in the Making of Modern Britain 1700–1920*. London: Routledge.

Lawson, E. (1993) *The Role of Smoking in the Lives of Low Income Pregnant Adolescents*. Kentucky: Department of Behavioural Science, University of Kentucky.

Lawton, J. (1998) Contemporary hospice care: the sequestration of the unbounded body and 'dirty dying'. *Sociology of Health and Illness*, 20(2): 121–43.

Lazarus, R. (1966) *Psychological Stress and the Coping Process*. New York: McGraw-Hill.

Leder, D. (1984–5) Toward a phenomenology of pain. *Review of Existential Psychiatry*, 19: 255–66.

Leder, D. (1990) *The Absent Body*. Chicago: Chicago University Press.

Leichter, H. (1997) Lifestyle correctness and the new secular morality, in A. Brandt and P. Rozin (eds) *Morality and Health*. London: Routledge.

Leiss, W. (1983) The icons of the marketplace. *Theory, Culture and Society*, 1(3): 24–35.

Ley, P. (1981) Professional non-compliance: a neglected problem. *British Journal of Clinical Psychology*, 20: 151–4.

Ley, P. (1989) Improving patients' understanding, recall, satisfaction and compliance, in A. Broome (ed.) *Health Psychology*. London: Chapman and Hall.

Liberman, R., Teigan, J., Patterson, R. and Baker, V. (1973) Reducing delusional speech in chronic paranoid schizophrenics. *Journal of Applied Behaviour Analysis*, 6: 57–64.

Lickey, M. and Gordon, B. (1991) *Medicine and Mental Illness: The Use of Drugs in Psychiatry*. New York: Freeman.

Lidz, T. (1963) *The Family and Human Adaptation*. New York: Harper and Row.

Lindemann, E. (1944) Symptomatology and management of acute grief. *American Journal of Psychiatry*, 101: 141–8.

Lindsay, S. and Powell, G. (1994) Practical issues of investigation in clinical psychology, in S. Lindsay and G. Powell (eds) *Handbook of Clinical Adult Psychology*. London: Routledge.

Lipsey, M. and Wilson, D. (1993) The efficacy of psychological, educational and behavioural treatment. *American Psychologist*, 48: 1181–209.

Locker, D. (1991) Prevention and health promotion, in G. Scrambler (ed.) *Sociology as Applied to Medicine*. London: Ballière-Tindall.

Loeser, J. (1980) Low back pain, in J. Bonica (ed.) *Pain*. New York: Raven Press.

Lord, J., Schnarr, A. and Hutchinson, P. (1987) The voice of the people: qualitative research and the needs of consumers. *Canadian Journal of Community Mental Health*, 6: 25–36.

Loro, A. and Orleans, C. (1981) Binge eating in obesity: preliminary finding and guidelines for behavioural analysis and treatment. *Addictive Behaviours*, 7: 155–66.

Lowy, E. and Ross, M. (1994) 'It'll never happen to me': gay men's beliefs, perceptions and folk constructions of sexual risk. *AIDS Education and Prevention*, 6(6): 467–82.

Luhmann, N. (1979) *Trust and Power*. London: John Wiley.

Lupton, D. (1994) *Medicine as Culture: Illness, Disease and the Body in Western Societies*. London: Sage.

Lupton, D. (1997a) Psychoanalytic sociology and the medical encounter: Parsons and beyond. *Sociology of Health and Illness*, 19(5): 561–79.

Lupton, D. (1997b) Foucault and the medicalisation critique, in A. Peterson and R. Bunton (eds) (1997) *Foucault, Health and Medicine*. London: Routledge.

Lupton, D. (1998) Psychoanalytic sociology and the medical encounter: a reply to Pilgrim. *Sociology of Health and Illness*, 20(4): 545–7.

Lyon, D. (1994) *Postmodernity*. Buckingham: Open University Press.

McCracken, L., Zayfert, C. and Gross, R. (1992) The pain anxiety symptom scale: development and validation of a scale to measure fear of pain. *Pain*, 50: 67–73.

McGuffin, P., Katz, R., Watkins, S. and Rutherford, J. (1996) A hospital-based twin register of the heritability of *DSM-IV* unipolar depression. *Archives of General Psychiatry*, 53: 129–36.

McIntyre, A. (1981) *After Virtue*. Notre Dame, IN: Notre Dame University Press.

McLeod, J. (1997) *Narrative and Psychotherapy*. London: Sage.

McNamara, B. (1998) A good enough death? pp. 1169–93 in A. Peterson and C. Waddell (eds) *Health Matters: A Sociology of Illness, Prevention and Care*. Buckingham: Open University Press.

McQueen, D. (1987) *Research in Health Behaviour, Health Promotion and Public Health*. Working paper. Edinburgh: Research Unit in Health and Behavioural Change, Edinburgh University.

Maddi, S. and Kobasa, S. (1984) *The Hardy Executive, Health Under Stress*. Homewood, IL: Dow Jones Irwin.

Main, T. (1957) The ailment. *British Journal of Medical Sociology*, 30(3): 129–45.

Marsh, A. and McKay, S. (1994) *Poor Smokers*. London: Policy Studies Institute.

Martin, E. (1993) *The Woman in the Body: A Cultural Analysis of Reproduction*. Buckingham: Open University Press.

May, C. and Sirur, D. (1998) Art, science and placebo: incorporating homeopathy in general practice. *Sociology of Health and Illness*, 20(2): 169–90.

May, C., Dowrick, C. and Richardson, M. (1996) The confidential patient: the social construction of therapeutic relationships in general medical practice. *Sociological Review*, 44: 187–203.

Mayer, M. (1994) *Examining Myself: One Woman's Story of Breast Cancer Treatment and Recovery*. Winchester, MA: Faber and Faber.

Melucci, A. (1996a) *Challenging Codes: Collective Action in the Information Age*. Cambridge: Cambridge University Press.

Melucci, A. (1996b) *The Playing Self: Person and Meaning in the Planetary Society*. Cambridge: Cambridge University Press.

Melzack, R. and Wall, P. (1965) Pain mechanisms: a new theory. *Science*, 150: 971–9.

Melzack, R. and Wall, P. (1982) *The Challenge of Pain*. Harmondsworth: Penguin.

Menzies-Lyth, I. (1960) A case-study in the functioning of social systems as a defence against anxiety. *Human Relations*, 13(1): 95–121.

Menzies-Lyth, I. (1970) *The Functioning of Social Systems as a Defence against Anxiety*. London: Tavistock.

Merleau-Ponty, M. (1962) *Phenomenology of Perception*. London: Routledge.

Milewa, T., Valentine, J. and Calnan, M. (1998) Managerialism and active citizenship in Britain's reformed health service: power and community in an era of decentralisation. *Social Science and Medicine*, 47(4): 507–14.

Minuchin, S. (1974) *Families and Family Therapy*. Cambridge, MA: Harvard University Press.

Mishler, E. (1984) *The Discourse of Medicine: Dialectics of Medical Interviews*. Norwood, NJ: Ablex Publishing Corporation.

Morgan, M., Calnan, M. and Manning, M. (1985) *Sociological Approaches to Health and Medicine*. London: Croom Helm.

Murray, M. (1999) The storied nature of health and illness, in M. Murray and K. Chamberlain (eds) *Qualitative Health Psychology: Theories and Methods*. London: Sage.

Murray, M. and Chamberlain, K. (1999) *Qualitative Health Psychology: Theories and Methods*. London: Sage.

Navarro, V. (1978) *Class Struggle, the State and Medicine*. London: Martin Robinson.

Nettleton, S. (1996) *The Sociology of Health and Illness*. Cambridge: Polity Press.

NHS and Community Care Bill (1989) London: HMSO.

NHS Executive (1995) *Priorities and Planning Guidelines, 1996–1997*. Leeds: NHS Executive.

Noll, P. (1989) *In the Face of Death*. Translated by Hans Noll. New York: Viking.

Nuland, S. (1994) *How We Die*. London: Chatto and Windus.

Oakley, A. (1984) *The Captured Womb*. Oxford: Blackwell.

Obholzer, A. (1994) Managing social anxieties in public sector organisations, in A. Obholzer and V. Roberts (eds) *The Unconscious at Work: Individual and Organisational Stresses in the Human Services*. London: Routledge.

Odets, W. (1995) *In the Shadow of the Epidemic: Being HIV Negative in the Age of AIDS.* Durham, NC: Duke University Press.

Ogden, J. (1996) *Health Psychology.* Buckingham: Open University Press.

Ogden, J. (1997) Diet as a vehicle for self-control, in L. Yardley (ed.) *Material Discourses of Health and Illness.* London: Routledge.

Osborne, T. (1995) On anti-medicine and clinical reason, in C. Jones and R. Porter (eds) *Reassessing Foucault: Power, Medicine and the Body.* London: Routledge.

Owens, G. and Payne, S. (1999) Qualitative research in the field of death and dying, pp. 148–64 in M. Murray and K. Chamberlain (eds) *Qualitative Health Psychology: Theories and Methods.* London: Sage.

Pancer, S. (1997) Social psychology: the crisis continues, in D. Fox and I. Prilleltensky (eds) *Critical Psychology: An Introduction.* London: Sage.

Parker, I., Georgaca, E., Harper, D., McLaughlin, T. and Stowell-Smith, M. (1995) *Deconstructing Psychopathology.* London: Sage.

Parkes, C. (1972) *Bereavement: Studies of Grief in Adult Life.* Harmondsworth: Penguin.

Parsons, T. (1975) The sick role and the role of the physician reconsidered. *Millbank Memorial Fund Quarterly,* 53(3): 257–78.

Payne, S., Horn, S. and Relf, M. (1999) *Loss and Bereavement.* Buckingham: Open University Press.

Peterson, A. and Bunton, R. (eds) (1997) *Foucault, Health and Medicine.* London: Routledge.

Peterson, A. and Lupton, D. (1996) *The New Public Health.* London: Sage.

Peterson, A. and Waddell, C. (eds) (1998) *Health Matters: A Sociology of Illness, Prevention and Care.* Buckingham: Open University Press.

Pilgrim, D. and Rogers, A. (1993) *A Sociology of Mental Health and Illness.* Buckingham: Open University Press.

Pilgrim, D. and Treacher, A. (1992) *Clinical Psychology Observed.* London: Routledge.

Pilnick, A. (1998) 'Why didn't you just say that?' Dealing with issues of asymmetry, knowledge and competence in the pharmacist/client encounter. *Sociology of Health and Illness,* 20(1): 29–51.

Polkinghorne, D. P. (1988) *Narrative Knowing and the Human Sciences.* Albany, NY: SUNY Press.

Pollock, K. (1993) Attitude of mind as a means of resisting illness, in A. Radley (ed.) *Worlds of Illness: Biographical and Cultural Perspectives on Health and Disease.* London: Routledge.

Potter, J. and Wetherell, M. (1987) *Discourse and Social Psychology: Beyond Attitudes and Behaviour.* London: Sage.

Powell, G. and Lindsay, S. (1994) An introduction to treatment, in S. Lindsay and G. Powell (eds) *Handbook of Clinical Adult Psychology.* London: Routledge.

Prilleltensky, I. and Fox, D. (1997) Introducing critical psychology: values, assumptions and the status quo, pp. 1–23 in D. Fox and I. Prilleltensky (eds) *Critical Psychology: An Introduction.* London: Sage.

Radley, A. (1993a) The role of metaphor in the adjustment to chronic illness, in A. Radley (ed.) *Worlds of Illness: Biographical and Cultural Perspectives on Health and Disease.* London: Routledge.

Radley, A. (ed.) (1993b) *Worlds of Illness: Biographical and Cultural Perspectives on Health and Disease.* London: Routledge.

Radley, A. (1994) *Making Sense of Illness: The Social Psychology of Health and Disease.* London: Sage.

Radley, A. (1997) What role does the body have in illness? pp. 50–68 in L. Yardley (ed.) *Material Discourses of Health and Illness.* London: Routledge.

Rappaport, J. and Stewart, E. (1997) A critical look at critical psychology, in D. Fox and I. Prilleltensky (eds) *Critical Psychology: An Introduction*. London: Sage.

Read, J. and Reynolds, J. (1996) *Speaking Our Minds*. London: Macmillan.

Reilly, D. (1983) Young doctors' views on alternative medicine. *British Medical Journal*, 287: 337–9.

Rhodes, T. (1998) Risk theory in epidemic times: sex, drugs and the social organisation of 'risk behaviour'. *Sociology of Health and Illness*, 4(2): 209–27.

Richardson, F. and Fowers, B. (1997) Critical theory, postmodernism and hermeneutics: insights for critical psychology, in D. Fox and I. Prilleltensky (eds) *Critical Psychology: An Introduction*. London: Sage.

Rippere, V. (1994) Depression, in S. Lindsay and G. Powell (eds) *Handbook of Clinical Adult Psychology*. London: Routledge.

Roberts, G. (1991) Delusional belief systems and meaning in life: a preferred reality? *British Journal of Psychiatry*, 159: 19–28.

Robinson, I. (1990) Personal narratives, social careers and medical courses: analysing life trajectories in autobiographies of people with multiple sclerosis. *Social Science and Medicine*, 30(11): 1173–86.

Rofes, E. (1998) *Dry Bones Breathe: Gay Men Creating Post-AIDS Identities and Cultures*. New York: Harrington Park Press.

Rogers, A., Pilgrim, D. and Lacey, R. (1993) *Experiencing Psychiatry: Users' Views of Services*. London: Macmillan, in association with MIND publications.

Rosch, E. and Lloyd, B. (eds) (1978) *Cognition and Categorisation*. Hillsdale, NJ: Erlbaum.

Rosenman, R., Brand, R. and Jenkins, C. (1975) Coronary heart disease in the Western Collaborative Group Study. Final follow-up experience of eight and a half years. *Journal of the American Medical Association*, 233: 872–7.

Rotter, J. (1966) Generalised expectancies for internal versus external control of reinforcement. *Psychological Monographs: General and Applied*, 80: whole issue.

Rowe, D. (1994) *Breaking the Bonds: Understanding Depression, Finding Freedom*. London: HarperCollins.

Saks, M. (ed.) (1992) *Alternative Medicine in Britain*. Oxford: Oxford University Press.

Salvage, J. (1990) The theory and practice of the new nursing. *Nursing Times*, 86: 42–5.

Sankaran, R. (1991) *The Spirit of Homeopathy*, Bombay: privately published.

Sankaran, R. (1994) *The Substance of Homeopathy*. Bombay: Homeopathic Medical Publishers.

Sarafino, E. (1994) *Health Psychology: Biopsychosocial Interactions*. New York: John Wiley.

Sartre, J.-P. (1956) *Being and Nothingness*. New York: Philosophical Library.

Saunders, C. and Baines, M. (1983) *Living with Dying: The Management of Terminal Disease*. Oxford: Oxford University Press.

Savage, M., Barlow, J., Dickens, P. and Fielding, T. (1992) *Property, Bureaucracy and Culture: Middle Class Formation in Contemporary Britain*. London: Routledge.

Scarry, E. (1985) *The Body in Pain: The Making and Unmaking of the World*. Oxford: Oxford University Press.

Scheier, M. and Carver, C. (1987) Dispositional optimism and physical well-being: the influence of generalised outcome expectancies on health. *Journal of Personality*, 55(2): 169–210.

Scheper-Hughes, N. and Lock, M. (1987) The mindful body: a prolegomenon to future work in medical anthropology. *Medical Anthropology Quarterly*, 1(1): 6–41.

Schildkraut, J. (1965) The cathecholamine hypothesis of affective disorders: a review of supporting evidence. *American Journal of Psychiatry*, 122: 509–22.

Schuchter, A. and Zisook, A. (1993) *Death and Dying*. Cambridge: Cambridge University Press.

Schutz, A. (1962) *Collected Papers I*. The Hague: Martinus Nijhoff.

Scott, A. (1998) Homeopathy as a feminist form of medicine. *Sociology of Health and Illness*, 20(2): 191–214.

Scrambler, A. (1998) Gender, health and the feminist debate on postmodernism, in G. Scrambler and P. Higgs (eds) *Modernity, Medicine and Health*. London: Routledge.

Seagrave, E. (1995) *Diary of a Breast*. London: Faber and Faber.

Sedgwick, P. (1982) *Psychopolitics*. London: Pluto Press.

Seeman, P. and Lee, T. (1975) Antipsychotic drugs: direct correlation between clinical potency and presynaptic action on dopamine neurons. *Science*, 188: 1271–9.

Shaffer, J., Graves, P., Swank, R. and Pearson, T. (1987) Clustering of personality traits in youth and the subsequent development of cancer among physicians. *Journal of Behavioural Medicine*, 10: 441–7.

Shapiro, A. (1997) *Vigil*. Chicago: University of Chicago Press.

Sharma, U. (1995) *Complementary Medicine Today: Practitioners and Patients*. London: Routledge.

Sheridan, C. and Radmacher, S. (1992) *Health Psychology: Challenging the Biomedical Model*. New York: John Wiley.

Shilling, C. (1993) *The Body and Social Theory*. London: Sage.

Shotter, J. (1993) *Cultural Politics of Everyday Life: Social Constructionism, Rhetoric and Knowing of the Third Kind*. Buckingham: Open University Press.

Simonton, O., Simonton, S. and Creighton, J. (1980) *Getting Well Again*. London: Bantam Books.

Skloot, F. (1996) *The Night-Side: Chronic Fatigue Syndrome and the Illness Experience*. Brownsville, Canada: Story Line Press.

Smith, J. (1995) Semi-structured interviewing and qualitative analysis, in J. Smith, R. Hare and L. Van Lagenhove (eds) *Rethinking Methods in Psychology*. London: Sage.

Smith, J. (1996) Beyond the divide between cognition and discourse: using interpretative phenomenological analysis in health psychology. *Psychology and Health*, 11: 261–71.

Smith, J., Flowers, P. and Osborn, M. (1997) Interpretative phenomenological analysis and the psychology of health and illness, in L. Yardley (ed.) *Material Discourses of Health and Illness*. London: Routledge.

Smith, M. (1994) Selfhood at risk: postmodern perils and the perils of postmodernism. *American Psychologist*, May: 405–11.

Smith, R. (1998) Renegotiating medicine's contract with patients: the GMC is leading the way. *British Medical Journal*, 316: 1622–3.

Smith, S. and Norton, K. (1999) *Counselling Skills for Doctors*. Buckingham: Open University Press.

Sontag, S. (1979) *Illness as Metaphor*. London: Allen Lane.

Spiro, H. (1986) *Doctors, Patients and Placebos*. New Haven, CT: Yale University Press.

Stainton-Rogers, W. (1991) *Explaining Health and Illness: An Exploration of Diversity*. Hemel Hempstead: Harvester Wheatsheaf.

Stein, H. (1985) *The Psychodynamics of Medical Practice: Unconscious Factors in Patient Care*. Berkeley: University of California Press.

Stein, H. (1990) *American Medicine as Culture*. Boulder, CO: Westview.

Stevens, R. (1996) *Understanding the Self*. London: Sage.

Stevens, R. (1998) Dimensions for distinguishing between theories in social psychology, in R. Sapsford, A. Still, M. Wetherell, D. Miell and R. Stevens (eds) *Theory and Social Psychology*. London: Sage.

Stroebe, M., Stroebe, W. and Hansson, R. (1993) *Handbook of Bereavement: Research and Intervention*. Cambridge: Cambridge University Press.

Sutherland, S. (1976) *Breakdown: A Personal Crisis and a Medical Dilemma*. London: Weidenfeld and Nicolson.

Sutherland, S. (1992) What goes wrong in the care and treatment of the mentally ill? in W. Dryden and C. Feltham (eds) *Psychotherapy and its Discontents*. Buckingham: Open University Press.

Sutherland, V. and Cooper, C. (1992) Job stress, satisfaction and mental health among GPs before and after introducton of new contract. *British Medical Journal*, 304: 1545–8.

Svartberg, M. and Stiles, T. (1991) Comparative effects of short-term psychodynamic psychotherapy: a meta-analysis. *Journal of Consulting and Clinical Psychology*, 59: 704–14.

Tait, R., Chibnall, T. and Krause, S. (1990) The pain disability index: psychometric properties. *Pain*, 40: 171–82.

Tajfel, H. (1982) *Social Identity and Intergroup Relations*. Cambridge: Cambridge University Press.

Taylor, C. (1989) *Sources of the Self: The Making of Modern Identity*. Cambridge: Cambridge University Press.

Taylor, S. (1983) Adjustment to threatening events: a theory of cognitive adaptation. *American Psychologist*, 38: 1161–73.

Taylor, S. (1989) *Positive Illusions: Creative Self-deception and the Healthy Mind*. New York: Basic Books.

Taylor, S. (1995) *Health Psychology*. New York: McGraw Hill.

Temoshok, L. and Fox, B. (1984) Coping styles and other psychosocial factors related to medical status and to prognosis in patients with cutaneous malignant melanoma, in B. Fox and B. Newberry (eds) *Impact of Neuroendocrine Systems in Cancer and Immunity*. Toronto: C. J. Hogrefe.

Thomas, K., Carr, J., Westlake, L. and Williams, B. (1991) Use of non-orthodox and conventional health care in Great Britain. *British Medical Journal*, 302: 207–10.

Tomm, K. (1990) A critique of the DSM. *Dulwich Centre Newsletter*, 3: 5–8.

Tuckett, D., Boulton, M., Olson, C. and Williams, A. (1985) *Meetings between Experts*. London: Tavistock.

Van den Berg, J. (1972) *The Psychology of the Sickbed*. New York: Humanities Press.

van Manen, M. (1998) Modalities of body experience in illness and health. *Qualitative Health Research*, 8(1): 7–24.

Verghese, A. (1994) *My Own Country: A Doctor's Story of a Town and Its People in the Age of AIDS*. London: Phoenix.

Vincent, C. and Furnham, A. (1996) Why do patients turn to complementary medicine? An empirical study. *British Journal of Clinical Psychology*, 35: 37–48.

Viney, L. and Bousfield, L. (1991) Narrative analysis: a method of psychosocial research for AIDS affected people. *Social Science and Medicine*, 32(7): 757–65.

Vrancken, M. (1989) Schools of thought on pain. *Social Science and Medicine*, 29(3): 435–44.

Waitzkin, H. (1991) *The Politics of Medical Encounters: How Patients and Doctors Deal with Social Problems*. New Haven, CT: Yale University Press.

Wakefield, J. (1992) Disorder as harmful dysfunction. A conceptual critique of *DSM-III-R's* definition of mental disorder. *Psychological Review*, 99: 232–47.

Wall, P. (1977) Why do we not understand pain? in R. Duncan and M. Weston-Smith (eds) *Encyclopaedia of Ignorance*, vol. 2. Oxford: Pergamon Press.

Warr, P. (1987) *Work, Unemployment and Mental Health at Work*. Oxford: Clarendon Press.

Watney, S. (1990) Safer sex as community practice, in P. Aggleton, P. Davies and G. Hart (eds) *AIDS: Individual, Cultural and Policy Dimensions*. London: Falmer Press.

Watson, D. and Clark, N. (1984) Negative affectivity: the disposition to experience negative emotional states. *Psychological Bulletin*, 96: 465–90.

Weber, M. (1964) *The Theory of Social and Economic Organization*. New York: Free Press.

Weinberger, D. (1995) Schizophrenia: from neuropathology to neurodevelopment. *Nature*, 346: 552–7.

Weiss, M. and Fitzpatrick, R. (1998) Challenges to medicine: the case of prescribing. *Sociology of Health and Illness*, 19(3): 297–327.

West, R. (1992) Alternative medicine: prospects and speculations, in M. Saks (ed.) *Alternative Medicine in Britain*. Oxford: Oxford University Press.

Wilkinson, S. and Kitzinger, C. (1993) Whose breast is it anyway? A feminist consideration of advice and 'treatment' for breast cancer. *Women's Studies International Forum*, 16: 229–38.

Williams, D. and Keefe, F. (1991) Pain beliefs and the use of cognitive behaviour strategies. *Pain*, 46: 185–90.

Williams, G. (1984) The genesis of chronic illness: narrative reconstruction. *Sociology of Health and Illness*, 11(2): 135–59.

Williams, S. (1998) Health as moral performance: ritual, transgression and taboo. *Health*, 2(4): 435–57.

Williams, S. and Bendelow, G. (1998) In search of the 'missing body'. Pain, suffering and the (post)modern condition, in G. Scrambler and P. Higgs (eds) *Modernity, Medicine and Health*. London: Routledge.

Williams, S. and Calnan, M. (1991) Key determinants of consumer satisfaction with general practice. *Family Practice*, 8(3): 237–42.

Winnicott, D. (1974) *Playing and Reality*. Harmondsworth: Pelican.

Woodward, K. (ed.) (1997) *Identity and Difference*. London: Sage.

Yardley, L. (ed.) (1997) *Material Discourses of Health and Illness*. London: Routledge.

Zborowski, M. (1952) Cultural components in response to pain. *Journal of Social Issues*, 8: 16–30.

Zola, I. (1972) Medicine as an institution of social control. *Sociological Review*, 20: 487–503.

Zola, I. (1977) Healthism and disabling medicalisation, in I. Illich, I. Zola, J. McKnight, J. Caplan and H. Shaiken *Disabling Professions*. London: Marion Boyars.

Index